NEW ASPECTS
of LEXICOGRAPHY

*Literary Criticism, Intellectual
History, and Social Change*

Edited by Howard D. Weinbrot

Southern Illinois University Press   *Carbondale and Edwardsville*
Feffer & Simons, Inc.   *London and Amsterdam*

To the Department of English
and the Riverside Campus
of the University of California:
with thanks for its generous intellectual
and financial support.

ec

Contents

The Nineteenth and Twentieth Centuries—
and Beyond

Preface

Dictionaries are hardly a novel or, many will argue, an exciting subject. Historians of lexicography, professional linguists and lexicographers, students of Samuel Johnson, the New Critics and their passion for the *Oxford English Dictionary,* and all their pertinent problems and quarrels have long been with us; but there has been little concerted effort to bring humanistic scholars together to discuss the values and limitations of the dictionary as an aid to literary studies and a guide to developments in culture. The former was the initial aim of the Riverside Conference on Lexicography which, at its inception, was titled "The Dictionary and Literary Studies." It soon became clear, however, that lexicography and literary criticism was only one of the relationships that the contributors and their audience were concerned with: we found ourselves dealing not only with how dictionaries can illumine poems, but how poems can illumine dictionaries; how Samuel Johnson theorized about lexicography and selected his illustrative quotations, and how Johnson himself changed in the process; how lexicography influenced style, and how style influenced lexicography; and, among other things, how the dictionary influenced the marketplace and computers, and how the marketplace and computers influence dictionaries. Moreover, we found ourselves engaged both in historical enquiry—how do dictionaries of today differ from those of the past—and in prognostication—how subsequent dictionaries should be made in order to be "authoritative" in some way.

The chronological scope of the papers presented here, then, extends from the medieval to the modern and near-future periods, and provides, as well, important insights into the uses and limitations of dictionaries in specific eras, examination of the personality, theory, and practice in Johnson's *Dictionary* (1755), an examination of the development of stylistics, and a brief overview of the development of American, English, and Continental lexicography. We hope both to contribute to discussion in well-established fields—Samuel Johnson, for example—and to be exploratory, to suggest new aspects of lexicography and its manifold relationships. That was a central aim of the Riverside Conference and is a central aim of this volume, which investigates some issues, and suggests the existence of others equally in need of such exploration.

For example, the two volumes of Samuel Johnson's *Dictionary* tell us much about the conservative nature of eighteenth-century English lexicography, the reading of a great man of letters, and the varied meanings of words in the middle of the century. If properly used, they also suggest the allusive nature of eighteenth-century poetry. Here, for example, are Johnson's second and third definitions of the verb *moralize:*

> **2.** In *Spenser* it seems to mean, to furnish with manners or examples. Fierce warres and faithful loves shall *moralize* my song. *Fairy Queen*, b. i. 3. In *Prior*, who imitates the foregoing line, it has a sense not easily discovered, if indeed it has any sense. High as their trumpets tune his lyre he strung,/And with his prince's arms he moraliz'd his song. *Prior* ["Ode to the Queen," 1706].

Johnson has done more than show us Prior imitating Spenser: he has also silently shown us Pope imitating both Prior and Spenser, and thus supplied the "source" for part of Pope's famous lines from the *Epistle to Dr. Arbuthnot* (1735): "not in Fancy's maze he wander'd long,/But stoop'd to truth, and moraliz'd his song" (ll. 340–41).

We hope to foster not merely the use, but the enlightened use of earlier dictionaries and encyclopedias, both of which tend to be conservative. Johnson admits that some of the words in his *Dictionary* were found only in other dictionaries, and not in life;

and Abraham Rees cautioned the readers of his *Cyclopedia* (1819) that "Science is progressive," and that his nineteen-volume work could not always keep up with that progress. This is also the case with the *Encyclopaedia Britannica*'s fourth and fifth editions, which are largely reprints of the third. Indeed, many of the articles in the third edition of 1788-97, also appear as late as the eighth edition of 1852-60. Clearly, one must be cautious before concluding that such a work embodies the latest or collective knowledge of its age.

Even with such limitations in mind, we should urge further research both with and into lexical and encyclopedic matters. These are a few of the issues and questions which might be raised: In what ways do the early editions of the *Encyclopaedia Britannica*, a product of the Scots Enlightenment, differ from Rees's London-based encyclopedia? How does the successive elimination of the Scots responsibility for the *Encyclopaedia Britannica* affect its development? To what degree is the *Encyclopaedia Britannica*, or Rees, for that matter, indebted to English forbears like Chambers, or Continental forbears like d'Alembert and Diderot? At what point in the development of lexicography do encyclopedias and dictionaries become different books with different names and purposes? Precisely how many, and of what nature, are the changes between Johnson's first and fourth editions of his *Dictionary*? Indeed, when will these and other relevant editions be collated, combined with unpublished manuscript corrections, and incorporated into a text showing Johnson's final, considered, opinions? How were the illustrative quotations for Johnson's *Dictionary* selected? What is the relationship between the rise of lexicography and the rise of travel and exploration? Can dictionaries of Christian terms and symbols offer the basis for appropriate "readings" of earlier literature? What are the advantages and disadvantages of using dictionaries of the past for today's literary criticism? How can future dictionaries be both reliable recorders of the flux of speech and the relative permanence of the written word?

These are some of the many questions which remain not merely unanswered but, in too many instances, not even raised or raised only within highly specialized and little publicized circles.

The following essays attempt to deal with a few of them, and to bring together literary historians, linguists, and lexicographers for the common purpose of lexicographic exploration.

Professor Howard proceeds inductively in his analysis of the charming medieval lyric *Levis exsurgit Zephirus.* He finds that the poem forces us to examine the word *languere* if we are properly to understand its meaning; but he also finds the frustrating quality of attempting to use dictionaries—largely inadequate for his purposes—to catch the subtle tones of an ingroup's use of a word, and stresses that the nuances of life must complement the categories of a lexicon. Recreating the consciousness of the past, Howard argues, is thus more in the realm of poetry than lexicography: "For it takes some amount of linguistic skill, imagination, and a critical sense to use a dictionary well—and poetry can cultivate that in us, as a dictionary cannot."

Professor Steadman also offers certain cautions in the use of lexicons, but his concern is not so much with creative as modern scholarly literature. He evaluates the current notion that classical dictionaries served both as omnipresent guides for Renaissance authors and readers and that they often replaced the primary classical text itself. Steadman focuses on the sort of evidence such dictionaries supply, and on whether that evidence should be employed in explication or source studies. He concludes that recent scholarship has overemphasized the value of dictionaries as sources, created an artificial distinction between primary and secondary materials and classical and Renaissance works, and arbitrarily separated lexicons and mythographical manuals. When put next to Howard's essay, two conflicting evaluations of the dictionary as a tool of literary research become clear, and we can see the appreciably different uses that lexicography has for different eras.

Professor Stewart's discussion of Marvell's "The Garden" offers yet another attitude toward the relationship of lexicography and literary criticism. He argues that the "new," psychoanalytic, or nonhistorical critic in general, is engaging in a contradiction in terms when he asks us to take the poem "on its own terms." We must have what Stewart calls "mediating evidence" drawn from the author's contemporaries. This evidence, he believes, is valuable in recreating an author's possible areas of meaning. Howard finds medieval dictionaries inadequate as glosses of *languere;* but Stewart finds Wilson's *Christian Dictionary* (1612) and its discussion of *green* (among other words in stanza 5 of "The Garden") invaluable in elucidating the spiritual background of Marvell's poem and in removing us from literary criticism as a form of prayer. Like Howard, Stewart argues that the serious critic actually builds "his own dictionary"; in the process he should be both enlarging the bounds of his lexicon and narrowing "the choices among the possible glosses with historical authenticity and critical tact."

The preceding group of three essays is concerned, among other things, with the efficacy of dictionaries for modern literary criticism. The following three are concerned with the eighteenth century, the technique, personality, and theory of Samuel Johnson, and the degree to which stylistics—as mirrored in lexicons—suggest trends in literary criticism.

Professor and Mrs. Kolb have examined every book that Johnson is known to have used in preparing his *Dictionary,* but for the present paper have concentrated upon South's *Sermons* (1692) and Watts's *Logick* (1745), and the letters *a, c, p,* and *u–v.* In the process they have been able to offer us some of Johnson's method in the "selection and use of the illustrative quotations in his *Dictionary.*" Among other things, the Kolbs find that (in their sample) less than half of the definitions Johnson marked finally appeared in the *Dictionary.* The quotations also show Johnson "preferring authorities of major rank" and his splendid economy of illustration, where one passage from an author may be used to illustrate as many as four different words. In the illustrations that did make it to the *Dictionary,* Johnson was often accurate; often compressed the beginning and ends of the passage; more often condensed internal sections, and in some cases altered a quotation so that it could illustrate two or more words. The Kolbs emerge with admiration for Johnson's ability to preserve the essential meaning of his author, and to provide a variety of authorities for his reader's illumination. Such lexicographic technique, they conclude, may be drudgery, but it is "imaginative drudgery" that inevitably increases our respect for Johnson.

In my own essay I discuss how Johnson's *Plan* (1747), dedicated to Chesterfield, and the Preface, devoted to the honor of his country, show his changed conceptions of lexicography, the lexicographer, and the world during seven years of epic battle against the intransigence of language and the nature of man. I argue that Johnson had, originally, sacrificed lexicographic reality to the social and economic reality of Chesterfield's name; but the Preface shows us the mature Johnson who has finished an immense task and made terrifying insights regarding the nature of human achievement. His attitudes toward the roles of patronage and authority, fixing of the language, the nature of the audience, and the character of the speaker himself in each work are given detailed comparison and contrast. All point toward Johnson's moving conclusion of the Preface, in which we see his awareness of "the infinite importance and infinite irrelevance of human achievement."

Professor Hansen also includes Johnson, but only as one of the many definers of the word *style* between (about) 1660 and 1800. He attempts to determine the important interrelations among critical, encyclopedic, and lexical definitions of *style;* shows how lexicographers and encyclopedists (the latter generally more prescriptive than the former) amplify the meaning of *style,* and how these amplifications indicate the antirhetorical trend in the criticism of English prose style. As the century progresses the word and concept emerge from the umbrella of *elocution,* take on a variety of new meanings and, by the end of the century, unite antirhetorical simplicity and perspicuity, with yet another "new" force—a demand for catholicity of taste which allows a synthesis of the plain and elegant styles. In his exhaustive survey Hansen thus—implicitly—examines eighteenth-century cultural change by means of a key literary term. His essay is a sort of bridge between the historically oriented papers that precede it, and to which it properly belongs, and the more "modern" essays which are so deeply concerned with our quality of civilization as mirrored in the quality of the dictionaries we use.

Professor Sledd's epitome of the rise of English, American, and Continental lexicography is both valuable in its own right, and serves as a foil for his discussion of what—alas—is going on in the world of the commercial American dictionary. The latter, he argues, has been so warmly embraced by the marketplace that it can no longer claim accurately to record language in its variety of spoken or written forms. Sledd also deplores the individualism of serious lexicographers and urges the creation of international pools of linguistic information. Until such pools are created, it is likely that "lexicographers at Oxford and Edinburgh and Ann Arbor and Madison and Victoria and Sydney [will] continue to work separately; and scholars elsewhere must still content themselves with expensive lexicons which record only a fragment of the available evidence and which can never be economically or efficiently revised." The Australian Language Research Centre has already begun such communication on its own. The current "crisis in descriptive lexicography," Sledd believes, can be lessened when scholars interested in making dictionaries work together to replace editors interested in making money.

Professor Baker writes not as a professional lexicographer or historian, but as a literary sociologist. He opposes the dominant linguistic interest in description of primitive languages or of the nonstandard aspects of American English. Instead, he insists, the Lockean empiricists should be replaced by the Cartesian-Leibnitzian advocates of innate ideas. Man needs to think, to reshape, to transcend the clumsiness of unrecorded thought and speech, and embody the "cognitive and cogitative side of language . . . by reading and writing." Baker opposes the fashionable McLuhanesque paeans—and dirges—regarding the death of the printed word, and opposes, as well, the "democratic empiricism" which he believes informs modern lexicography. In reading Baker one is aware not only that the philosophical basis of argument regarding *Webster's Third New International Dictionary* is very much alive, but also that there is an inherent paradox involved in permanently recording transient speech.

In Dr. Gove's essay we read the words of the man who knows more about W3 than anyone else in the world. He thus outlines W3's aims, suggests how computers will aid lexicographers in the future, anticipates problems for the editors of W4—many years away from publication, he warns—and deals with the appropriate tools that can help the dictionary maker of the future. In the process, Gove draws on directives he issued to the editors of W3, insists—contrary to Baker—that the tendency of language is to improve, not decay, and praises the extraordinary vigor and intelligence of modern linguistic study. And that, as Gove sees it, will be the chief source for the improvement of the dictionary of the future—"the methodology of linguists" which sometimes goes astray by producing absurd sentences that are utterly foreign to sane speech, "is inadvertently piling up a mass of information about linguistic behavior that must someday be a direct contribution to lexicography. . . . The lexicographer of the future who neglects to tap these valuable contributions will do so at his peril."

It is clear that the group of essays here collected offer both unity and diversity: the former in each contributor's commitment to an examination of the value and function of lexicography in literary criticism, intellectual history, or social change, and the latter in the sometimes overlapping but often disparate approaches taken. Howard, for example, is convinced that there are psychological nuances in the living word which a dictionary cannot catch; Baker is equally convinced of the richness of recorded history that the spoken word cannot supply. Steadman illuminates the limits to be placed on the lexicons of the past in analyzing relevant literature, while Stewart and Hansen illuminate the value of lexicons for understanding, respectively, a specific poem of a specific year, and a century-long change in attitude toward stylistics and, by implication, the act of writing itself. Gove sees the dictionary of the future as inescapably and profitably indebted to the linguistic renaissance of our own age, but Sledd believes that unless such studies are coordinated on an international scale a scholarly dictionary of modern English, long ago called for by Craigie, will never appear. Finally, Kolb's intense examination of Samuel Johnson's practice in the selection and use of his illustrative quotations, may be set against my own comparison and contrast of Johnson's changing theories regarding lexicography, and his consequent change in attitude toward Lord Chesterfield.

There are, of course, numerous—one might say innumerable—other problems in lexicography that the student will wish to investigate; those mentioned and pointed to here, however, can at least suggest some of the literary intellectual, and social aspects of lexicography that, we hope, will stimulate subsequent inquisitors.

It is a pleasure to thank my former colleagues in the English Department at the University of California, Riverside, and the secretarial staff, particularly Mrs. Joan Ruth, for innumerable acts of aid and assistance. Special thanks are due to Dean Carlo Golino, whose encouragement and financial support made the Conference possible, and to Dean Norman Better and the Convocation Speakers' Fund. The Conference was also enhanced by the shorter papers, on Samuel Johnson's *Dictionary*, by Donald J. Greene (Southern California), James Edmund Congleton (Findlay College), Paul K. Alkon (Minnesota), and Paul J. Korshin (Pennsylvania).

Howard D. Weinbrot

Madison, Wisconsin
June 1, 1971

Notes on Contributors

The following notes are limited to identification of the contributor by title, present affiliation, and citation of the books by which he is known. Each has also written numerous articles which, lamentably, we can not list here.

SHERIDAN W. BAKER, Professor of English at the University of Michigan, is author of *The Practical Stylist* (New York: Crowell, 1962), *The Complete Stylist* (New York: Crowell, 1966), *Ernest Hemingway: An Introduction and Interpretation* (New York: Holt, Rinehart & Winston, 1967), and a research anthology on Alan Paton's *Cry, The Beloved Country* (New York: Scribner's, 1968).

PHILIP B. GOVE, editor in chief of *Webster's Third New International Dictionary*, is also author of *The Imaginary Voyage in Prose Fiction* (New York: Columbia Univ. Press, 1941), and editor of *The Role of the Dictionary* (Indianapolis: Bobbs-Merrill, 1967).

DAVID A. HANSEN is Assistant Professor of English at the University of California, Riverside, and recently completed a book-length study of eighteenth-century prose style.

DONALD R. HOWARD, Professor of English at the Johns Hopkins University, is author of *The Three Temptations: Medieval Man in Search of the World* (Princeton: Princeton Univ. Press, 1966), coeditor of *Critical Studies of Sir Gawain and the Green Knight* (Notre Dame: Notre Dame Univ. Press, 1968), editor of Lothario dei Segni (Pope Innocent III), *On the Misery of the Human Condition* (Indianapolis and New York: Bobbs-Merrill, 1969), and *Chaucer: Canterbury Tales, A Selection* (New York: New American Library, 1969).

GWIN J. KOLB, Professor of English at the University of Chicago, is co-author of *Dr. Johnson's Dictionary: Essays in the Biography of a Book* (Chicago: Univ. of Chicago Press, 1955), editor of *Rasselas* (New York: Appleton-Century-Crofts, 1962), coeditor of *English Literature, 1660–1800: A Bibliography of Modern Studies Compiled for Philological Quarterly* (Princeton: Princeton Univ. Press, 1962), and editor of *Rasselas*, forthcoming, in the *Works of Samuel Johnson* (New Haven: Yale Univ. Press).

RUTH A. KOLB is Professor Kolb's collaborator on his article in this book, on other Johnsonian matters, and in life.

JAMES A. SLEDD, Professor of English at the University of Texas, Austin, is coauthor of *Dr. Johnson's Dictionary*, author of *A Short Introduction to English Grammar* (Chicago: Scott, Foresman, 1959), and coeditor of *Dictionaries and That Dictionary* (Chicago: Scott, Foresman, 1962), and *English Linguistics* (Chicago: Scott, Foresman, 1970).

JOHN M. STEADMAN is Professor of English at the University of California, Riverside, Senior Research Associate of the Henry E. Huntington Library, and Editor of the *Huntington Library Quarterly*. His books include *Milton and the Renaissance Hero* (Oxford: Clarendon Press, 1967), *Milton's Epic Characters: Image and Idol* (Chapel Hill: Univ. of North Carolina Press, 1968), and *The Myth of Asia* (New York: Simon and Schuster, 1969; London: MacMillan & Co., 1970).

STANLEY STEWART, Professor of English at the University of California, Riverside, is author of *The Enclosed Garden: The Tradition and the Image in Seventeenth-Century Poetry* (Madison: Univ. of Wisconsin Press, 1966), *The Expanded Voice: The Art of Thomas Traherne* (San Marino: The Huntington Library, 1970).

HOWARD D. WEINBROT, Associate Professor of English at the University of Wisconsin, Madison, is author of *The Formal Strain: Studies in Augustan Imitation and Satire* (Chicago: Univ. of Chicago Press, 1969), and organizer of the Riverside Conference on Lexicography.

Medieval and Renaissance

Lexicography and the Silence of the Past

DONALD R. HOWARD

§ 1

WHAT DOES "languish" mean? The Latin word, *languere*, occurs in the last line of a famous and haunting medieval lyric, *Levis exsurgit Zephirus*. Raby, conjecturing that the poem was of French or Italian origin, called it the first dramatic lyric of the Middle Ages.[1] It is found in a manuscript collection of Latin poems now in the Cambridge University Library (Gg.5.35, ff. 432^r–441^v). The codex was formerly possessed by the monastery of St. Augustine in Canterbury; an Englishman, it is thought, copied it about 1050 from a Rhenish manuscript. Its forty-nine poems may have come from the repertory of a "goliard," a wandering scholar or Latin-speaking minstrel of some kind; or from the collection of an arch-bishop or abbott with a taste for songs;[2] or from a cathedral school with humanistic leanings.[3] Its poems are of every conceivable kind —some in quantitative and some in accentual verse, some snippets of classical authors, some religious, and four of them lewd enough to have been scraped off the page by a prude of a later time. The poem in question consists of six riming quatrains:

Levis exsurgit Zephirus,
et sol procedit tepidus,
iam terra sinus aperit,
dulcore suo diffluit.

Light Zephirus arises
and the warm sun comes forth,
now earth bares her bosom
and pours forth her sweets.

Ver purpuratum exiit,	Purple Spring comes out
ornatus suos induit,	and puts its finery on,
aspergit terram floribus,	scatters the earth with flowers,
ligna silvarum frondibus.	the trees in the woods with leaves.

Struunt lustra quadrupedes	Animals build their lairs
et dulces nidos volucres,	and the sweet birds their nests;
inter ligna florentia	among the blossoming trees
sua decantant gaudia.	they sing their joys.

Quod oculis dum video	All this, while I see it with my eyes
et auribus dum audio,	and hear it with my ears,
heu pro tantis gaudiis	alas, for so many joys
tantis inflor suspiriis.	I am filled with as many sighs.

Cum mihi sola sedeo	When I sit, a woman alone,
et hec revolvens palleo,	and think of these things, I pale,
si forte capud sublevo,	and if I chance to raise my head
nec audio nec video.	I do not hear, I do not see.

Tu saltim, Veris gratia,	You at least, for Spring's sake,
exaudi et considera	hear and care about
frondes, flores et gramina,	the leaves and flowers and grass,
nam mea languet anima.[4]	for my soul languishes.

The poem divides itself neatly into two parts. The first three stanzas are a conventional description of the coming of Spring. There is the West Wind, the sun, the flowers and foliage, the animals and birds; the colors are purple and green; the tactile sensation is of warmth; the noise is of singing. The last three stanzas are an interior monologue. The speaker hears and sees this lushness but heaves as many sighs as Spring has joys; only in the fourth stanza do we get the single indication that the speaker is a woman—and she proceeds to say that she herself loses color, neither hears nor sees. In the last stanza she gives over the care of leaves, flowers, and grass because her soul "languishes." The "you" she addresses is unidentified, unless it is the reader, or Spring itself (*Veris gratia* can be, and often is, translated "grace of Spring"). The poem expresses, it may be, the inexplicable weariness, the "spring fever" we sometimes feel when the snow melts and the trees turn green; and perhaps a more existential state of mind, the world-weariness and apathy we may experience even in the face of the world's effulgence, the sense of death and emptiness which life itself implies.

Such a feeling is what draws me to the poem, at any rate, and I think its power to move me, almost a thousand years after it was written, is an important fact about it. But it is not, of course, what the poem *means;* it may be one level of meaning, and I would not quarrel with him who thought it the most important. Yet this poem always leaves me with a feeling that something is missing in my reading of it: I remain doggedly curious to know who the speaker is, why she feels so out-of-it just when the weather is picking up, and what is wrong with her when she says her soul languishes.

It is possible the poem is an allegory. It could for example be an allegory based on traditions of biblical exegesis. An interpretation of this kind would argue that spring traditionally referred to the Resurrection;[5] the foliage, flowers, and grass would be symbols of virtues or grace;[6] purple, being the royal color, would suggest Christ the King.[7] The joys would then be those of salvation, and the languishing lady whose eyes and ears are closed would be a human soul deprived of God's grace—in other words, a sinner.[8]

Or the poem could be a much simpler kind of allegory: an allegory of the seasons. The subject being Spring, the speaker would be Winter: as Spring bursts forth Winter pales, loses its senses, and languishes. "Winter" in Latin, *hiems,* is a feminine noun; and there is an off chance that *anima* is used in its oldest sense, the wind or north-wind, though this is unlikely in a medieval work. The feeling evoked would be the feeling prompted by the passing of time or the revolving of the years; in the Middle Ages this feeling suggested the moral lesson of *contemptus mundi* to be drawn from all time past with its apocalyptic and eschatological implications for time future; spring would suggest again the Resurrection and spiritual rebirth.[9]

Neither of these allegorical interpretations appeals to me very much because neither explains why I find the poem so lustrous and so subtly disturbing. Medieval readers would have brought to such a lyric emotions different from ours, I know; but unlike so many medieval lyrics, this one still has the power to move us deeply, and that fact cries out for explanation no less than the poem itself.

The reading which satisfies me best is the most literal one, that the speaker is simply an unidentified woman. Why she falls into such gloom in springtime is not explained, and whom she addresses is not specified. But let me suggest a reason for her mood: *her lover has left her.* Thus abandoned, she finds the bursting of spring in the world a reminder of the emptiness in her heart. This must on the surface seem the most fanciful explanation—one might as well believe a hundred other things about her, that she is ill (which is what *languere* fundamentally means) or that somebody has died (which the elegiac tone might suggest). One scholar interprets it only by saying "Her love, or her baby, or her faith is dead." [10] But this idea, that her lover has left her, is the opinion of an expert on such poems, Peter Dronke.[11] He argues that the poem is a Latin adaptation of a Mozarabic *kharja*, and is a conventional lament of a woman abandoned by her lover.[12] The chance of influence from Moorish Spain in the Rhineland early in the eleventh century seems farfetched, but is not impossible. The parallels with those examples of the *kharjas* he cites are indeed striking. And he cites a similar Latin poem found in the same manuscript which begins *Nam languens amore tuo,* translating it as follows:

> Languishing
> for love of you
> I arose
> at dawn
> and made my way
> bare-footed
> across the snows
> and cold,
> and searched
> the desolate seas
> to see if I could find
> sails flying in the wind,

or catch sight of the prow
of a ship.[13]

Poems which describe such a circumstance in springtime are not
unknown in the Middle Ages. For example, a thirteenth-century
Middle English lyric, "Now springeth the spray," depicts a young
girl abandoned by her love in the spring; the fact is stated ballad-
fashion in the verses, and implied in the refrain:

Now spryngeth the spray,
Al for love I am so sik
That slepen I ne may.

But do such sources and analogues explain anything? If the
lament of a woman abandoned by her lover was conventional
among the Spanish Christians in Moorish Spain, *they* would have
understood the situation implied in this kind of poem; but if such
a poem were imitated in Latin somewhere in Germany, would
anyone there have known this background? The author, adapter,
or translator might have known it, and the minstrel or goliard (if
there was one) might have explained it before or after he sang
or recited; but the poem does not bring with it in its language the
culture of Moorish Spain, and if it had an appeal in Latin Christen-
dom it must have had that appeal for other reasons. Perhaps indeed in Germany they thought it a Christian allegory or an allegory
of the seasons; or perhaps they were simply intrigued, as I am,
by its mysterious qualities. What *we* see in a Japanese *haiku* translated into English is something very different from what a Japanese sees in the original, and indeed part of what we see is "the
mysterious East" or "the inscrutable Oriental mind," but I doubt
this counts for much in Japan. What then did its readers in Germany and England see in this poem? There are a thousand reasons
why a woman may be pale and abstracted, and I find nothing to
give a clue—nothing except, perhaps, the last line. If we could
be sure what it meant to "languish," we might find that the poem
springs on us, in its last line, a specialized sense of the word
which explains the mystery it has posed. We would normally
understand the word from the context, but in this instance we

cannot be sure what kind of context it is unless we understand the word. And this, brings us to the dictionary.

§ 2

There were a few medieval Latin lexicons before the fifteenth century, but they are hard to come by and scarcely worth the trouble.[14] The dictionary is after all a modern conception: the word, *dictionarius,* is thought to have been used first c. 1225 by John of Garland, who made a list of Latin words a student should know; but only a few of them are glossed in English, and they are arranged by subject, not alphabetically. Because the medievals presumed a constituted relationship between words and things, such reference books as they had, for example Isadore's *Etymologies,* are really encyclopedias and specialize in nouns. The medievals preferred authority to experience, and old books to new observations, so they would have preferred to discuss, as many people still do, what a word was supposed to mean or was said to mean. What an individual really meant when he used a word was of no concern to the medieval mentality; because they believed that every man's reason was obscured by ignorance through original sin, they might have supposed, as many still do, that words were in large part used "incorrectly." They believed, as many still do, that etymologies indicated the "real" meanings of words; and they made up fanciful etymologies, as many still do, to support their preconceptions. The result is that whatever they said about the meanings of words must be used with caution if not disdain; it is perhaps a good thing they said so little. Of *languere,* I should add, I have found nothing.

Dictionaries of medieval Latin made in modern times are not much more help. I can summarize in a paragraph a whole afternoon spent languishing in the Johns Hopkins Library. The big lexicons of the Latin language are interested in classical Latin and ignore the Middle Ages. The great one, *Thesaurus linguae latinae* (Leipzig, 1900–), is only up to *M* and has somehow managed to omit *L,* I hope only for the time being. I get basic meanings from Forcellini (rev. ed., Prato, 1865): "languish; be sick, feeble, or faint; fade, droop, become languid or weak. . . . Used of the sea when no wind moves it ["an inconvenience to sailors," the lexicographer adds]. . . . Used of sick people. . . . Often refers to the soul . . . grow listless . . . grow dull or heavy." A shelf of dictionaries specialized in medieval Latin gives me little more. DuCange, *Glossarium mediae et infimae latinitatis* (rev. ed., Paris, 1937–38) gives for *langor* "labor, cura, sollicitudo," an Italian cognate, and two unprepossessing citations. From Habel, *Mittellateinisches Glossar* (Paderborn, 1931), "matt sein, krank sein; schlafen; verkümmern, schlaff werden, ermüden." Souter, *Glossary of Later Latin to 600 A.D.* (Oxford, 1949) coughs up the solitary meaning "to be ill." A promising new dictionary, *Mittellateinisches Wörterbuch*, ed. O. Prinz (Munich, 1967–) has barely arrived at *C*. But another new one, *Novum glossarium mediae latinitatis*, ed. F. Blatt (Copenhagen, 1957) has conveniently started production with *L* and *M*. It gives these definitions: "être faible—souffrir, faiblir, pécher; montrer sa faiblesse; dormir." Among the citations it seems to give just what I have been looking for: *amor languet cum abest quod amatur*. The author, however, is St. Bernard of Clairvaux, the work his sermon on the Song of Songs. So the one reference to love in any dictionary is to Christian love, which is to me a disappointment.

While browsing in the stacks I flush a covey of biblical materials, among them a concordance to the Latin Bible. It is an ancient, coverless volume, as fragile as the Dead Sea Scrolls, but I manage a peep into the *L*'s. Nine biblical uses of the verb reveal nothing strange—it is used in the usual senses, most often referring to sickness or lassitude; but there is one usage which strikes me, occurring twice in the Song of Songs (2:5, 5:8), the phrase *quia amore langueo*. This is exactly what I am after—some evidence of a connotation clinging about the word which suggests love. I remember that Dronke hinted in an offhand way at an allusion to Solomon's bride. But, upon reflection, there is no reason why *nam mea languet anima* should be an echo of *quia amore langueo* any more than an echo of any other biblical use—Dronke thought the poem a love-poem because he saw a similarity to the Mozarabic *kharjas*, and thus interpreting the last line "to languish with love" saw in it an echo of the Song of Songs; but that

is surely a circular argument. Besides, even if it were an echo of
the Song of Songs, we would be obliged to recall that the Song
of Songs was read throughout the Middle Ages as an allegory of
the marriage between Christ and His Church, so that the allusion
would as easily push the meaning in the direction of Christian
allegory as in the direction of love-longing.

So far, then, dictionaries are silent about a suggestion of
physical love attached to this word. I must at least prove such
a sense possible and, better yet, probable. And there is nothing
for it but to make a dictionary entry of my own.

§ 3

Given the problem of dating Latin poems of this period, and of
finding printed editions or manuscripts of them, such a task might
take a year. Fortunately, though, the manuscript of the Cambridge
poems itself provides two such uses. One is the poem I have already mentioned, which begins *Nam languens amore tuo*,[15] in
which the sense is "longing" and the association with love. The
other is one of those lyrics which were scraped off the page, and
perhaps a fragment at that; with Dronke's reconstruction and
without the jolly *oh*'s and *ah*'s which punctuate the lines, it reads
as follows:

Veni, dilectissime,	Come, my dearest one,
gratam me invisere;	and visit me, a lovely girl;
in languore pereo;	I'm perishing with languor,
venerem desidero;	and what I want is loving;
Si cum clave Veneris	If [you come] with Venus' key
mox intrare poteris.[16]	you will get in soon.

The sense is clear enough—*languor* here is sexual desire pure and
simple.

We can take these two uses as anecdotal evidence that the
word could, at the time of our poem, refer to feelings prompted
by love. So much for the possibility. But we have as yet only a
poor shard of a usage: the probability that the word refers to love

would be pushed along nicely if we could find many such usages. I could perhaps find others by leafing through the more than 21,000 entries in Hans Walther's *Initia carminum* (Göttingen, 1959), but only if the word occurred in the incipit, that is, in the opening line of a poem. Then there is a catalogue of Latin *Sprichwörter* in five large volumes by the same industrious German (Göttingen, 1963–67); of eleven entries which begin with *languere* or its derivatives four have reference to love—over a third, if that is any indication; but then how do you date a *Sprichwort?* Beyond this there remains for the scholar only the hapless task of reading Latin works of the period helter-skelter in search of more citations.

But let me add to my entry two poems of the thirteenth century. One of these, the splendid lyric *De ramis cadunt folia,* is so much like *Levis exsurgit Zephirus,* so much a counterpart to it, that it is hard not to suppose some relatedness between them, even though they are in different verse forms. The setting of this poem is autumn rather than spring, and as the world grows cold and barren the speaker, a man in this case, finds himself not languishing but warm and indeed burning because of his love for a young girl. Her power over him makes the flame inextinguishable, and he calls himself miserable; yet he is not abandoned or even neglected—far from that, the fire inside him is fed by her kisses, her touch, and her eyes. In short he is quite enjoying his misery, for what we have here is the "sweet pain" and the "hot and cold" so familiar in the literature of courtly love. The poem, like *Levis exsurgit Zephirus,* is in six stanzas, the first three a description of the season and the last three an interior monologue. The speaker, then, reveals his love in the fourth stanza:

Modo frigescit quidquid est,	Now whatever is, is freezing,
Sed solus ego caleo;	I alone am hot inside;
immo sic mihi cordi est	nay, things stand so in my heart
quod ardeo;	that I am blazing;
hic ignis tamen virgo est,	and this fire of my anguish
qua la[n]g[u]eo.[17]	is a girl for whom I languish.

If I am right that this poem is modeled on *Levis exsurgit Zephirus* or belongs to a genre of poems like it, we can take it as evidence that *languere* was a conventional word for being lovesick in such poems, at least in a later century.

The conventionality of the word is further suggested by one of the *Carmina burana*—the poems collected and written down in the late thirteenth century at the monastery at Benediktbeuren in Upper Bavaria. This is the song *Vacillantis trutine*; it consists of two seven-line, two ten-line, and two five-line stanzas, with a four-line refrain as follows:

> O langueo!   O I languish! And I see
> Causam languoris video   my languor's cause, and yet, ah me,
> nec caveo   I take no care;
> videns et prudens pereo. seeing, and being fully aware,
>   I perish.

There is something suspiciously jaunty about this menacing sentiment, and the tone is explained by the situation. The speaker is a university student, and his mind is wavering back and forth (he says) like the pointer on a scale. Reason tells him that he absolutely must study, but Love counsels him otherwise. He is like a lost ship, he goes on, and can't make up his mind; but in the end he peremptorily exiles Reason in favor of Venus, and all his languishing and perishing by this time comes to sound like quite a lot of fun. The verse, with its multiple rimes, its jaunty alliteration, and its ironic refrain about languishing and dying, gives us a nice view of university life before it got so cheerless as it has now become; the very texture of the verse makes the point by itself:

> Sicut in arbore
>   frons tremula,
>   navicula
> levis in equore,
> dum caret ancore
>   subsidio,
>   contrario
> flatu concussa fluitat:
>   sic agitat,

> sic turbine sollicitat
> me dubio
> hinc Amor, inde Ratio.

> O langueo!
> Causam languoris video
> nec caveo,
> videns et prudens pereo.

In the end, Love triumphs over Reason:

> Nam solari
> me scolari
> cogitat exilio.
> sed, Ratio,
> procul abi! vinceris
> sub Veneris
> imperio.[18]

§ 4

So far we know that in the late Middle Ages *languere* sometimes meant to be "lovesick" or to suffer sexual frustration or desire. It was used both of men and of women, and was appropriate to a serious or to a funny context. The sense included its basic meaning "to be sick, feeble, faint, listless" and so on, for of course love was often described as a malady, a pain, or a wound—this caused by the lady (the lover's "sweet foe") and able to be cured by her (his "physician"). Everyone knows that this kind of parlance was conventional; that it was used sometimes in dead earnest, sometimes with delicate irony, and sometimes with wild humor. Many believe that it started in Provence with the troubadours in the late eleventh century. So we still have to face the question whether in the early eleventh century it already suggested "languishing with love" strongly enough to affect the meaning of a poem which contains no other suggestion of this kind. Could any dictionary be much help in answering such a question? The usage is only one of many; it belonged to an argot, to the terminology of an ingroup who used it and understood it with reference to their own attitudes and values. No dictionary could afford it much space; even the *Oxford English Dictionary*, which lavishes almost seven columns on English "languish" and its cognates and derivatives, gets no closer to a sexual sense than "to droop in spirits; to pine with love, grief, or the like"—or, under "languishment," "sorrow caused by love or by longing of any kind; amorous grief or pain." Still, I believe a full dictionary of medieval Latin would need to include a definition such as this: "in the literature of love, the depression of one unsatisfied or disappointed in love, his listlessness and hopelessness, accompanied by such symptoms as faintness, sighing, weeping, indecision; metaphorically, the sickness of love; sexual frustration; lust."

But was it an argot word in the early eleventh century? If so, it was a very early instance of such a usage, an instance which precedes in Germany the "courtly love" of Provence and may reveal a hint of its unknown or disputed antecedents. In order to get the full force of its meaning we have to imagine what it feels like to hear a new argot word: we have to imagine a milieu and a mystique too new to have a name, and then imagine an ordinary word picked up by such a milieu. Perhaps in our own time the word *relevance* is that kind of word: it means just what it has always meant, but to one free-floating segment of the population it has become mixed up with an ideology. It takes its argot meaning from a shared feeling, one which we can grasp with our own feelings and which does help us understand the usage if we can but articulate what we feel. *Relevance* is still a useful word and has not been supplanted by its argot sense or undergone semantic specialization; in its argot sense, depending on who hears it, it can be inflammatory, or comical, or meaningless. Such a word, it may be, was *languere* in the eleventh century; we do not know. There have always been songs about love's joys and sorrows, but this need not alter the fact that in the late eleventh century a particular *combination* of preexisting ideas about love took shape, and with it a mystique, perhaps a cult. Whether this amounted to a "revolution in human sentiment," whether it was a heresy, or a doctrine, or a sensibility, what its origins and antecedents were—these matters are all debated endlessly. The feelings themselves, and whatever changes took place in them or in the expression of them, were so subtle, so conflicted, and so various that we will probably never understand them very fully. But that is no reason for concluding that such feelings have always been the same. Probably a man of the eleventh century, however au courant, could not have explained them better than we can; but he would have known and felt them in ways that we do not.

Can any dictionary ever give us as clear a sense of a dead word in a dead language as the full experiential sense men possess of their own living words? Of course not. No dictionary can re-create experience or consciousness. Hence no dictionary can supply the mysterious meeting of minds between author and reader which takes place through and because of a text. No dictionary can give us contexts for citations—an anthology would have to be compiled for every word. And even a vast computerized dictionary, multilingual, synchronic and diachronic, some phantasmagoria of lexicography which stored every use of every word ever written down, could recreate consciousness only as far as the edges of imagination, fantasy, emotion. Probably poems are of more use to dictionaries than dictionaries are to poems. For it takes some amount of linguistic skill, imagination, and a critical sense to use a dictionary well—and poetry can cultivate that in us, as a dictionary cannot.

To return to *Levis exsurgit Zephirus,* I think that *languere* here only partially suggested love, that its real emphasis was just where our present dictionaries suggest—on an abstract feeling of sickness, faintness, and depression; it could have suggested as well the hopelessness of a lost soul, and I believe it did evoke the feeling, as undefinable then as now, of emptiness which overtakes us strangely when the world turns warm and green. The emphasis falls where the basic meaning of the word falls—on the feeling, not on the reason for that feeling. In the same way, the "you" of the last stanza might be Spring itself, or the absent lover, or just anyone other than the speaker herself: the desolation which that stanza expresses is so intense that the ambiguous "you" is perfect. When we truly languish in this way it matters very little who we talk to or who cares about anything. In the end I accept Dronke's interpretation that it is a love poem, that these thoughts "reveal the extent of her loneliness to the woman who speaks them," that "loneliness is to know all this but not know it for oneself, to take it in with all one's senses and at the same time be unable to hear or see it at all." [19] But the wonder is that the poem is so much more than merely a love poem.

That is a wonder of language, and chiefly of one word as best we can grasp its real meaning. We are all of us worried sick half the time about the "real" meanings of words, and so we are always snatching at an etymology, or scurrying through a dictionary after numbered senses, or building a house of index cards to supply a tradition, or a convention, or a background. But words as they are really used are most often ambiguous and confused just because they express the chaos that goes on in people's heads. And yet we understand them. Words are noises; but the real meaning of the words we use is inarticulate and silent—it is not in the words but in our culture and our minds, in our hearts, and in our bones. As the great linguist Vigotsky said: "Consciousness reflects itself in words, like the sun in a drop of water. A word is related to consciousness like a small world to a big one, like a living cell to the organism. It is a small world of consciousness. The meaningful word is the microcosmos of human consciousness." [20] In the silence of consciousness the true and full meanings of words burst upon us, and the poets most of all hear the message of that silence; yet it is the secret of that inner silence which we ask a dictionary to reveal.

Renaissance Dictionaries and Manuals as Instruments of Literary Scholarship
The Problem of Evidence

JOHN M. STEADMAN

IN A SATIRE written near the close of the sixteenth century, John
Marston pilloried a rival satirist for obscurity. Precisely whom he
was satirizing and whether or not the charge was really justified
need not concern us here. The significant point is that Marston
pretended to seek enlightenment from popular reference books.

> I'le leaue the white roabe, and the biting times
> Vnto our moderne Satyres sharpest lines;
> Whose hungry fangs snarle at some secret sinne.
> And in such pitchy clouds enwrapped beene
> His *Sphinxian* ridles, that old *Oedipus*
> Would be amaz'd and take it in foule snufs
> That such *Cymerian* darkness should inuolue
> A quaint conceit, that he could not resolue.
> O darknes palpable! Egipts black night!
> My wit is stricken blind, hath lost his sight.
> My shins are broke, with groping for some sence
> To know to what his words haue reference.
> Certes (*sunt*) but (*non videntur*) that I know.
> Reach me some Poets Index that will show.

Imagines Deorum, Booke of Epithites,
Natales Comes, thou I know recites,
And mak'st Anatomie of Poesie.
Helpe to vnmaske the Satyres secresie.
Delphick *Apollo,* ayde me to vnrip,
These intricate deepe Oracles of wit.
These darke Enigmaes, and strange ridling sence
Which passe my dullard braines intelligence.[1]

This passage has been frequently quoted in recent years (sometimes quite out of context) by students of Renaissance mythography.[2] In their opinion it throws indubitable light on contemporary methods of literary composition and interpretation. It provides
definitive evidence as to how Renaissance poetry was originally
written and how it was originally read. It offers an authoritative
commentary on the nature, sources, and techniques of poetic and
iconographic allusion. And (perhaps most important of all) it
illuminates the relationship between the poet and his audience.
The Renaissance poet might speak in cryptograms, but with a
modicum of patience and a good library his readers might decipher them. With a little labor and intent study they could break
his code. For in actuality the same systems of allusive shorthand,
the same cryptographic codes were available to the poet and his
audience. Within convenient reach—on the library shelf—lay the
indispensable tools: the manuals of mythography, the handbooks
of epithets, the dictionaries and lexicons. Between the enigmatic
poet and an audience that delighted in enigmas stood that useful
intermediary, the lexicographer.

The Renaissance poet (as these scholars view him) was no
congenital horseman. He did not mount Pegasus at one bound and
soar instinctively toward whatever altitudes his talents merited—
Olympus, the Empyrean, the Paradisus Stultorum. Far from it.
Instead of vaulting boldly onto his feathered steed, he climbed his
way painfully into the saddle, teetering precariously on a stack of
accumulated handbooks. He wrote with ears attuned to the Muse,
eyes focused on reference manuals.

If his readers desired to follow him, they too must mount by
the same humble but indispensable footstool. It was from the lexi-

cographers that they must learn the difficult techniques of equitation—the art of mounting among the "feathers of imagination" and (once mounted) managing to stay safely on. Shod *in Musarum incude* at second or third heat, the Renaissance Pegasus reeked (it would seem) not so much of the stable as of the oil lamp and the forge.

In recent years sweeping claims have been made for the direct influence of dictionaries and similar reference books on Renaissance literature and art. Such an influence undoubtedly did exist, and it can hardly have been negligible. In certain instances it has been established with reasonable certitude. In others, it remains a strong probability, if not a historical fact. In many cases, however, it is little more than a remote, though tempting, possibility. Before accepting at face value the recent claims made for these lexicons and manuals, we must first evaluate the evidence on which such claims have been based. In some instances this seems very tenuous indeed; the quotation with which we began is a case in point.

Marston's lines may conveniently serve as an introduction, if not an epigraph, to this discussion of the use and abuse of lexicography for they provide a clearcut example of the misuse of evidence. Though they are really concerned with the abuse of poetry, recent scholarship has sometimes detached them from their satiric context and applied them literally to the use of dictionaries and handbooks. Here, for example, is Jean Seznec's comment. The writings of Conti, Cartari, and perhaps Ravisius Textor are, in his opinion, "the works which Marston call[ed] upon spontaneously to help him resolve the enigmas posed by contemporary poets." "It would seem," Mr. Seznec adds, "that Marston had all these works conveniently at hand ('reach me') on his library shelves—proof that they were currently consulted at the time, and that they served as indices not only for poets, but for their readers as well." [3]

Even the most conscientious scholar may occasionally stretch his evidence beyond the breaking point. If one is not altogether convinced by Mr. Seznec's "proof," it is because—like several other commentators before or after him—he has mistaken an artificial dramatic situation for literary history. Marston was, of course, writing a satire, not a library catalogue. Seznec's argument hinges apparently on the phrase "reach me"; these words refer, however, only to the fictional situation deliberately created by the satirist, not (surely) to bibliographical detail or to autobiographical fact. They do not indicate that Marston himself really possessed these books or that he himself normally made a practice of consulting them. He is, after all, speaking in the *persona* of the satirist, not *in propria persona*. The phrase "poets index," in turn, can conceivably be interpreted literally, but it may well be simply a trope, intended to heighten the satire against the abuse of poetry. It would conform, therefore, to the principles of ironic, not bibliographical description. The notion that these manuals served as "indices for poets" is admittedly explicit in the text, but it must be appraised through yellow spectacles; for it reflects the characteristic colors, the jaundiced vision, of the satirist. On this point we should accord Marston the charity of poetic faith, not the strict justice of historical assent.

Similar protests against obscurity in literature are (as we well know) fairly common today. Having grown thoroughly accustomed to them, we are usually cautious about accepting them at face value. A critic might well complain that he required a copy of the *Summa Theologiae,* several annotated anthologies of Irish ballads, and a street map of Dublin in order to make the most of *Finnegan's Wake*; yet we should hardly take him at his word. Still less should we interpret his remarks (as Seznec does Marston's) as proof positive that these were common "indices" for poets and readers.

For Seznec unfortunately insists on this point. Marston's satire does (he argues) provide demonstrable "proof" for the formative influence of mythographical manuals on the Renaissance poetic imagination. Yet in fact these lines offer no solid evidence for the major generalizations he extracts from them. We may agree with him that they constitute "evidence of the highest interest concerning the popularity of Cartari and Conti in the late sixteenth century," but that is all. In and of themselves they throw very little light on how poets or readers actually utilized these manuals.

Finally, there is considerable room for doubt as to how relevant these particular authors are to the problem that Marston describes. The charge of obscurity had frequently been leveled against Roman satirists—especially Persius and to a lesser extent

Juvenal and even Horace. It is scarcely appropriate, however, to Joseph Hall's *Virgidemiae,* commonly regarded as the target of Marston's invective. Although Marston presses the same charge against his opponent in other satires,[4] Hall himself complains that he has been accused not of being too obscure but of being too plain and outspoken:

> Some say my Satyrs ouer-loosely flow,
> Nor hide their gall inough from open show:
> Not ridle-like obscuring their intent:
> But packe-staffe plaine vttring what thing they ment:
> Contrarie to the Roman ancients,
> Whose wordes were short, & darkesome was their sense.[5]

To a modern reader Hall's assertion that his satires are more "open" than those of "blindfold" Juvenal, "darke" Horace, and "rough-hew'ne" Scaliger seems justified.[6] Marston has boldly given his opponent the lie by flatly denying Hall's insistence on his clarity. This disingenuous rhetorical maneuver may be effective as satire, but it tends to undermine Marston's value as literary evidence. The reference works to which he appeals (ironically) for aid would, moreover, have been of negligible value in enabling him to decipher Hall's meaning. As Hall makes little use of classical mythology in his satires, these manuals would have thrown scant light on his "ridling sence." They would have been highly appropriate, on the other hand, had Marston directed his satire against Chapman; the latter did in fact draw heavily from Conti and perhaps Cartari.

In pressing the charge of obscurity, Marston made use of a variety of convenient commonplaces—the proverbial ambiguity of several Latin satirists, the abstruse allegories of contemporary mythological poets, and possibly the riddling enigmas of Renaissance emblem-literature. ("Egipts black night" might well serve as a label for some of the fashionable hieroglyphics of the period.) None of these references was strictly relevant to Hall's *Virgidemiae,* but they could effectively remind the reader of notorious forms of ambiguity he had encountered elsewhere, either in art or in poetry. As critics we may admire Marston's tactical audacity. As scholars we must question the authority that Seznec and other commentators attribute to him. His lines belong rather to the history of satire than to the history of manuals and dictionaries. They demonstrate rather the type of abuse Renaissance satirists heaped on one another than the use they actually made of the manuals.

Finally, in two of the three references Marston gives us we have no real evidence that he had any specific work in mind. As Seznec himself points out, "many other manuals" of epithets existed beside Textor's.[7] *Imagines deorum* were likewise fairly numerous. Du Verdier's Latin translation of Cartari's book was known by this title, but so was Philostratus' *Icones*. Several Renaissance authors cite du Choul's unpublished *De imaginibus deorum;* nor should we forget the two medieval works that circulated under this title—the *Liber imaginum deorum* and the *De deorum imaginibus libellus*.[8] Though it is unlikely that Marston had the latter works in mind, we should not rule out the possibility that he may be referring to Philostratus instead of Cartari—to a classical manual rather than a Renaissance work. (Burton, for instance, refers to the work of both authors as *Imagines deorum*.)[9]

The same tendency to inflate the limited evidence concerning the mythographers and their general influence appears in recent discussions of other sixteenth- or seventeenth-century writers. Though Chapman and Jonson allude to the manuals—and are in fact even more deeply indebted to them than they acknowledge— they are not altogether representative of their period. Jonson was one of the most learned poets of his day, Chapman one of the most obscure; both achieved—and perhaps literally enjoyed—a contemporary notoriety for pedantry. Nor is the influence of the manuals apparent in their works as a whole. In both cases it is limited by generic considerations—the allegorical and iconographical demands of the Jonsonian masque, the Orphic darkness of Chapman's esoteric hymns. This is hardly sufficient evidence to establish the general influence of the manuals on Renaissance poetry.

Burton's allusions to the mythographers have similarly been cited as evidence for their widespread diffusion. He does indeed refer on occasion to Boccaccio, Conti, Giraldi, and Cartari, but he also alludes to older mythographers and iconographers, such as Philostratus and Phornutus [Cornutus], or lists them alongside authorities of a very different nature: Guicciardini, Ficino, Pompo-nazzi, Delrio, Weyer, and Cornelius Agrippa.[10] Burton was too omnivorous a reader, and too generous an annotator, for us to attach much weight to his passing references to the mythographers. Though his footnotes demonstrate that he had read the manuals, they do not permit us to draw any major conclusions about their general influence.

At this point one would like to add a word of warning. One is not contesting either the general or the specific influence of the manuals, but rather the type of evidence that has all too frequently been adduced in order to demonstrate or prove such influence. Scholars have tended, all too often, to interpret dubious or un-representative cases of specific influence as valid proof of general influence, or (conversely) to argue from general to specific in-debtedness. Both types of influence can (one feels) be taken for granted; yet both are hard to demonstrate, and the evidence adduced for them is sometimes profoundly disturbing.

Thus far one has refrained, moreover, from drawing a sharp distinction between dictionaries and other types of compendia—mythographical manuals, emblem-books, iconologies, and the like. Though this distinction may be highly significant in other contexts, it can become misleading when applied to the Renaissance mytho-graphical tradition. The boundary line between the dictionary and other forms of reference works has been fluid, not fixed; it has shifted constantly, and one does not wish to take up the com-plex question of riparian rights. The chief reason for avoiding a clearcut distinction, however, is that the same claims have been advanced for both genres. They share, not infrequently, the same subject matter; and they have been credited with the same type of influence on the same authors. Scholars have sometimes blurred the distinction between dictionaries and manuals in examining Renaissance mythological poetry, or else treated these categories more or less on a par, as rivals. So far as the transmission of classi-cal myth is concerned, a sharp dichotomy between lexicographical and mythographical works would not be a functional distinction.

We might well bear in mind, therefore, that convenient, though equivocal, category (still preserved in library catalogues)—Dictionaries and Encyclopaedias.

Recent scholarship on these references works has stressed their importance as intermediaries between classical mythology and Renaissance poetry and painting. Controversy has centered largely on channels of transmission, on the secondary sources, medieval or Renaissance, that conditioned a writer's interpretation of his primary sources (the classics themselves) and sometimes served as a convenient substitute for them. For well over a half-century, scholars have demonstrated an increasing awareness of the specifically Renaissance context of the mythological themes so prominent in the literature and art of the period. Since Henry Green's pioneer researches into the influence of emblem-books on drama (nearly a century ago) both iconographers and literary scholars have achieved clearer insights into the complex nature of the "Renaissance Tradition" underlying the presentation and interpretation of classical mythology. The problem of Milton's, or Spenser's or Jonson's, indebtedness to the ancients is not, as we now realize, quite so simple as eighteenth- and nineteenth-century critics often believed. We owe, therefore, an incalculable debt to twentieth-century researches on Renaissance iconography and mythography.[11] Though this is not the place fully to assess their contribution, I shall like to emphasize two points in particular that we owe especially to them: first the value of these manuals and lexicons for the reevaluation of earlier source studies; secondly, their usefulness as glosses on obscure or difficult passages in Renaissance poetry or art. As materials for source studies they have provided a significant, though limited, basis for "revisionist" views. Except in a few notable instances—such as Chapman's hymns and Jonson's masques—these manuals and dictionaries are chiefly useful to us as negative evidence, for refutation rather than confirmation, and for denial rather than assertion. By emphasizing specifically Renaissance channels of transmission, they may make us more skeptical of earlier studies which stressed classical sources at the expense of Renaissance contexts. They effectively challenge the methods and conclusions of nineteenth-century source-hunters, but (again with a few notable exceptions) they rarely enable us to ascertain specific indebtedness to specific sources. There is a world of difference between considering these reference works as possible sources and accepting them as actual sources. It is the difference between the skeptical and the gullible mythographer.

In the present state of source studies (which is far more complex than a half-century ago) the second approach would appear to be the more profitable of the two. The parallels we encounter in these reference books are primarily significant as analogues rather than as immediate sources. They represent a tradition that they themselves helped to diffuse and popularize. In emphasizing a poet's or painter's general indebtedness to a tradition we are on relatively safe ground. When we argue for his specific indebtedness to a particular passage in a particular work, on the other hand, we venture on more treacherous terrain.

A principal merit as well as a major danger of recent studies of the manuals and lexicons lies (it would seem) in their bearing on source studies. Nineteenth-century criticism often tended to stress primary sources at the expense of secondary materials; in investigating Milton's or Spenser's, Mantegna's or Correggio's indebtedness to the ancients it seemed sufficient to cite analogues in classical texts, without considering secondary channels of transmission or the various ways in which classical motifs had been sifted and combined, allegorized and moralized, transformed and perhaps deformed by medieval and Renaissance accretions. Despite its obvious limitations, however, this approach produced results that (with proper qualifications) are still valid today. Nor was its method quite so anachronistic as it may seem; its own classical bias tended to coincide with that of the Renaissance. In stressing primary sources rather than more recent channels of transmission, it fostered perhaps the very impression a Renaissance poet or painter would have liked to make. Finally, it is still a fairly reliable method as long as one recognizes its limitations. In many cases it is extremely difficult to identify immediate secondary sources with precision; to identify primary sources is sometimes less hazardous, provided one does not mistake these for immediate sources.

To this approach the recent emphasis on specifically Renaissance sources has been a healthy restorative, though not an infallible cure. To its credit, it succeeded in viewing Renaissance classicism in a distinctively Renaissance context. Cinquecento and seicento mythography (as it justly observed) was an eclectic and synthetic tradition, sometimes less faithful to the classics themselves than to the encyclopedic preoccupations of more barbarous ages. Collecting, organizing, and diffusing classical allusions and motifs, imposing upon pagan superstitions the categories of classical and Christian ethics or medieval science, Renaissance mythographers made these motifs readily available to poets, artists, and laymen in an intelligible and readily comprehensible form.

The importance of these manuals and lexicons, in the eyes of recent critics, can be summarized briefly as follows. First, they constitute possible sources for classical allusions or quotations that Renaissance authors conceivably encountered in the classics themselves but which they might, with equal or greater probability, have encountered in contemporary reference works. Secondly, in selecting and combining classical allusions on particular themes, these reference books encroached on the poet's own domain. They usurped, to a degree, the eclectic and synthetic prerogatives of the poetic imagination. (In some instances, Renaissance poets have been praised for achieving a synthesis that they probably owed to mythographers or lexicographers.) Thirdly, by moralizing and allegorizing classical motifs, these works further aided the poet or artist by suggesting the interpretation or application he might appropriately give them; here again they provided the spadework for the creative imagination. Finally, these reference works helped to create or diffuse a common stock of ideas and symbols that the poet or painter might share with his audience.

Though we are indebted to recent scholarship for emphasizing these functions, we must be cautious in applying them in specific instances. While there is no doubt of the important general influence of these reference books, it is still hard to demonstrate their particular influence on particular authors. Indeed several major scholars who have attempted this task acknowledge its difficulties, if not its dangers. "When we attempt to specify the precise role and influence of the manuals," Seznec observes, "it is difficult to find evidence. The books that everyone consults and keeps constantly at his elbow are never, or hardly ever, mentioned; by reason of their popularity, they soon become anonymous handbooks; no one quotes a dictionary." Starnes and Talbert similarly find it "extremely difficult" to demonstrate "indebtedness to the lexicons on the part of a writer who was continually reading the classics." [12]

A further reason has also been advanced for the apparent dearth of evidence. In an age that prized erudition in poetry and painting alike, perhaps the artist consciously concealed his dependence on secondary sources? "A writer or artist who wishes to display his erudition is not particularly eager," Seznec suggests, "to reveal the source of the learning that he has acquired with so little expenditure of time or energy: those who owe the most to Giraldi, Cartari, and Conti are *usually careful not to acknowledge* their indebtedness" (italics mine). Starnes and Talbert make similar charges in discussing E. K.'s gloss on Flora in Spenser's March Aeglogue: "Flora, the Goddesse of flowres, but indede (as saith Tacitus) a famous harlot . . . whom the Romans called not Andronica, but Flora."

On the basis of certain verbal parallels in this passage, Starnes and Talbert argue that E. K.'s "immediate source" was Cooper's *Thesaurus*. On this point they may well be correct. They are less convincing, however, when they attempt to explain away apparent discrepancies between Cooper's and E. K.'s accounts: "E. K.'s insertion of the parenthesis, 'as saith Tacitus,' and the name 'Andronica,' may [they declare] be designed to mislead, since there is no such comment in Tacitus and no Andronica notorious as a harlot." [13] Like Seznec, these critics resort to ethical rather than logical proof in order to explain away the paucity of reliable data. Like Seznec, they accuse the Renaissance author of consciously concealing his debt. If the evidence for his immediate sources seems insufficient, it is (they suggest) because the artist or writer has deliberately suppressed it.

Admittedly the Renaissance was the age of Machiavelli, but perhaps we have exaggerated Machiavellism in the arts. The Renaissance poet or painter was certainly capable of disingenuousness; but one suspects that this is not really the principal issue here. If we approach the problem of evidence in terms of its Renaissance context, the point at issue is actually the question of authority rather than the question of immediate sources. On questions of mythology, the highest authority clearly belonged to the ancients themselves; after all, they had made, transmitted, and "in part believed" the archaic myths. Whatever authority the moderns might possess in this field was clearly secondary to that of the ancients themselves. It is hardly surprising, therefore, that the Renaissance writer should have preferred to cite primary rather than secondary sources; the former were, in his opinion, the real and ultimate authority. In stating his authority for a Virgilian or an Ovidian detail he had encountered in some reliable manual or dictionary, he was surely justified in adding "*dixit Virgilius*" or "*legitur in Ovidio*" instead of "*apud Stephanum*" or "*dixit Comes.*" One finds, in fact, little evidence that he deliberately concealed his debt to other moderns. When he does actually cite them, moreover, it is usually as authorities rather than as sources. Desiring to refer his reader to an extended and systematic discussion of a particular myth, to a detailed allegorical interpretation, or to a definitive iconological description, he may allude explicitly to Cartari or Conti or Ripa. In such cases he is not as a rule confessing a debt; he is adducing support for his own statements, and perhaps saving space by citing a standard reference work instead of printing an extended footnote. Where the authority of the ancients will not stretch, he appeals to modern authorities.

Our own approach, we should remember, is in large part anachronistic and, unless we bear this fact in mind, we are apt to misconstrue the intent and methods of Renaissance poets and their early commentators. In examining their use of mythological themes, we look for sources; they were, on the whole, concerned with authorities. For us, the significant question concerning a borrowed detail is its channel of transmission, its immediate derivation. For them, the significant point was its original provenance, its antiquity, its classical sanction.

In tending to think in terms of sources and influences rather than authorities and precedents, we are apt to create an artificial tension between the Renaissance reference books and the classical materials to which they refer. In mythography at least there is no real "quarrel of ancients and moderns." These Renaissance manuals and dictionaries were, after all, tools of classical scholarship; not surrogates for the classics, but guides to them. Bringing together in systematic form themes and motifs, fables and quotations that lay scattered and dispersed throughout the corpus of classical literature, they subjected these allusions to rational order and discipline. The manuals were, in short, mythology methodized. Far from being substitutes for direct knowledge of the classics, they were convenient instruments for the rhetorical or icongraphic exploitation of classical learning. Like the topics of invention, the collections of *exempla,* the mnemonic tables and commonplace-books so dear to humanist educators, they served a practical end. They enabled orator, poet, and painter to draw at will on an organized, comprehensive body of classical learning—aiding invention, assisting memory, embellishing style. They did not represent learning for learning's sake so much as learning for the sake of communication. Ancillary to the spoken rhetoric of poetic discourse and the silent rhetoric of painting, they served the ends of verbal and visual persuasion. If we view these manuals primarily against the background of the Renaissance rhetorical tradition—as handbooks designed to assist composition and description; as guides for making the most effective practical use of classical materials rather than as rival or alternative sources—we shall not, in my opinion, be far wrong.

The Renaissance ideal of imitation, as Bolgar has justly observed, entailed not only close "analytical" study of classical texts, but also the preparation of rhetorical aids for composing in the classical manner: lists of idioms, proverbs, or *exempla* compiled under convenient headings or *topoi.* The "notebook and heading method" was advocated by numerous Continental educators—Guarino of Verona, Agricola, Vives, Erasmus—and later by British schoolmasters Brinsley and Hoole. Many of the standard reference works—florilegia, compendia of proverbs and epithets, and dictionaries—were in fact to serve essentially the same functions as the more primitive phrase-lists and commonplace-books kept by schoolboys. Erasmus's *Copia verborum* and *Copia rerum* were a direct outgrowth of the "methodical" and "historical" notebooks of Guarino's school.[14]

As an instrument of persuasion, mythology too might serve rhetorical ends. Cartari's work was expressly designed to provide "inventions"—arguments, topics, and themes—for artists and poets. Allegorized myths could easily serve as *exempla* of virtues and vices; they could be readily adapted to deliberative or demonstrative rhetoric, to exhortation or dehortation, encomium or diatribe. Iconographic details, meticulously moralized, were in themselves rhetorical arguments. Extensive quotations from the classics in many of the manuals assisted "imitation" in diction as well as in imagery and in allegorical symbolism.

The statements of Renaissance schoolmasters concerning the value of these reference manuals in training the student to imitate the ancients offer, it would seem, little warrant for the current tendency to treat the Renaissance compilations as rivals of the classics themselves and to weigh the relative claims of lexicons and manuals as alternative sources. The student was generally expected to use these works more or less simultaneously, reading the classical texts with the aid of commentaries, lexicons, and mythographies and drawing therefrom examples and topics, images and idioms to be exploited in his own Latin prose or verse. Hoole directs the student to a variety of sources: aids to versifying (Textor, Buchler, Henrich Smet); mythographical manuals or annotations (Conti, Cartari, Ross, Bacon, and Sandys's translation and commentary on Ovid); and of course the classics themselves ("the best means of arriving at excellence in poetry").[15]

While recent scholarship has effectively cast doubt on some of the older types of source study, it has not, on the whole, succeeded in displacing them. If eighteenth- and nineteenth-century critics sometimes exaggerated a poet's direct debt to the classics, recent scholars frequently show an equal tendency to underestimate his knowledge of, and reliance on, classical authors. Brandishing Ockham's razor with the zeal of a Demon Barber, several of the new mythographers boldly excise the primary sources, or many of them, as "unnecessary principles." Since so much that Milton allegedly derived from Virgil and Horace and Seneca was already conveniently at hand in Conti, the law of parsimony would, they suggest, designate the *Mythologia* as his immediate source. That this sort of argument has been turned against its advocates is merely poetic justice. For Starnes and Talbert, as we have seen, the manuals themselves would appear to be, in certain notable cases, unnecessary principles. Instead of consulting the chief Italian mythographers—Conti, Cartari, Giraldi—English poets could have found the material they needed much closer at hand in their own language, in the lexicons of Elyot and Cooper and Thomas.

To establish a probable case for the general influence of the manuals has not been difficult; in spite of the shaky evidence sometimes adduced for such influence, bibliographical evidence alone indicates their widespread diffusion on the Continent and in England. To prove their specific influence, on the other hand, has been much more difficult, except in the cases of writers like Chapman and Jonson, who sometimes acknowledged their debt. The new mythography has successfully challenged earlier efforts to trace specific debts to the ancients, but it has not, on the whole, succeeded in demonstrating specific debts to the moderns.[16] In some instances it has resorted to circular arguments. (The specific influence of the manuals in the case of Jonson and Chapman demonstrates their general influence; their general influence, in turn, is a cogent argument for their specific influence on other writers.) All too frequently, moreover, scholars have weakened their case by mixing solid and dubious evidence, piling doubtful examples on sound ones, like Pelion on Ossa, and overwhelming the "skeptical reader" by sheer volume and quantity of parallels.

The problem of sources has, in fact, become far more complex during the last half-century. Examination of the manuals forced reappraisal of previous source studies oriented primarily towards the classics. Scholarship on the lexicons and dictionaries, in turn, led to reevaluation of the role of the manuals. And perhaps more intensive study of other types of reference works—emblem-books, florilegia, hieroglyphics, and natural histories—may compel us to reappraise the role of the dictionaries themselves.

Patterns of influence are clearest, perhaps, among works of the same genre. The scholar can demonstrate with reasonable certitude Giraldi's influence on Conti, Valeriano's impact on Cartari, Stephanus's debt to Calepine and Torrentinus or his influence on English lexicographers. Arguments for the influence of one dictionary on another are usually far more successful than attempts to identify lexicographical elements in Renaissance literature. While Professor Starnes's brilliant studies of the English lexicographical tradition have placed us permanently in his debt, attempts to treat the dictionaries as sources of particular passages or motifs in literary works are far less convincing.[17] One is reluctant to attach much weight to parallels like Spenser's "Lybicke ocean" and Stephanus's "mari Libyco" or to such familiar commonplaces as the twinship of Castor and Pollux, the pride of Tarquinius Superbus, the Minotaur's association with the Cretan Labyrinth, or "the voluptuousness or lustfulness of the sirens." Nor is one able to find the analogy between Shakespeare's poem and Cooper's reference to "the noble and chaste matron Lucrece [quite] so significant" as recent scholars regard it. "Cooper's concise summary," they suggest, "could indeed have served as an outline, which the poet filled in with suggestions from various other sources and with his own invention." For "in the first sentence of the dictionary account Cooper presents Lucrece as a model of Chastity; so in the first stanza of his poem Shakespeare refers to 'Lucrece the chaste.' . . . Chastity indeed, as emphasized in the preliminary argument and as the leitmotif of the whole poem, may well have been inspired by the initial statement of the Lucretia sketch." [18]

This type of source-hunting—utilizing commonplaces as evidence of direct borrowing, and alleged borrowing as evidence for a poet's method of composition—constitutes, one feels, a grave danger in the lexicographical approach to literary studies. The authors achieve less sensational, but more significant results when they stress "the value of the dictionaries and other current reference works in an explanatory and illustrative capacity," utilizing them less as probable sources than as representative glosses for annotating "important passages" in sixteenth- and seventeenth-century poetry.[19]

If patterns of indebtedness are clearer within the strictly lexicographical tradition than within the broader literary tradition, they are also, on the whole, easier to trace in prose than in verse. The poet does not necessarily attempt to achieve literary fidelity to his sources; selecting and altering his material, he paraphrases it in accordance with narrative or metrical demands. He amplifies or diminishes his borrowings, with the license rhetoric has traditionally afforded him, altering and embellishing them with schemes and tropes. One cannot always rely on verbal parallels, therefore, to establish a poet's sources or the extent of his indebtedness to them.

Indeed, in tracing the influence of the manuals and lexicons on Renaissance poetry, modern scholars have been compelled to draw much of their more reliable evidence not from the poetry itself but from marginal glosses and commentaries. In Muret's commentary on Ronsard, Goulart's commentary on DuBartas's *Sepmaine,* Chapman's notes on his own nocturnal hymns, and Jonson's annotations to his own masques, the influence of the manuals is more easily demonstrated than in the poetry itself. Even in these cases, however, the source-hunter is sometimes largely dependent on the charity of the early commentators. Without the lead they had given him, by occasionally identifying one or more of their sources, his task would have been far more difficult.

The evidence concerning the influence of the manuals sometimes raises far more questions than it answers. What are we to make, for instance, of the striking parallels between Vasari's and Cartari's descriptions of the goddess Ops? Iconologists have noted their point-by-point resemblances both in iconographical details and in allegorical interpretations. "Even if we did not have [Vasari's] *Ragionamenti,*" Seznec comments, "Cartari's text would apply perfectly to [Vasari's] Palazzo Vecchio goddess, and would account for her slightest attribute." Nevertheless, as Seznec himself observes, this parallel presents certain difficulties. Though Cartari's *Imagini* was published in 1556—two years before the completion of Vasari's frescoes—the "painting of the Camera di Opi was begun before the first publication of the book." [20] As Seznec justly observes, "no final conclusions as to the influence of the *Imagini* can be drawn from this parallel." Instead we are confronted with a confusing multiplicity of hypothetical alternatives. Had Vasari seen part of the *Imagini* in manuscript? Had he and Cartari consulted a common source or enlisted the aid of the same humanistic authorities? (Other authors sought iconographical information from contemporary scholars, and we know that Vasari relied heavily on letters from Cosimo Bartoli.) Or did Vasari rely on other sources for his painting of Ops and afterwards turn to Cartari for aid in compiling his commentary? If the last alternative seems at all probable, one wonders how many other Renaissance poets or painters may have followed a similar procedure—relying on the mythographers more heavily in writing the commentary than in composing the actual poem or picture. We cannot always accept an allusion in a footnote as the actual source of the poet's verses; and we should be especially cautious when the commentary has been written by another author, eager to display the poet's erudition—and his own.

To conclude, the chief weaknesses of recent scholarship in this area are (it would seem) threefold. First, an overemphasis on sources. These are usually hard to establish, since the parallels adduced frequently involve commonplaces. Secondly, the tendency to create an artificial dichotomy between primary and secondary materials, classical and Renaissance works. These were, on the whole, interdependent and were, in fact, usually studied together. Thirdly, the tendency, apparent in at least one standard work on this subject, to draw an arbitrary distinction between the lexicons and dictionaries, on the one hand, and the mythographical manuals and related types of reference works, on the other. It would be wiser and more fruitful, one feels, to avoid such sharp distinctions between lexicographical and mythographical works or between classical and Renaissance materials, and to subordinate the quest for specific sources, whether primary or secondary, to the elucidation of contemporary commonplaces. Rightly handled, the dictionaries and manuals can be useful aids for the literary scholar. But they are not precision tools, and to employ them effectively he must be aware of their limitations. In the hands of the source-hunter they are especially dangerous and, like other hunters, he is apt to be injured by his own weapons.

But surely the open season on sources is long past. The bounties are negligible, and the trophies themselves sometimes a greater tribute to the taxidermist's art—his skill in stuffing and padding—than to the hunter's expertise.

Paradoxically, the very factors that make these reference works dangerous tools for the source-hunter can make them useful instruments for the explicator. As collections of commonplaces (and I use the term in its rhetorical sense) they assisted the Renaissance poet and artist; perhaps it is in this respect, moreover, that they may prove most helpful to the modern scholar. Though we should not deny their potential yet limited value for source studies, they are primarily useful to us as representative statements of a tradition. Men of the Renaissance employed them as sources of "inventions": we may employ them as glosses.

Thomas *Wilson's* Christian Dictionary *and* the *"Idea"* of *Marvell's* *"Garden"*

STANLEY STEWART

WE HAVE ALL HEARD that the most effective literary criticism meets the poem "on its own terms," without the use of "mediating evidence." And we are very likely familiar with spokesmen for this view, who regard the locution "the poem on its own terms" as an immeasurably helpful guide to one's critical perceptions. Vexing though this view may be in its complacency, up to a point, we cannot even quarrel with it: after all, it is apparent that when we explicate a poem like Marvell's "The Garden," we regard it as distinct, say, from "Leda and the Swan." But experience suggests that critics insinuate much more by their use of the two terms I have singled out. Proponents of such critical language normally assume that "the poem" and "on its own terms" are readily analyzable notions, and that, in the fuller context of their discussion, "mediating evidence" and "the poem on its own terms" designate logically exclusive categories.

If it is true that we perceive the text and the poem more or less simultaneously,[1] it is also true that something other than the text of the poem is required for a sufficient perception of the poem (as distinct from a sequence of phonemes). Otherwise, we would all be able from birth, intuitively, to enjoy the poetry of every language, having been freed both from the restrictions of language and from the responsibilities of rational interpretation. In such a marvelous domain of solipsistic interpretation, we would have no need for dictionaries, and criticism, like language itself, would have no function beyond the purely decorative. Yet, it seems only reasonable to assume that we currently lack such intuitive knowledge; and, as frequent critical controversy suggests, in practice, scholars assume a disjunction between perception of the text and construing of the poem. Furthermore, most modest critics admit to using the *Oxford English Dictionary* as a legitimate tool of criticism, an admission which bears important theoretical consequences, since no linguistic artifact is less like Marvell's "Garden" than the *OED*. When the critic resorts to the counsel of the lexicographer, he does not seek the poem on its own terms; he hopes to turn up relevant, mediating evidence. Critics may argue about the meaning of "a green Thought in a green Shade," but they will not be silenced by discovering that particular use solemnly recorded in the *OED*; for, if that were so, we could eliminate the problem of meaning, at least for literary critics, by simply proliferating entries in the dictionary to include every literary use. Accordingly, when the reader closes the dictionary with satisfaction, and not before, only then has the dictionary effectively fulfilled its linguistic function. At times, of course, even after an exhaustive perusal of every potentially relevant grouping, the user is forced to close the *OED* with the sense that he has not acquired sufficient information about the poetic use in question.

It seems to me, however, that one who objects to use of mediating evidence in criticism cannot logically explain any dissatisfaction, because he has already eliminated the relevance of the mediating evidence found in dictionaries. Yet without mediating evidence we are left with a definition of Marvell's "Garden" as the product of collision between the text and—all too often— the vagaries of one's autobiography. Certainly, Marvell criticism provides evidence for this view. Consider analyses of the celebrated stanza 5 of "The Garden":

> What wond'rous Life in this I lead!
> Ripe Apples drop about my head;

The Luscious Clusters of the Vine
Upon my Mouth do crush their Wine;
The Nectaren, and curious Peach,
Into my hands themselves do reach;
Stumbling on Melons, as I pass,
Insnar'd with Flow'rs, I fall on Grass.[2]

(*Ll.* 33-40)

In these lines one critic perceives the garden as a giant fleshly orchid, poised to devour man; this interpreter, in turn, defends his subsequent description of the tone of this delightful passage as "ominous":[3] the text as Rorschach inkblot. Similarly, in the most influential of all essays on "The Garden," William Empson writes: "The chief point of the poem is to contrast and reconcile conscious and unconscious states, intuitive and intellectual modes of apprehension; and yet that distinction is never made, perhaps could not have been made; his thought is implied by his metaphors." [4] From a lexicographical point of view, this is an interesting assertion: Empson claims not only that Marvell's thought is implied by the metaphors in the text, but also that these express the "Puritan ambivalence" toward pleasure, along with a distinguishable variation on a theme of return to the womb. The question is: How should such propositions be regarded in the nonclinical context of literary criticism? How can any type of ambiguity be present in a poem if the meanings we impute are not possible in the language of the time? I have not found a single contemporary discussion of "Puritan ambivalence" toward pleasure; the meaning of the term "ambivalence" is also unclear (it has not yet found a place in such a modern repository as the *OED*). Even if the chief point of Marvell's poem *had* been made (instead of being, presumably, detoured somewhere shy of its destination in the language of the poem), it is hard to see how we can establish the validity of our case in the absence of mediating evidence. We need not conceive of the text of any poem as a Rorschach, in which the meanings of poetry become functions of one's autobiography. We may prefer to assert that the implications of Marvell's text did not change with the expanding vocabulary of psychoanalysis, but that, instead, only the range of inference increased.

I am not here advocating abolition of anachronistic criticism; we all know it is often far more diverting—and we ought to grant that it can be clinically more useful—than its historical counterpart. On the other hand, judging from the tone of at least one critic, we might suspect that abolition is favored in some quarters. In a fit of ungenerosity, Pierre Legouis chastises the critics who approach Marvell's "The Garden" with anachronistic methods:

> I wonder why nobody has yet (to my knowledge) given a psychoanalytic explanation of these "melons": in Greek they are apples, Mr. Empson reminds us, and in French "pommes" is sometimes applied, in a very informal style, to those globular charms that have made Marilyn Monroe and Gina Lollobrigida famous in our time. As a result no doubt of repression, the English Puritans, probably in a dream, find these instruments of the Fall of Man enticing them to "fall on grass." [5]

We might make the same point about this "ominous" flesh-eating orchid. The word "orchid" comes from Latin, and was not introduced into English until 1845, when it appeared in a school textbook on botany. It derives, finally, from the Greek ὄρχις, so-called probably because the plant was thought to resemble sections of the male generative organs. In 1562, in *The Second Parte of W. Turners Herball*, we find: "There are divers kinds of orchis . . . the other kinds ar in other countress called fox stones or hear stones, and they may after the Greke be called dog-stones" (*OED*). So as we can see, with reference to stanza 5 and this carnivorous ὄρχις, either the critic is mistaken, or Marvell was badly mixing his metaphors.

Though his tone may be punitive, Legouis makes a good point. To what extent is all the business in recent criticism about ominous ambivalences, sexual guilts, and castration anxieties a projection of twentieth-century preoccupations rather than a correct elucidation of the text on the terms offered by the language of the seventeenth century? Modern criticism, even in its most

fashionably deranged modes, can profit from the various species
of linguistic helps available. Indeed, it may do so easily, and
without so much as the loss of a single amount of *angst*. There is
no longer any serious question of crass historicism in dialectical
opposition to exquisite sensibility, and vice versa. We need only
revive the insights of the past to see that we have and perhaps
even need both personal impressions and linguistic aids. Modern
criticism would be helped, I believe, by reconsideration and
adoption of certain methodological distinctions and practices employed by scholars and lexicographers of Marvell's time. Thomas
Wilson was such a man; in an important reference work of the
period, *A Christian Dictionary* (*1612–1678*), he and his colleagues
expressed the firm conviction that not all interpretations exert
equal claims to assent. It seems to be that reconciliation between
intuition and the history of language begins here: not all insights
into the word are actually insights. Edward Calamy, principle
editor of the revised eighth edition of Wilson's *Dictionary*, observes: "*it cannot be denied, but that there are many who, Spider-
like, suck the poyson of sin and error out of these sweet and
precious flowers* [of Scripture]." One must be aware of linguistic
aberrations: "*There are many* [he says] *that are* unlearned and
unstable who (*as the Apostle saith*) wrest Scriptures unto their
own destruction" (sig. A5ʳ).[6]

Calamy makes these remarks in appreciation of the good of-
fices of Thomas Wilson, author of the *Dictionary*. Wilson was an
extraordinary man, a clergyman, a man of letters, and an industrious lexicographer. The last of his collaborators, Andrew Symson,
who continued work on the *Dictionary* long after Wilson's death
in 1622, describes him in this fashion: "Amongst *others*, the faithful and painful Labourers in the Lords Vineyard, this our Author
was of Special note, eminent in his time, famous in that Generation. Ordinarily, he preached *thrice* every Week (above an hundred and fifty Sermons yearly), often *every day*. As he was of a
strong *constitution*, so he was of a *good memory*, retaining what
he had read, and able even on the sudden to make use thereof
for the edification of others" (8th ed., sig. A3ʳ). Despite his remarkable memory, Wilson spent years compiling and revising a
lexicon for his own and others' use. He assumed that memory was

not a thoroughly reliable repository of relevant materials for the interpretation of language. With all the advantages of his wide reading, and after taking pains to formulate a dictionary, at no time does Wilson ever associate the garden or the lovely shade of the apple tree with fear, with ambivalence toward pleasure, with flesh-eating orchids or returns to the womb. Yet surely his notions about such figures are potentially relevant to interpretation of Marvell's text, for not only is his work a contemporary source, but Wilson's *Christian Dictionary* was an enormously successful one; it went through many editions in the seventeenth century, and in fact the response of readers was so generous that Wilson expressed gratitude for it in a later work.[7]

We have already seen that many readers would deny, a priori, the relevance to Marvell's poem (or to any other poem) of Wilson's *Dictionary*. It is only fair to admit the rhetorical advantages of their position: it is more democratic to suppose that no rules exist by which to measure the claims of one man's inner lexicon against another. The question is whether right-thinking critics export this admirable ideal of equality and permissiveness to other disciplines, to lexicography, for instance. Wilson believed that some interpretations were of lesser value than others, and that some were patently wrong. Without stated or implied rules for decision no such judgment can be made. Yet without such rules the lexicographer could not operate; he would be unable to number the various entries under "green," for in so doing he implicitly decrees the ground rules for distinguishing the homonyms from the synonyms. The groupings in the *OED* imply direct imperatives, such as "Look again." But by what warrant, implied or stated, does the lexicographer (or critic) say that this is or is not an apposite utterance, relevant or not to some other piece of language? What are the rules governing such decisions? Does Wilson believe in such rules, and, if so, does he consider the same rules binding in all cases?

According to Wilson, the "most difficult and ambiguous speeches" require the reader to search out not only other examples (hence, to consult such artifacts as dictionaries), but also to encounter more numerous examples for more complex utterances. By expanding the number of examples one provides the user with a wider base for the comparative judgment required in deciding on the appropriate interpretation. It would follow, then, that by increasing the number of potentially relevant examples one increases the potential usefulness of his lexicon. On this sound principle Wilson revised his *Dictionary* by expanding both the number of the entries and the material of examples for entries retained. At the same time, he explicitly recognized the arbitrariness of the limits established in publishing even this expanded lexicon:

> Finally if in the draught . . . of this . . . Dictionary, I have failed in any thing (as no doubt but I have, being but a man; and therefore subject to errour, from which no Booke is priviledged, saving the Booke of Bookes,) I do earnestly intreate thee to cover my slips by love, either amending them, or admonishing me of them: doing unto mee, as in the like case thy selfe wouldest bee done unto. (Sig. ¶ 6ᵛ)

The reader can perceive in this golden rule for lexicographers (which might even apply to literary critics) something more than gratuitous piety. Wilson understands human nature, and is therefore looking ahead to criticism of his work. All interpretations are subject to human error; his *Christian Dictionary* will be no exception to this rule, since the rule admits of only the one exception. For Wilson, the same rules apply to all interpretive efforts; they are always made by men, and therefore all interpretive claims must be limited, like his. Wilson invites an attitude of generosity in his critics, and he reinforces his invitation with a promise to cooperate in the further revision of his work. The nature of language is such that the lexicographer's work is never done.

Just as Wilson invites the constructive advice of his critics, he likewise offers some of his own. Couched in the language of charity is a hard challenge to competitors. It is not enough that critics maintain the same sense of love and dedication in their criticism as he has shown through the lengthy process of building a dictionary. Wilson requires that his critics perform an act of lexicography too: they are to cover his slips, or to help him cover them; they are to contribute as he has. The most effective form of criticism would be construction of a better dictionary. In this sense, as he revises his work, Wilson functions as his own most responsible critic. He effectively applies his categorical imperative, and his critics are to emulate him, "ever remembring, that it is much easier to dislike, then to do the like. The former will cost thee nothing; but the latter trust me, will cost thee paines, unto sweate & wearinesse, if thou wilt but endevour to do what I have done before thee" (sig. ¶ 6ᵛ). This passage is from Wilson's "Preface to the Table," a kind of grid distinguishing the three sorts of words found in scripture, and he ends the "Preface" with a somewhat dramatic "Farewell" (sig. ¶¶ 2ᵛ). Perhaps the plaintive tone here is endemic to lexicographers; the greatest of the species would make a similar complaint. And, like Samuel Johnson, Wilson both proclaims and complains that the lexicographer's job is not only onerous but (ultimately) quite secondary in importance. Wilson considered his efforts as a lexicographer to be an adjunct of his teaching function: "The end of Teaching is to cause others to learn." This heuristic conception underlies Wilson's implied criterion for judging both his work and that of his future critics. The lexicographer approaches meaning in one of the two possible ways open to man; finally, he sees the nature of language as such that meaningful criticism is restricted to the methods of the lexicographer.

In a section prefixed to the *Christian Dictionary*, Charles Evars touches the crux of this matter. Given the nature of language and of fallen man, only two methods of explicating scripture exist: preeminently the most prestigious of these is the first, namely, prayer. Evars writes: *"the Keyes of the house of* David, *to open the wits and understanding of such as be blinde by Nature"* issues forth from man's *"humble faithfull prayers,"* which *"most instantly"* open the reader's eyes to the wonders of the text. In this way, insight into scripture is epiphanic, like spiritual conversion; it is characterized by a telescoping of time (*"most instantly"*), which bears important lexicographical consequences. This telescoping of time markedly differentiates the first from the second method of understanding: *"to wit, the Interpretation of Scriptures, eyther by vocall preaching or by sound writing of such Scribes as bee skilfull too pen the word of the Kingdome."* Now, the second so-called "ministeriall" strategy of interpretation is the handiwork of natural man; *"full of labour,"* Evars writes, "the

naturall man" (he is referring to the lexicographer) does not compete with—he supplements—the silent and superior intuitions of
prayer. While prayer is the private responsibility of the entire
congregation, the mediating, *"Ministeriall"* practices of the lexicographer require the prolonged (and sometimes tedious) public
service of the scholar (sig. ¶ 2ʳ).

Because of the nature of the text under consideration, Wilson
limits the claims for his *"Ministeriall"* achievement. The English
language is largely an imperfect vessel for transmitting "divine
language." Hence, prayer must remain the more effective and
reliable of the two methods: "I would," he wrote, "have none to
thinke that my meanings were to give an exact definition of everything"—a splendid example of lexicographical modesty (sig. A7ʳ).
The value of Wilson's work inheres partly in this modesty; he
purports to remove only the accessible parts of the mystery surrounding the word. His method will be to render "true and
familiar glosses" of the most striking or significant words in biblical
discourse. For Wilson, lexicographical truth and familiarity are
parallel and closely related values. He seeks correspondence between the scope and form of his work on the one hand and the
actualities of language on the other. In so doing, he readily accepts the limits of his discipline, which he recognizes to be those
of the collector and author merging with the necessary limits of
man. Though he admits that his "explications . . . may differ in
tearmes from such . . . as [one may] finde in other mens writings
of the same words," he does so apologetically, and not without
adding that "for the most part," they will show "agreement in
substance of trueth" (sig. A7ʳ). His point, surely is that the value
of the lexicographer does not stem from his power to tell one how
he ought to understand the text, but from his willingness to organize in an accessible and useful way pertinent examples of the manner in which language is actually used. For this reason he apologizes for any disparity between his grouping and the realities of
usage in contemporary discourse.

As Willard Quine has pointed out, the logic of the lexicographer's groupings are not actually prescriptive.[8] The lexicographer
does not insist that the user stop at a particular number beneath
"green," pause, or read more carefully. He does not tell the user

when to close the dictionary, or which of the numbered sections
to ignore. The groupings are merely a heuristic device, not an
ideological pose or statement. The *OED* does not seek legislation
against anachronism, nor even against the warm human institution
of the malapropism. The lexicographer is the people's servant,
laboring "in the Lord's Vineyard" with Thomas Wilson, perform-
ing a service for the well-meaning user of his lexicon. His aim is
to confront the reader with the richest possible set of potentially
relevant utterances. In just the same way, many critics attempt to
formulate appropriate contexts for poetry, especially in cases where
available dictionaries seem too stingy in their range of examples.
When the critic undertakes such a task he functions in many ways
like the lexicographer, and he also encounters many of the same
problems. How, for instance, will he decide which examples are
relevant?

Wilson's *Christian Dictionary* provides us with helpful clues.
Wilson believed (and I am on his side here) that proper explication depends partly on selection and arrangement of uses employed in actual discourse. With this general rule in mind he
sought to provide the maximum value to users of his dictionary,
and he did so by acting on certain assumptions. His practice suggests that the lexicon of any large domain of discourse is actually
composed of a theoretically unknown but very large set of smaller
dictionaries. This is the clear implication of the formal arrangement which he imposed on his material, an arrangement which
he retained in all editions issued under his control, and one which
disappeared only long after his death. Wilson divided his work
into four discrete lexicons, bound in one volume, and subsumed
under the single title, *A Christian Dictionary*.

I have chosen to discuss this particular work because it provides a convenient paradigm of the way in which critical assertion
of the relevance of one context rather than another bears directly
upon the "idea" of what the text of a poem means. For example,
based on *A Christian Dictionary* alone, we may think of four distinct "ideas" of Marvell's "Garden," each imbedded in a particular
lexicon. The relation between the text and this lexicon provides
the "idea" of the poem with its claim to historical validity; this
relation, in turn, answers what Hirsch calls "the criterion of legiti-

macy." [9] With this theoretical point in mind, examination of Wilson's *Dictionary* may easily address itself to the criteria for deciding upon the relevance of meanings, all of which are historically possible. As analysis of the structure of the *Christian Dictionary* shows, Wilson's implied system of explication involves more than the simple proliferation of examples. It embodies a sophisticated sense of the problems of decision involved in explication.

The first and largest dictionary purports to canvass all the most important words and phrases of scripture, with accurate definitions and exegeses. The three smaller lexicons treat of particular books of the Bible: the Apocalypse, the Epistle to the Hebrews, and the Song of Songs. This arrangement is, in effect, like the groupings in the *OED*. The question is, which dictionary is relevant to the passage in Marvell under consideration: "a green Thought in a green Shade"? Grounds for decision are not lacking. For example, consultation of the dictionary, "For the Epistle to the Hebrews," would be useless, since we find no entry for the operative word "green." If we may legitimately eliminate this title, only three dictionaries remain as potentially relevant. In the largest of these we find these examples:

> [**Greene.**] Flourishing and prosperous. Psal. 37, 35. *Like the Greene Bay Tree.* . . .
> [**Greene tree.**] An innocent and unguilty person. Luke 23, 31. *If this bee done to the Greene tree, what will be done to the dry?* . . . what greevous judgements will fall upon impenitent sinners, who are like dry stickes, apt and meere to burn in the fire of Gods wrath? (P. 247)

In the lexicon entitled "For the Revelation of S. John," we read:

> [**Greene Grasse**] The Fruites of the earth, of all sortes, . . . Revel. 8, 7. *And all Green grasse was burnt up.* Some do understand this spiritually, of the great Famine and scarsity of the word, and of Christians in shew, which have taken no sound roote, but were (as Greene grasse) soone scorched and sindged with the heat of persecution. (P. 739)

And "For the Canticles or Song of Salomon," lists:

> **Greene Bed.** See Bed. (P. 834)
>
> [**Our Bed is greene**] The procreation of Children unto God in Christ, in that spirituall birth, by the immortall seed of the word. For the Church is so a Virgine, as she is the Mother of all Gods Children. Cant. 1, 15. *Our Bed is greene.* (P. 825)

Placed in the shifting contexts of these examples, Marvell's text shifts in meaning. Hence, the thought and shade of Marvell's poem may be "green" in the sense of "Like the Green Bay Tree," or, again, green in the sense of moist or innocent, as with the greenness of the grass before it is burnt. And the lexicon for the Canticles provides still further possibilities: associations of the nuptial bed (in the diction of motherhood), procreation, immortality, spiritual birth, fecundity, virginity, and so on.

We return to our major question: How do we distinguish the synonyms from the homonyms? That is, how do we choose definitions relevant to Marvell's "Garden"? Evidently, the occurrence in the dictionary for Revelation can be excluded: the immediate context of "The Garden" suggests that the figure of burning grass is not relevant to this particular use. In Marvell's poem, heat is identified with the single branches attained by pursuit of "mortal Beauty," and with the frenetic competition of the toiling men of stanza 1. The use rendered in this lexicon is antithetical to the greenness of the thought and shade of stanza 6, which is the problematic figure under consideration. If we eliminate this dictionary we have narrowed the potentially relevant sets to two: the general lexicon and the dictionary for the Canticles. Moving on, comparison between these lexicons will show entries for other items in the text. For example, both dictionaries list "garden." Thus, in the larger dictionary, we read:

> [**Garden.**] A place of pleasure for hearbes and flowers, to delight our sences withall. Mat. 26, Gen. 2, 8. In the Hebrew it signifieth a fenced place, because Gardens use to be fenced

with hedges, and because they bee places of pleasure, thence
called Paradises.

2 The Church, wherein the righteous which bee the Lords
Plants do grow, having excellent graces, and bringing forth
excellent workes (as spices & fruit) to delight Christ withall,
that he may love to walke and abide therein. Can. 6, 10. *I went
downe to the Garden of Nuts. Can.* 4, 15.16 and 5, 1. (P. 219)

Though the slight eroticism of the second entry seems to fit Marvell's text, and though this entry might both fit and shed some
light on the idea of "Sacred Plants" growing only among "the
Plants" (of stanza 2), actually the reader would have no reason
to eliminate the entry from the larger dictionary. But notice: the
second entry is drawn from the Song of Songs. This means that of
the three *"materiall"* uses preserved in the larger dictionary, the
user may understand one in the context of the smaller dictionary.
In other words, of the two possible ways of understanding the
word "garden" within the larger culture of biblical discourse (as
rendered in this single source) one is restricted to discourse in or
on the Song of Songs.

Turning to the lexicon for the Canticles, we read as follows:

[Garden]
THE Kingdome of Heaven, where Christ (as man) remaineth
in glory till the last judgment, when the marriage betweene him
and his Church shall be accomplished fully. Cant. 5, 1. *I am
come into my Garden, my Sister, my Spouse.*

2 The true Church heere upon earth, which with firme
faithfulnesse keepes her-selfe onely to Christ, (like an enclosed
Garden) admitting none other to enter, reserving all the fruites
for him. *Can.* 4, 12. *My Spouse is as a Garden enclosed.* (P. 833)

We find that the larger dictionary asserts that "garden" may be
understood within the context of one of its smaller members, and
that in that narrower context, interpretation of the text hinges
upon direct quotation and paraphrase of a single sentence from
the Song of Songs. Hobbes would be likely to say that these as-

sociative links between figures have a kind of logic to them; the "Trayne of Thoughts" linking the various figures and ideas together may appear to us arbitrary or even absurd, especially to one untrained in religious tradition and vocabulary.

According to Hobbes, connections between words and ideas may appear absurd, but, with effort, one may find "out the way of it." In this view, Hobbes and Wilson are in accord: individuals can misconstrue a text. What both men sought was a method applicable in ordinary discourse for dealing with the problem of language. Perhaps every reader has his own reading, his own idea of Marvell's "Garden." But, as Wilson points out, it is when interpretations are made public—"vocall or preaching"—that checks are called for. For "the poem on its own terms" appears to mean the text as I construe it without the chastening and potentially useful mediation of linguistic evidence. One need not surrender the private experience to see and act upon what Wilson is getting at: the public pronouncement. Not someone's idea of Marvell's text, but what the text means, in the context of the most pertinent examples available.

But Wilson's method seems to me to hint in the right direction. We must destroy the idea that we can limit the set of dictionaries. The expanding nature of the work reminds the critic that he can build his own dictionary, he can acquire a knowledge of the language used by the artist of the culture he is studying. Apropos of this point, Wilson specifically attacks the distinction between definition and exegesis; he insists that we are always talking about the potentialities of language as it is actually used by men. There is nothing sacrosanct about the term dictionary. We may easily multiply examples of the kind found in Wilson. For instance, in Wilson's dictionary for the Song of Songs, we read:

[**Greene Bed**] See Bed.
[**Our Bed is greene**] The procreation of . . . *Our Bed is greene*. (See previous extract taken from Wilson, p. 825.)

And in *An Open Paraphrase upon the Song of Solomon,* Bishop Hall writes:

The Church

My wel-
beloved, be
hold, thou art
faire & plea-
sant: also our
bed is greene.

Nay then (O my sweet savior and spouse) thou alone art that faire and pleasant one indeed, from whose fulnesse I confesse to have received al this little measure of my spiritual beauty: and behold, from this our mutuall delight, & heavenly conjunction, there ariseth a plentifull and florishing increase of thy faithfull ones, in all places, & through all times.[10]

The point is that we have more avenues to "mediating evidence" than dictionaries, in the formal sense of the word. Once we admit that our impressions may need supplements and checks, we have the riches of the "Lord's Vineyard" at our command. "In the beginning was the Word," and it looks as if the word will be with us at the finish, too. That being the case, it seems to me not overly generous for us to make room (among the more fashionable readings of the text) for Marvell's "idea" of "The Garden." In order to do this, we must know what uses are possible, and, hence, we must expand our body of potentially relevant examples: we as critics cannot evaluate uses of whose existence we are unaware.

Wilson's *Christian Dictionary* enhances the decision-making process in at least two ways. First, by discriminating among various lexical sets Wilson draws attention to the particular associations of each; he reminds the reader that the Song of Songs was a "*darkesome* Booke" whose language concerned "*the most sweete and straight conjunction betweene Christe and his Church*" (p. 823). With respect to the color "green," Wilson's glosses produce a configuration of mystical and ecstatic associations applying to a set of related figures: green, shade, bed:

[Bed of Spices] The church, where graces (like sweet Spices in a Bed) do grow. Cant. 6, 1. *He is gone into the Bed of Spices.* (P. 825)

Green refers one to "greene bed," which in turn relates to "Bed of Spices," and hence, to ecclesiastical as well as erotic associations. Closely linked to these figures, also, are those of oral indulgence.

In stanza 5 of Marvell's poem the garden does not devour man. Quite the opposite, it offers itself to the passive speaker in a series of self-immolating acts. The speaker experiences the pleasure of the garden in the form of enjoyment in eating and drinking of fruit and wine. In the context we are discussing numerous associations would occur:

> [To Eate pleasant fruite] To be present with the Church, to feast and make merry with her, in communicating of her graces. *Cant.* 4, 16. *Let my welbeloved come to his Garden, and Eate his pleasant fruite.* (P. 831)

The oral satisfactions of the Spouse was thought to represent the spiritual transport of the mystical state. In Robert Crofts' *The Lover* (1638), the Beloved invites his Spouse into "his faire garden, to eate, drinke, . . . bee merry, and to enjoy his presence forever, Cant., 5." [11] And in *A Treatise of Mentall Prayer* (1627), Alonso Roderigues suggests that in this eating and drinking the Spouse becomes "inebriated . . . taken, and absorpt in God" in such a way that all awareness of the present world disappears. Further, he sees in this eating and drinking the emblematic traces of the three stages of mental prayer:

> In this most speciall kind of *Prayer*, and *Contemplation*, S. *Bernard* placeth three degrees. The first, he compareth to *Eating*, the second to *Drinking* (which is done with more facility & delight than *Eating*, for there is no trouble in the chewing) and the third, in being *Inebriated*. And he brings to this purpose, that of the Spouse in the *Canticles, Comedite amici, & bibite, & inebriamini charissimi.* He sayth first, come *Eate;* secondly, come and *Drinke;* and thirdly, come and *Inebriate* your selves, with this Love.[12]

One element always stressed in such examples is the passivity of the speaker in this perfect enjoyment in love. Here, there is no press or rush or heat, such as that depicted in stanza 4 of "The Garden":

> When we have run our Passions heat,
> Love hither makes his best retreat.

> The *Gods,* that mortal Beauty chase,
> Still in a Tree did end their race.
> *Apollo* hunted *Daphne* so,
> Only that She might Laurel grow.
> And *Pan* did after *Syrinx* speed,
> Not as a Nymph, but for a Reed.
>   (*Ll.* 25–32)

The full irony of this passage unfolds in the contrast between this overheated and frustrating physical approach to love and the marvelous rewards of passivity depicted in stanza 5. Marvell draws upon the traditional associations of the Canticles tradition, with its image cluster of garden, shade, fruit, tree. In this context the passivity of the Spouse is the appropriate emotional stance of one who was thought to be the type of heaven's Bride. As she enjoys herself beneath the tree she was thought to represent the recipient of the shade of Grace:

> [Shaddow] Jesus Christ, from whom the faithfull receive rest, peace, and refreshing against hot persecutions of the world, the fiery temptations of Sathan, and burning heat of guiltinesse for sinne . . . are refreshed by the Shaddow of a Tree. *Cant.* 2, 3. *Under his Shadow had I delight, and sate down.* (P. 844)

Analogues to this passage are numerous in the literature and iconography of the Renaissance and seventeenth century. In Quarles's *Emblemes* (1635), for example, an engraving based on the same text depicts the Spouse, seated beneath an apple tree, gazing up at Divine Cupid, who is nailed with arms outstretched to the boughs of the tree. This tree was thought to shade man from the oppressive "Sun of the Law":

> See, here's a Shadow found; The humane nature
>   Is made th'Umbrella to the Deity,
> To catch the Sun-beames of thy just Creator;
>   Beneath this Covert thou maist safely lie:
>   Permit thine eyes to climbe this fruitfull Tree,

> As quick *Zacheus* did, and thou shalt see
> A Cloud of dying flesh betwixt those Beames and thee.[13]

As we can see, then, the graphic representation of Bride and Bride-
groom, with its sacramental overtones, brings together associations
of both Old and New Testament events and meanings, which
merge with the established ideas of erotic sensuousness.

So the second major value of a work like Wilson's *Dictionary*
is that it guides the reader to the larger repository of the Canticles
tradition, from which its own expanding number of examples are
drawn. In this context the "idea" of Marvell's "Garden" assumes a
range of associations which might escape even the most patient
modern reader. We find, for example, that the contrast in the text
between heat and shade is a subtle handling of a traditional theme,
juxtaposing garden and wilderness, sun and shade. The theme re-
emerges in stanza 9, with its reminder that the sun in this "fragrant
Zodiack" is a "milder Sun," a fact which reinforces the thematic
treatment of time. For "the skilful Gardner" who has drawn this
particular "Dial" has made a floral invention entirely "new." All of
time and all of human activity have been redefined, seen in a new
perspective:

> How well the skilful Gardner drew
> Of flow'rs and herbes this Dial new;
> Where from above the milder Sun
> Does through a fragrant Zodiack run;
> And, as it works, th' industrious Bee
> Computes its time as well as we.
> How could such sweet and wholesome Hours
> Be reckon'd but with herbs and flow'rs!
>
> (*Ll.* 65–72)

The heat of competition ends only in the single branch or "short
and narrow-verged shade." The heat of the Law, and of a purely
secular understanding of man's place in nature, contrasts with the
cool repose of Grace ("Here at the Fountains sliding foot/Or at
some Fruit-trees mossy root"). But in a subtle shift, competition is

replaced by productive industry; the speaker is passive in relation
to the garden forms, not intrinsically slothful. Further, the once
admired solitude of the early stanzas has subtly been replaced.
Implicitly, the speaker lays claim to the communion with God
enjoyed by Adam before the creation of Eve: "Such [as described
in stanzas 5 through 7] was that happy Garden-state,/While Man
there walk'd without a Mate." Though it was beyond the purely
"Mortal's share" to enjoy such company, the speaker has experienced it nevertheless. He does so by relying not on his own physical prowess, like the pagan gods in their pursuit of "mortal Beauty,"
or like the vain because "busie Companies of Men." Human solitari-
ness, when properly directed, populates the universe. And this is
more than a statement about the powers of the imagination. In the
final stanza Marvell suggests that his speaker has reordered his
understanding of creation itself. He is like "th' industrious Bee"
because he invests his time as well as the bee, but also as well as
someone else: the use of "we" is not royal (notice the "I" of stanzas
1, 2, 3, and 5, and the "My" of stanza 7). Rather, it restates the
implicit assertion of stanzas 5 through 8, namely, that the speaker
enjoys communion and satisfactions of an extraordinary nature.
Partly, this is a statement with allegorical significance declaring the
speaker's presence for all eternity with the congregation: the
Church as Bride. But the more pertinent application of appropriate
associations concerns the anagogic meaning of these garden figures.
Marvell's speaker enjoys the same passivity of St. Teresa's, in *Conceptions of the Love of God* (1571–73). St. Teresa is writing in
paraphrase on the text, "I sat down under his shadow with great
delight, and his fruit was sweet to my taste," which for her describes the highest state of mystical union: "A person in this state
has no need for any purpose, to move her hand, or to rise (I mean
by this to practise meditation), for the Lord is giving her the fruit
from the apple-tree with which she compares her Beloved: He
picks it and cooks it and almost eats it for her." [14]

In the context of the Song of Songs, the self-immolation of the
garden forms (overlooked by critics of the Freudian, Jungian,
Riechian, and Rogerian schools) represents the felt belief that the
Sacrifice bestowed on man—freely and fully—benefits he could not
earn with his natural powers. Critics have noted that the speaker

seems to long for death, and that, in fact, in stanza 7 he appears to experience a desired separation of soul from body:

> Here at the Fountains sliding foot,
> Or at some Fruit-trees mossy root,
> Casting the Bodies Vest aside,
> My Soul into the boughs does glide:
> There like a Bird it sits, and sings,
> Then whets, and combs its silver Wings;
> And, till prepar'd for longer flight,
> Waves in its Plumes the various Light.
>
> (*Ll. 49–56*)

During the poem the soul's movement from contact with the world (stanzas 1 and 2) ends in the fantasy of transport into the branches of the tree itself. This is that mystical death, thought to entail a suspension of awareness of the surrounding world. The soul sheds its clothing of flesh, and "like a Bird it sits, and sings." The emotional content of the thematic development was traditionally one of regeneration; in the soul's ascent was a miniature history recapitulating the Passion. Wilson glosses the figure in this way:

> [**Birds singing**] Pleasant and delightfull times, such as be to the body, the spring time after Winter, when Birds make melody, chirp, and sing sweetly; and to the Soule, the times which follow effectuall vocation to Christ, when the bitter and sharpe winter of an unregenerate estate being over, the Soule is all replenished with comfortable graces and motions of the holy Spirit. Cant. 2, 12. *The time of the singing of Birds is come.* Peace and joy in the Holy Ghost. (P. 825)

The material of the closing stanzas depicts the speaker's subsequent safe return from ecstasy; but he returns to a renewed awareness of the emblematic world around him. Death is followed by transfiguration. This sharpened consciousness is the emotional and moral (or tropological) understanding of the "milder Sun" of Grace. In the "green Shade" of that "Sun" all men may see their "hopes as in a Glass." The final "we" refers not only to a generalized community to which the speaker belongs, but also to an apprehension shared by speaker and audience. The enclosed garden of the soul is at once microcosm and macrocosm, "Annihilating all that's made/To a green Thought in a green Shade."

I am not suggesting that Marvell had all or only associations from the Canticles tradition in mind when he wrote "The Garden." (We must learn to distinguish the meaning of an author's text from the psychic acts coincident with its generation; the former is open to rational inquiry, the latter is not.) Nor does the approach to explication suggested in this essay logically preclude a critic's interest in personal impressions based on one's autobiography. It attempts rather to offer an alternative to dependence on the arbitrary limits of autobiography. We possess our biographies by the simple fact (as distinct from virtue) of our existence; we all have our own "meanings" and fantasies and aberrations. With this thought in mind I suggest that in the system outlined by Wilson such a statement as, "Marvell's 'Garden' means so and so," need not occur. Indeed, coming as it so often does with suspicious swiftness, without the steadying influence of "mediating evidence," it is subject to the limits of the first of Wilson's two approaches to language: prayer. We can if we wish reserve unmediated visions for angels and saints, and for the silent reflections of Everyman. The critic's public service involves (often oppressive) temporal delay, as he awaits acquisition and processing of information, and determination on what materials are relevant and what not. Father Ong has written that print is the "word literally locked in space." [15] His assertion is especially relevant to a period like the seventeenth century, with its strong interest in the emblem. We may add to Father Ong's remark that print always locks a particular word in a particular context, and that the resulting gestalt is a miniature but particular event. Though locked in the space of the page, the word nevertheless moves in time, subject to the vagaries of shifting contexts, temperaments, and intellectual vogues. As the word passes through time it is subject to the contaminations of anachronistic interpretations: "it cannot be denied, but that there are many who, spider-like, suck the poyson" of twentieth-century obsessions from the "sweet and precious flowers" of Marvell's stanza 5, and from many other texts, which are locked helplessly in the silence of the page. But this is no cause for despair. For just as the word passes through time, subject to certain dangers, so also does it come with the potential power to enrich. Surely that power is more accessible to us if, with Wilson, we both enlarge the boundaries of our lexicon, and narrow our choices among the possible glosses with historical authenticity and critical tact.

Samuel Johnson
and the Eighteenth Century

The Selection and Use
of the Illustrative Quotations
in Dr. Johnson's Dictionary

GWIN J. *and* RUTH A. KOLB

OF THE BOOKS which Dr. Johnson marked up while compiling his *Dictionary* (1755), at least eleven whole or partial works are known to survive. They include: Bryan Duppa's *Holy Rules and Helps to Devotion both in Prayer and Practice* (1675);[1] Robert Burton's *Anatomy of Melancholy* (1676); Sir Matthew Hale's *Primitive Origination of Mankind* (1677); Izaak Walton's *Life of Dr. Sanderson . . . to Which is added some Short Tracts . . . Written by the . . . Bishop* (1678); one volume of Robert South's *Sermons* (1692);[2] John Norris's *Collection of Miscellanies: Consisting of Poems, Essays, and Letters* (1699); Sir Francis Bacon's *Works* (1740);[3] Isaac Watts's *Logick* (1745); William Warburton's edition (1747) of Shakespeare's plays;[4] Michael Drayton's *Works* (1748); and one volume of *The Works of the Most Celebrated Minor Poets* (1749), containing the verse of Dorset, Halifax, and Garth.[5] Taken as a group, the volumes form a valuable, hitherto neglected source of information about the creation of the great lexicon. A complete examination of the materials would involve a recording of all the words which Johnson singled out for inclusion in the *Dictionary,* a notation of all the other comments and markings he made in the volumes, a check of all the words and contextual passages against those in the *Dictionary*, and a comparison of every illustrative quotation with its counterpart in the published version of the lexicon.

The present essay, which is offered as an earnest of a more comprehensive study, derives from a sharply limited, though substantial, undertaking. We limited our investigation to six of the eleven works named above—specifically, Duppa's *Holy Rules and Helps to Devotion*, Burton's *Anatomy of Melancholy*, Hale's *Primitive Origination of Mankind*, South's *Sermons*, Watts's *Logick*, and *The Works of the Most Celebrated Minor Poets*. We recorded all the words distinguished by Johnson in these volumes together with all his incidental comments and markings. The total number of words comes to almost four thousand and includes entries under every letter of the eighteenth-century alphabet except *X*, which, so Johnson declared under *X* in the *Dictionary*, "though found in Saxon words, begins no word in the English language." After alphabetizing our cards, we compared each word (as well as its author reference[s]) beginning with *A*, *E*, *P*, *and U–V* with the corresponding parts of the *Dictionary*. Finally, we concentrated our attention on approximately a hundred passages in South's *Sermons* (scattered rather evenly among the four letters we had selected) and some forty (also divided fairly equally) in Watts's *Logick* which made their way into print, and carefully examined the reception accorded them by Johnson or his amanuenses or his printer. These narrow, unscientific samplings comprise, then, the basis for our tentative generalizations about Johnson's selection and use of the illustrative quotations in his *Dictionary*.

First of all, as he "applied" himself, with "sluggish resolution," "to the perusal" of English writers,[6] Johnson established and maintained a systematic procedure for indicating the words and passages to be copied by his assistants. As earlier commentators have pointed out,[7] he underlined the specific words, drew short, perpendicular lines to denote the beginning and end of the illustrative passages, and wrote the first letters of the words in the margins of the books. Later when they had finished their transcriptions, the amanuenses presumably struck through these letters. Sometimes Johnson noted, by the use of parentheses, deletions within the individual passages; once in a while he apparently forgot to underline a word (or phrase) or to mark off a passage or to place a first letter in the margin.

His reading was obviously attentive and evidently rapid. He rarely stopped to gloss portions of his text. Of the six volumes we have examined, only Hale's *Primitive Origination of Mankind* elicited several extended responses. Four examples (out of a total of six) will serve to show the range and character of his annotation. Affected by the incongruity between Hale's insistence on the absolute power and goodness of God and the comparable quality of some but not all of his creations (The Almighty, says Hale, "hath made some Beings of that perfection, that Omnipotence it self cannot make them one grain perfecter, that they are but in the very next degree of perfection to himself, and cannot have the addition of one grain more to the excellence of their nature"), Johnson jotted in the margin, "It will follow that he hath made all so" (p. 92). Again, reflecting on the implications of remarks in Hale on the eternal duration of the world (part of the specific passage reads: "if the World were not eternal, but created in some certain *Epocha* or Period, it could never have been at all, because an eternal duration must necessarily have anteceded the first production of the World; and that Supposition excludeth the possibility of such its production"), he reacted tersely: "This argument will hold equally against the writing which I now write" (p. 97). A third comment discloses his awareness of conflicting notions regarding geological formations and changes. Whereas Hale posited a daily increase of "more dry Land" on the Earth, with "the Seas" growing "narrower and deeper," Thomas Burnet, as Johnson averred in his marginal note "This is contrary to Burnet" (p. 187), expressed an opposing view in his *Sacred Theory of the Earth* (2d ed. [1691]: Book 1, chap. 10), which, like Hale's work, was also a source of quotations in the *Dictionary*. And a fourth comment displays still another sort of attention and knowledge. Discussing the relationships between new settlers and the old inhabitants of a country, Hale stated that "where the Accessions are but thin and sparring, and scattered among the Natives of the Country where they come, and are driven to conform themselves unto their Customs for their very subsistence, safety and entertainment, it falls out that the very first Planters do soon degenerate in their Habits,

Customs and Religion; as a little Wine poured into a great Vessel of Water loseth it self." In Johnson's opinion, precisely "This happened to the English in Ireland, they made court to the Natives by imitating them. Spenser's Dacius [?]" (p. 197).

Such extra-professional musings, to repeat, however interesting to later readers and typical of him, were quite exceptional for the lexicographer who initially "resolved to leave neither words nor things unexamined" [8] but who subsequently was forced to set decidedly strict bounds to his work. Few and far between, too, were his other unusual scribbles: four corrections of patent errors in printing ("son of son" for "son of God" and "idtrude" for "intrude," for instance), three strike-throughs revealing second thoughts about words to be transcribed (*mouldy*, for example), two lonely x's opposite passages that seemingly held special significance for him. On a number of other occasions, he made clear his choice of spellings—"spite" instead of "spight," "clue" rather than "clew," and the like.

The principles underlying Johnson's selection of quotations appear, on the foundation of our restricted induction, to coincide rather closely with the summarizing statements he made in the Preface about his practice. Everywhere he seems to have kept pretty firmly in mind his announced intention of proving, wherever proof could be secured, the existence of words in the ample middle range of the complete English vocabulary—with emphasis on "the diction of common life," as he called it in describing Shakespeare's language[9]—and of demonstrating the variety and subtlety of the senses conveyed by these words. Furthermore, he regularly chose passages that, as he says, contained either formal definitions of terms being elucidated or explanations "equivalent" to definitions; and, to anticipate our later remarks and again in consonance with his own comments,[10] he employed these quotations as supplements to his own definitions—sometimes, in fact, as the sole means of discriminating particular meanings. Many passages from Watts's work—the urge to call it a logical choice is irresistible—exemplify this habit. We cite, for instance, the entry under *argumentation* in the *Dictionary*, which reads: "Reasoning; the act of reasoning"; and then immediately on the next line: "*Argumentation* is that operation of the mind, whereby we infer one proposition from two or more propositions premised. Or it is the drawing a conclusion, which before was unknown, or doubtful, from some propositions more known and evident; so when we have judged that matter cannot think, and that the mind of man doth think, we conclude, that therefore the mind of man is not matter. *Watts's Logick.*" And we can mention, in addition, the entries under *apprehension* and *essence,* where, instead of attempting a definition himself of the most general sense of the term, he simply writes "1." and inserts an explanatory passage from Watts.

Moreover, in his selections Johnson was often concerned, as he asserted in the Preface, to make an illustrative quotation serve a double purpose—first and foremost, of exhibiting the significa-tion of a word; second, of conveying some kind of refreshment or instruction to his presumed reader; he had hoped, it will be re-called, to include "all that was pleasing or useful in *English* litera-ture." [11] Not surprisingly, many of the marked passages in South's *Sermons* exhibit forthrightly the precepts of prudence and piety he was intent on garnering from the divine branch of English letters. "Does any thing shine so bright as *Vertue,* and that even in the Eyes of those who are void of it? For hardly shall you find any one so bad, but he desires the Credit of *being Thought,* what his Vice will not let *him be*" (p. 31). Or: "let every Believer comfort himself in this high Privilege, That in the great things, that con-cern his eternal Peace, he is not left to *stand* or fall by the uncertain directions of his own judgment" (p. 93).

So ambitious an aspiration regarding the scope of his word-book brought thousands upon thousands of extracts in its train. The eight authors we mentioned at the outset of this paper, none of them, unlike Shakespeare, Dryden, Milton, the Bible, and Pope, among the most lavish contributors to the work, nevertheless afforded Johnson almost 4,000 passages, as we've already noted. Our examination of the four sample letters *A, E, P,* and *U–V* shows, too, that letter by letter less than half of the quotations finally appeared in the *Dictionary*—only 477 of the total of 1,031, to be exact. Extrapolating these proportions and applying them to the entire project, one can quickly understand why Johnson, initially the indefatigable collector, might eventually decide that "the bulk of my volumes would fright away the student." [12]

A simple analysis of the figures comprising the entire number of passages under discussion here also suggests the operation of additional if subordinate principles in Johnson's selection of illustrative quotations. Excepting—and definitely puzzling exceptions they are—the passages (only 52 altogether) from Burton's *Anatomy of Melancholy*, "the only book," of course, "that ever took him out of bed two hours sooner than he wished to rise," [13] and those from Duppa's *Holy Rules and Helps to Devotion*, about which no information is apparently available, the relative number of quotations from our eight authors correlate significantly (even when we take into account the differences in the length of their writings) though not universally, on the one hand, with his intention of preferring authorities of major rank and, on the other, with what we know about his subsequent critical estimates of these specific men. Remarks in the *Lives of the Poets* disclose his measured evaluation of the poetical productions of Dorset ("the effusions of a man of wit"), Halifax ("of which a short time has withered the beauties"), and Garth ("No passages fall below mediocrity, and few rise much above it"),[14] which are drawn on for 40, 53, and 354 passages, respectively. Also in the *Lives* and elsewhere[15] he revealed his warm esteem for Isaac Watts's prose publications, including the book on *Logick*, which he marked for 1012 quotations. *The Primitive Origination of Mankind* contributed almost 300 more, 1,302; its author, Matthew Hale, Johnson once described as a "great lawyer" who "knew a great many other things, and has written upon other things." [16] Finally, Robert South, according to Johnson's assessment, belonged in style, despite notable defects, to "the best" of English pulpit writers; and the substance of his sermons, as is well documented, exercised a powerful attraction on the lexicographer.[17] His contribution was 1,202 passages. Perhaps of consequence, it may be added, South is the only author in our four-letter sample whose extracts in the published *Dictionary* outnumber those (the precise figures are 201 as against 110) eliminated during its preparation. From the same evidence, it might be possible to infer that Johnson, as he occasionally implies in the *Plan* and Preface,[18] was perpetually a moralist as he went about the job of choosing and later discarding quotations for his *Dictionary*.

Though he nowhere alludes to it, still another standard operates so often in his selection—and subsequent use—of passages as to deserve at least brief recognition. This criterion, which may be dubbed a principle of lexicographical economy or efficiency, helps to explain how he was able to do the work of forty Frenchmen in eight or nine years; and it consists of the display of two words or more in a single quotation. We observed repeated instances of the practice while noting the nearly four thousand words included in our larger survey and again, with a sharply reduced frequency, when we were checking selected passages from South and Watts against relevant items in the *Dictionary*. The same quotation from the former, for example (reading: "how often may we meet with those, who are one while courteous, civil, and obliging . . . but within a small time after, are so supercilious, sharp, troublesome, fierce, and exceptious, that they are not only short of the true Character of Friendship, but become the very Sores and Burthens of Society?" [pp. 97–98]), is used to illustrate the senses of four different words, namely, *courteous, exceptious, sharp,* and *supercilious;* another passage serves to exhibit the meanings of three different words; and fourteen other extracts clarify the senses of twenty-eight other entries.

Before turning from Johnson's choice of quotations to his treatment of those that actually appear in the wordbook, we should stress the patent fact that, his remark in the Preface notwithstanding,[19] he did not always drink deep from *"the wells of English undefiled."* Robert Burton is the solitary Renaissance man in our sample group of eight, and his *Anatomy,* as we have pointed out, is the repository of only 52 of the approximately 4,000 quotations we have brought together. Our collection is accidental and rather arbitrary, to be sure; nonetheless, its claim to partial representativeness is supported by the preeminent positions of Dryden (especially), Pope, and Swift[20]—to list only three post-Renaissance authors—as sources of passages in the *Dictionary*.

What now can be said of the usage given the authorities whose gems of eloquence and elegance were marked for inclusion in the lexicon? Part of the answer to this question has been suggested already: a very large number of the extracts—more than half, perhaps, of the total collection—never saw the light of print, their sole visible sign being the extraordinarily well-stocked mind that so delights the readers of Boswell's *Life* and Johnson's other works today. Along with the discarding of quotations went the loss of a fair number of words; we have noted, for example, the absence of *eloquently, preferrible, peripateticism, viciousness, unaccessible,* and *unexcusable* in the published work. Of those passages which did survive the ordeal of "expunging," as Johnson labeled it,[21] many offered explanations that were supplementary to the lexicographer's own definitions, and a sizable percentage performed individually the duties of midwifery for the senses of two or more words.

Another part of the answer to the question is provided by various remarks in the Preface, particularly those which assert the continued interspersion of "verdure and flowers" among "the dusty desarts of barren philology," defend the "multiplicity" of examples by reference to complex "diversities of signification," and acknowledge candidly the "mutilation" of authorial meanings produced by necessary alterations and "hasty truncation." [22] And still a third part of the answer, mostly but not entirely confirmatory of Johnson's own statements, results from our comparison of sample passages in South and Watts (altogether about 140, to repeat) with the versions of the same passages that appear in the *Dictionary*.

Remembering Johnson's emphasis on his dismemberment of quotations, we were pleasantly surprised, first of all, to discover complete identity, excluding italics and capitalization (it will be recalled that only proper nouns within quotations in the *Dictionary* are capitalized) but including punctuation, between some marked and published passages—for instance, in the passage (illustrating *Apostle*) from Watts (p. 48) which reads (in the *Dictionary*): "We know but a small part of the notion of an *apostle,* by knowing barely that he is sent forth"; and in another (Watts, p. 81; illustrating *Enrichment*) which runs (in the *Dictionary*): "It is a vast hindrance to the *enrichment* of our understandings, if we spend too much of our time and pains among infinites and unsearchables." We were impressed, too, by the striking resemblances between a larger number of original passages and *Dictionary* versions; in this group (we cite as examples the extracts from Watts [pp. 10, 359, 58] under *essence, parenthesis,* and *univocal;* and the quotation from South [p. 644] under *undauntedly*), only a very few words or a short phrase prevents the original and the printed forms from being substantively identical.

Nevertheless, Johnson's general warning in the Preface about his compression and modification of the illustrative passages is fundamentally accurate. Aside from the minor kind we have just described, the changes he made fall into four distinct groups, three of them easily predictable. First, he frequently eliminated the opening portion—sometimes short, sometimes long—before granting it his approval. Thus, at one extreme, he cut only the initial *So* in this extract (under *Unit*) from Watts (p. 117): "So *Units* are the integral Parts of any large *Number*"; at the other extreme, he shortened this passage (under *Perpetuity;* from South, p. 516)—"It is indeed a real Trapan upon it; feeding it with Colours, and Appearances, instead of Arguments; and driving the very same Bargain, which *Jacob* did with *Esau*: A *Mess of Pottage* for a *Birth-right;* a present Repast for a Perpetuity"—to simply the aphoristic "A mess of pottage for a birth-right, a present repast for a *perpetuity*." Secondly, as can be quickly guessed, he performed the same surgery at the end of a passage. Thus, the extract under *Etymology* from Watts (p. 50) reading "If the Meaning of a Word could be learn'd by its Derivation or Etymology yet the original Derivation of Words is oftentimes very dark and unsearchable" appears in its printed form minus the "and unsearchable." Likewise, this sentence from South (p. 373) illustrating one sense of *Parabolical*—"The whole Scheme of these Words is Figurative, as being a Parabolical Description of God's vouchsafing to the World the Invaluable Blessing of the Gospel, by the Similitude of a *King*, with great Magnificence, Solemnizing his *Son's Marriage*"—ends in the *Dictionary* with the word *King*. We assume, it should be said here, but have no evidence to prove that Johnson also simply cut both the beginnings and ends of some quotations.

Thirdly, and this sort of change occurs more frequently than any other in our sample, Johnson deleted and sometimes recast substantial internal sections of the passages he had earlier marked for transcription. His alterations usually consist of extensive, artfully devised omissions. For instance, this passage from Watts (pp.

344-45; illustrating *Economical*)—"in *moral, political, aeconomical* Affairs, having proposed the *Government of Self*, a *Family*, a *Society* or a *Nation*, in order to their best Interest, we consider and search out what are the *proper Laws, Rules* and *Means* to effect it"—is pared to the uncluttered "In *economical* affairs, having proposed the government of a family, we consider the proper means to effect it." Similarly, this one from South (pp. 615-16; under *Alteration*)—"I am sure, no other *Alteration* will satisfie *Dissenting Consciences*, no, nor this neither, very long, without an utter Abolition of all that looks like Order or Government in the Church"—becomes the crisp "No other *alteration* will satisfy; nor this neither, very long, without an utter abolition of all order." Now and then the editorial revisions include a little rewriting, all of it, presumably, by Johnson himself. For example, a passage (under *Plenary*) from Watts (p. 355) which reads—"The Method of treating a Subject should be *plenary* or *full, so that nothing may be wanting;* nothing which is necessary or proper should be omitted"—becomes in the *Dictionary*: "A treatise on a subject should be *plenary* or full, so that nothing may be wanting, nothing which is proper omitted." Again, another quotation from the same author (p. 122; under *Page*) reading—"So if a *Printer* were to consider the several Parts of a *Book*, he must divide it into *Sheets*, the *Sheets* into *Pages*, the *Pages* into *Lines*, and the *Lines* into *Letters*"—is condensed in its published form to: "A printer divides a book into sheets, the sheets into *pages*, the *pages* into lines, and the lines into letters."

The fourth and final group of changes varies from the third only because in them Johnson adjusted each of the original extracts to illustrate the meanings of two or more words. He evidently made his alterations at different times when he was considering different parts of the alphabet; for only this kind of hypothesis seems to explain the otherwise curious fact that none of these double- or triple-functioning passages closely resembles its counterpart(s). A quotation from South (p. 575), for example, which displays both *Even* and *Reckoning*, appears thus in its authorial version: "It is with a Man and his Conscience, as with one Man, and another; amongst whom we use to say, that *Even*

Reckoning makes *lasting Friends;* and the way to make Reckonings *even,* I am sure, is to make them often." Here is the version included under *Even:* "*Even* reckoning makes lasting friends; and the way to make reckonings *even,* I am sure, is to make them often." But the version under *Reckoning* is something else again: "It is with a man and his conscience, as with one man and another; even *reckoning* makes lasting friends; and the way to make *reckonings* even, is to make them often." A much more elaborate—and longer—instance of the same sort of revision is provided by the quotation from South (p. 246) which clarifies the meanings of three words, *harmlessness, mischievousness,* and *pliableness.*

In examining at restricted secondhand this mass of editorial labors, we have not noticed any violent wrenching of the senses of illustrative passages, although Johnson, of course, proclaimed such distortions in the Preface[23] and although we therefore believe that certain perversions must have occurred. On the contrary, we have been consistently struck by the deftness, the sure touch, the striking faithfulness to the original sentiments, of Johnson's revising hand. His admirers have always known that, both in his talk and in his writings, he was a master of the pithy, epigrammatic maxim; the same rare gifts are often manifest, we are happy to testify, in his manipulation of other men's prose. Our scrutiny indicates moreover, it should be stressed, a steady—and usually successful—effort to embrace as many authorities as possible in his illustrative quotations: when faced with alternative extracts for one or more senses of the same word, he appears to have chosen unhesitatingly quotations by different writers rather than several by one person.

Summarizing briefly, in conclusion, our sober yet scarcely impartial view of Johnson's selection, treatment, and ultimate use of the illustrative quotations in the *Dictionary,* we should say, first, that, on the whole, he did what he said he did—and several noteworthy things besides; and, second, that, since in the Preface he failed to do full justice to himself as collector, chooser, and reviser, modern investigators are bound to return from a visit to his reconstructed workshop with enhanced respect and admiration for the imaginative drudgery of the Great Lexicographer. Back in

1955 James Sledd and Gwin Kolb wrote at the end of their book on the *Dictionary*: "The magnitude of his achievement remains." [24] In 1971, after an examination of some of his illustrative passages, we are inclined to change "remains" to "increases."

Samuel Johnson's Plan *and* Preface *to* The Dictionary: *The Growth of a Lexicographer's Mind*

HOWARD D. WEINBROT

THE RECEPTION of Johnson's *Plan of an English Dictionary* (1747) was largely favorable.[1] Dodsley's *Museum*, no. 36 (1747), observes that it "has excited great Expectation," and has given "universal Satisfaction" not only to the generality of readers, but to its generous and noble patron so elegantly complimented therein.[2] The Earl of Orrery tells Thomas Birch that he has just read the *Plan* "addressed to Lord Chesterfield" and was "much pleased with" it. He regards it as "one of the best that I have ever read," and observes that "the language . . . is good, and the arguments . . . properly and modestly expressed."[3] Boswell insists that "the 'Plan' has not only the substantial merit of comprehension, perspicuity, and precision, but that the language of it is unexceptionably excellent," that it is "altogether free from . . . inflation of style," and that, regarding the passages addressed to Chesterfield, "never was there a more dignified strain of compliment."[4]

Significantly, each of these commentators mentions both Johnson's language and the presence of Chesterfield in the *Plan*. Indeed, those with less happy feelings for it often mention language and Chesterfield as well. Thomas Birch labels its style "flatulent,"[5] and Daniel Wray, who wrote a critique of the *Plan*, alludes to its style as one of "high-scented Flowers." [6] Sir John Hawkins is harsher, insists that Chesterfield is "a smatterer in learning, and in manners a coxcomb," discusses his apparent influence on the *Plan*, observes that Johnson "was betrayed to celebrate [Chesterfield] as the Maecenas of the age," and adds that "the stile and language of that address which his plan includes are little less than adulatory." [7]

Hawkins's estimate of Johnson's prose and attitude toward Chesterfield seems to me accurate. I conjecture that Johnson was in fact betrayed, probably by his own pride and wishes for financial success, and that, partially as a result of the presence of Chesterfield, the *Plan* is unsuccessful as a rhetorical and lexicographical document. I further conjecture that shortly after publishing the *Plan* Johnson realized his error, disliked Chesterfield, his own moral compromise, and some of the beliefs regarding language that were a function of his temperament and circumstances while writing the *Plan*. Consequently, in the later Preface, he disowned several of the concepts and much of the rhetoric of the *Plan*, and certain aspects of his character that allowed the plea to Chesterfield in the first place. Much of this takes place between February of 1749 and February of 1755, when Johnson wrote his "Celebrated Letter" to Chesterfield.

§ 1

In 1755 Chesterfield remarked that he was so used to flattery that he could no longer respond to it.[8] When one examines some of the dedications of works written to him, one can see why. The anonymous author of *The Triumph of Wisdom* (1745) tells Chesterfield that he is inspired and beloved by Wisdom and Poetry; as Lord Lieutenant of Ireland he will bring boundless virtue, harmony, and plenty to the country. Hence, if he should "raise the Poet's Genius to his Theme" the poem will necessarily be "Sacred to TRUTH, to PLATO's, STANHOPE's Praise!" [9] Samuel Madden's long panegyric, *Boulter's Monument* (1745) was not only known to Johnson, but (for the second edition, which never appeared) corrected and improved by him. There Johnson read that

Chesterfield's arrival in Ireland was like an inscribed *"Tablet* from the *Sun,"* that he is "the *Muses* mighty *Lord,* and *Friend"* who would save the country from death and be, at once, a ministering angel, a sweetly singing David, and a powerful Saint "indulg'd by Heav'n" and thus capable of removing ills and restoring health. All nature will conspire to bring the Earl to Ireland, and *"welcome* hither that *exalted Mind!/*The *Friend* of *Merit,* and of *Human-kind!"* [10] Even this praise was modest when compared to that with which Madden graced Chesterfield in 1748, before the first Canto of an as yet unidentified poem. "As to the Dedication," Chesterfield wrote to Madden upon receiving a copy, "I must tell you very sincerely, that I heartily wish you would lower it. . . . The few light, trifling things that I have accidentally scribbled in my youth . . . do by no means entitle me to the compliments which you make me." [11] The author of *The History of the Rise, Progress, and Tendency of Patriotism* (1747) is hardly less discreet than Madden. This writer regards Chesterfield's sole fault as that of monopoly of all the good traits and virtues of "Learning and Politeness, all the talents natural and acquired." Chesterfield is thus a greater orator than Cicero or Demosthenes, and as a poet rivals Horace in his odes.[12] By 1750 this growing group addressing itself to Chesterfield included Teresia Constantia Phillips Muilman, the notorious "Con Phillips" mentioned in 1, vi of Fielding's *Amelia* (1751) as "not least" among courtesans and shrewish women of some repute. In 1721 she accused Chesterfield, in print, of having seduced, impregnated, and abandoned her; her popular *Apology* appeared between 1748 and 1750 and relumed this episode; and in 1750 she published her *Letter* to Chesterfield, a thinly veiled reiteration of her earlier charge regarding Chesterfield's paternity of her child.[13] This *Letter,* according to "a Lady" attempting to refute it, "is universally read." [14]

Not even William Warburton's relatively modest praise—which Chesterfield enjoyed but also rejected as too lavish—can alter the nature of this dedicating mob of largely inferior poets, politicians, and others.[15] Even in 1747, it is odd to find Johnson in such company; but it is odder to find that the speaker of the *Plan* sometimes sounds like Samuel Madden rather than Samuel Johnson, for Johnson is flattering a man whose literary merits he must at least have suspected, if not positively known, were over-rated, whose politics he had probably come to mistrust,[16] and whose serious interest in language was spurious. For instance, considering his relationship with Dodsley in 1747, he may have known that several of Chesterfield's pleasant but flimsy occasional poems would be published in the second edition of Dodsley's *Collection* (1748), the volumes in which his own *London* (1738) and "Prologue Spoken by Mr. Garrick at the Opening of . . . Drury Lane" (1747) also reappeared.[17] And, whether or not he had read these poems at the time, he would have realized that Chesterfield's literary efforts were both meager and trifling. Furthermore, considering Chesterfield's remarks on the manuscript of the *Plan*,[18] he would probably have been aware of what is clear on reading Chesterfield's relevant letters concerning language, and his subsequent numbers of the *World* puffing the *Dictionary*: namely, that the Earl's interest in language was largely a social rather than intellectual matter.[19] Thomas Sheridan's plea to Chesterfield (in 1756) to become an "establisher" of the language and the founder of an academy to *"correct, ascertain, and fix"* the language, was more congenial to Chesterfield's thought than Johnson's.[20] Moreover, though Johnson probably would not have agreed with Horace Walpole's depreciation of Chesterfield as a debater, he probably would have agreed that Chesterfield's talents were overpraised. Samuel Johnson wrote all eight of the speeches attributed to Chesterfield between 1741 and February 1743. These appeared in the Parliamentary Debates of the *Gentleman's Magazine* between 1742 and 1744; upon seeing Chesterfield's *Works* in 1778, Johnson was amused to find that two speeches ascribed to Chesterfield were actually by him: "and the best of it is, they have found out that one is like Demosthenes, and the other like Cicero." [21] Professors Sledd and Kolb have shown that the "Ciceronian" Chesterfield made eight minor suggestions for revision of Johnson's *Plan*, and conclude that "Chesterfield's reputation as a man of wit and sense will not be enhanced" by them.[22] These remarks, Johnson later told Boswell, were solicited only because of Dodsley's urging and his own laziness, and not because of Chesterfield's natural role as patron of those concerned with the English language.[23]

This evidence supports the following hypothesis: in the process of puffing his projected dictionary, Johnson's unwarranted praise of Chesterfield served as a source of compromise, humiliation, and anger against both Chesterfield and himself. Hawkins, for example, reports that "Johnson was so little pleased with his once supposed patron, that he forebore not ever after to speak of him in terms of the greatest contempt." Some of this contempt, Hawkins continues, resulted from their discussions "on the subject of literature, in which [Johnson] found [Chesterfield] so deficient as gave him occasion to repent the choice he had made, and to say, that the labour he had bestowed in his address to Lord Chesterfield resembled that of gilding a rotten post." [24] We can thus see several reasons for Johnson's break from Chesterfield: though Johnson was beginning to emerge from the class of literary hack, he nevertheless joined an undistinguished group seeking noble patronage; he was led to have great literary and financial expectations from a patron who soon emerged as meager of both intellectual and monetary reward; yet shortly after receiving inappropriate praise, the patron apparently refused to see his charge. To the compromise of a proud and scrupulous man, was added compromise for no reward or purpose.

Sledd and Kolb conjecture that about early February of 1749 Johnson had decided not to wait upon Chesterfield any longer.[25] Perhaps as a result of this decision, the *Rambler*, no. 163 (1751), attacks patrons who encourage "expectations which are never to be gratified," and laments the consequent "elation and depression of the heart by needless vicissitudes of hope and disappointment." [26] In the final *Rambler*, no. 208 (1752), Johnson insists that he will not attempt "to overbear [the censures of criticism] by the influence of a patron" (as he seemed to do in the *Plan*), and adds that "having laboured to maintain the dignity of virtue, I will not now degrade it by the meanness of dedication." [27] Indeed, Johnson had already rejected another patron, since, sometime between late March and early May 1750, he refused Bubb Dodington's offer of friendship.[28] Furthermore, *The Vanity of Human Wishes* (1749) was to be reprinted in the fourth volume of Dodsley's *Collection* (1755), much of which was apparently gathered by September 29th, 1753, when Dodsley wrote to Shenstone seeking his contribution and saying: "I am now thinking of

putting my Fourth Volume of Poems to Press." [29] It may have
been within a few months of this date that Johnson changed line
160 of the *Vanity*'s description of the scholar's ills from "Toil,
envy, want, the garret, and the jail," to "the patron and the jail." [30]
And it was probably in mid-May of 1753 that Johnson wrote his
double-edged definition of *patron:* "One who countenances, supports, or protects. Commonly a wretch who supports with insolence, and is paid with flattery." The animus here is directed at
Johnson as well as Chesterfield. This is suggested (among other
ways) in the definition of *flattery* written sometime in late 1749:
it is "False praise; artful obsequiousness; adulation." [31] In the definition of *patron,* I suggest, Johnson is punishing Chesterfield for
his insolence and himself for artful obsequiousness in the *Plan*
(and, perhaps, if Hawkins is correct, at their private meeting?),
an obsequiousness which, given the "defensive pride" Johnson ad-
mitted to,[32] was bound to trouble him. He confesses as much in
the opening paragraphs of the *Plan,* when he characterizes his
pre-Chesterfield conception of the *Dictionary* as a labor which
would not "throw in my way any temptation to disturb the quiet
of others by censure, or my own by flattery." [33] In the "Celebrated
Letter" Johnson again admits his earlier pride in seeking Chesterfield's patronage: "[I] could not forbear to wish that I might boast
myself Le Vainqueur du Vainqueur de la Terre, that I might obtain that regard for which I saw the world contending." He concludes with a contrasting thought: "I have been long awakened
from that Dream of hope, in which I once boasted myself with so
much exultation, My Lord, Your Lordship's most humble Most
Obedient Servant." [34] The last time Johnson thus wrote to Chesterfield was in the *Plan* of the *Dictionary,* part of which included,
Johnson makes clear to Chesterfield and himself, an ephemeral
dream, an empty boast, and false exultation.[35]

When writing the *Plan,* then, Johnson was flattering in order
to acquire the rewards due to the conqueror of the conqueror of
the fashionable world. Republication and redistribution of the
Plan in 1755 was commercially wise but, since Johnson long disowned it, personally embarrassing; and Chesterfield's allusion to
it in his papers in the *World* probably added further embarrass-
ment, particularly since, in the forthcoming Preface to the *Dic-*

tionary Johnson had overtly rejected much of the *Plan*.[36] For instance, he found that his initial notion that "every quotation should be useful to some other end than the illustration of a word," might be morally enlightening, but would require several lifetimes and several tomes. "Such is design, while it is yet at a distance from execution," and so, in the present volumes, the reader will find only "some passages" which will instruct and please him (p. 313). Shortly thereafter, he again portrays the enthusiastic novice and the tones of the *Plan*: when he began this work, he says, he hoped to examine words, things, and ideas, amass huge treasures of learning, triumphantly display his acquisitions to mankind, and thereby cause his dictionary to replace all others. "But these were the dreams of a poet doomed at last to wake a lexicographer" (p. 317). Similarly, he admits that he had formerly "flattered" himself with the possibility of fixing the language and stopping "those alterations which time and change have" previously made in language. Now, however, he fears that he has "indulged expectation which neither reason nor experience can justify" (p. 319). Major parts of the *Plan* dedicated to Chesterfield, Johnson thereby admits, were excessive in their demands on the lexicographer, the products of pride and self-flattery, recordings of a dream, and indulgences of the irrational and naïve.

Moreover, substantial parts of Johnson's audience were encouraged—by Chesterfield—to reread the *Plan* and regard it as a definitive statement of the *Dictionary's* guiding principles. In *The World*, no. 100 (1754), Chesterfield insists that Johnson's *Plan* is a proof of his ability to bring the work "as near to perfection as any one man could do. Nothing," he continues, "can be more rationally imagined, or more accurately and elegantly expressed. I therefore recommend the previous perusal of it to all those who intend to buy the dictionary." [37] Apparently Dr. Matthew Maty, already a protégé of Chesterfield, did apply the *Plan's* theory to the *Dictionary's* practice as portrayed in the Preface, and duly noted Johnson's overlapping yet clearly different attitudes in the two works. In his *Journal britannique* for July–August of 1755, he insists that Johnson should have reprinted the *Plan* at the head of the *Dictionary*, and accuses him of attempting to disparage his former patron:

Dès l'année 1747, on peut voir le plan qu'il se proposait de remplir, dans une lettre addressée à Mylord Chesterfield. Les vues neuves et approfondies, que contenoit ce projet, prévinrent en faveur d'un travail entrepris sous de tels auspices et dirigé par de telles régles. On a lieu d'être surpris que cette pièce ne se trouve point à la tête du dictionnaire, dont elle contenoit l'annonce. Elle eût épargné à l'Auteur la composition d'une nouvelle préface, qui ne contient qu'en partie les mêmes choses, et qu'on est tenté de regarder comme destineé a faire perdre de vue quelques unes des obligations, que M. Johnson avoit contracteés, et le Mécène qu'il avoit choisi.[38]

We are, then, justified in adapting Johnson's subdued and Maty's overt device of comparison and contrast of the two documents, and determining some of their essential differences, strengths, and weaknesses. In so doing, Chesterfield's role and influence will be important.

§ 2

According to the terms of its own rhetoric, Chesterfield exerted a great influence on Johnson's conception of the *Plan*. Though lexicography is a menial task, it was, Johnson says, regarded as a "safe" and "useful" performance which would keep life "innocent . . . would awaken no passion, engage [him] in no contention, nor throw in [his] way any temptation to disturb the quiet of others by censure, or [his] own by flattery." Though "princes and statesmen" of earlier ages were said to protect those who improved the tongue, he could only regard "such acts of beneficence as prodigies" (pp. 121–22). Johnson thus establishes two aspects of time-past: his own innocent and safe occupation, and an earlier golden age of the nobles' interest in language. Both are changed when Johnson's time-present is altered by Chesterfield, whose protection establishes him as a prodigy and Johnson as the possible center of controversy and concern; hence he becomes anxious lest Chesterfield's patronage "should fix the attention of the public too much upon me, as it once happened to an epic poet of France" (p. 122). The earlier lonely and lowly but useful toil is transmuted into an epic task performed under public scrutiny. Near the end of the *Plan* the lexicographer's efforts which once were "not splendid" but "useful" now are discussed in terms of "the difficulty" and "importance of philological studies" (p. 135). But this change is not the earned result of Johnson's revaluation of the lexicographer's role: it is the result of the scheme now being "prosecuted under your Lordship's influence" (p. 122). Consequently, Johnson is publishing this *Plan* in order to gain suggestions or approbation from those who will surely *now* regard it as important, since it is "a design that you, my Lord, have not thought unworthy to share your attention with treaties and with wars" (p. 122). One of Chesterfield's roles in the *Plan,* then, is significantly to heighten both the public's regard and the lexicographer's anxiety and fame.

Chesterfield appears again briefly when Johnson observes that the Earl is aware of Britain's unsettled orthography. Since this is hardly an observation original to Chesterfield or particularly distinguished in its own right, we are surprised to find that in Chesterfield's next appearance, he is likened to no less a figure than Caesar.

> Ausonius thought that modesty forbad him to plead inability for a task to which Caesar had judged him equal. . . . And I may hope, my Lord, that since you, whose authority in our language is so generally acknowledged, have commissioned me to declare my own opinion, I shall be considered as exercising a kind of vicarious jurisdiction, and that the power which might have been denied to my own claim, will be readily allowed me as the delegate of your Lordship. (P. 137)

Chesterfield, once among princes and statesmen, is now exalted to the level of emperor who silences dissent against his powerful decrees and rewards the man of letters faithful to him. This example both overpraises Chesterfield and places Johnson among those who rise by the patronage of the great. Moreover, Johnson is not speaking with his own voice or authority, but merely as a mouthpiece for Chesterfield. At first Chesterfield as Caesar was the emperor Gratian who aids Ausonius; he soon becomes the emperor Claudius invading England, and Johnson becomes one of "the soldiers of Caesar" looking on Britain "as a new world, which it is almost madness to invade," but during which invasion the process of civilization may at least begin. Whatever the outcome, even if the invasion should fail, Johnson "shall not easily regret" the attempt, which has procured him "the honour" of appearing publicly as his Lordship's most humble servant (pp. 138–39).

Johnson's subservient attitude toward Chesterfield cannot be dismissed merely as the conventional and irrelevant nod to power, since it shows Johnson sharing some of Chesterfield's values regarding language. In the rough draft of the *Plan*, called "A Short Scheme for compiling a new Dictionary of the English Language" (1746), Johnson observes that orthography is now "settled with . . . propriety." [39] In the *Plan* Johnson reverses his opinion—or at the very least substantially changes his emphasis—and says that "according to your Lordship's observation, there is still great uncertainty among the best critics" (p. 125). Chesterfield's concern with fixing the language also appears in Johnson's *Plan*. This difficult task is both desirable and largely achievable. Since "the first change" in language "will naturally begin by corruptions in the living speech," Johnson hopes to supply new "rules for . . . pronunciation" and thereby "to provide that the harmony of the moderns may be more permanent." This is consistent with one of the lexicographer's "great" ends, fixing the language; because "a new pronunciation will make almost a new speech, . . . care will be taken to determine the accentuation of all polysyllables by proper authorities" (p. 127).

The need to stabilize language appears throughout the *Plan*. It is, for example, "necessary to fix the pronunciation of monosyllables" in order to avoid "the danger of . . . variation" (p. 127). Moreover, by tracing every word to its etymon, "and not admitting, but with great caution, any of which no original can be found, we shall secure our language from being over-run with *cant*" (p. 129). Johnson does tell Chesterfield that one cannot properly expect permanence in words, since "language is the work of man, of a being from whom permanence and stability cannot be derived"; but he also wonders who "can forbear to wish" that the "fundamental atoms of our speech might obtain the firmness and immutability of the primogenial and constituent particles of matter" (p. 130). Hence it is not surprising to hear him insist that "barbarous or impure words and expressions . . . are carefully to be eradicated wherever they are found," and to liken his work "to the proposal made by Boileau to the [French] academicians" to review their best authors and expunge their impurities, lest they contribute "to the depravation of the language" (p. 136). He begins his peroration by telling Chesterfield that in his "idea of an English Dictionary . . . the pronunciation of our language may be fixed, and its attainment facilitated, by which its purity may be preserved, its use ascertained, and its duration lengthened." Undertaking such a task may be an act of near-madness, but it surely will be undertaken and, with Chesterfield's patronage, will at least make it easier for another lexicographer "to reduce [the English, and hence their language] wholly to subjection and settle them under laws" (p. 138).

Much of the force of the invading soldiers comes from Caesar's authority—and in the *Plan* that authority is often alluded to and generally external to Johnson. It is, chiefly, Chesterfield's for Johnson insists that he is but "the delegate of your Lordship" (p. 137). He will also find "proper authorities" for pronunciation and will recognize that the different sounds of some words are "equally defensible by authority" (p. 127). His use of etymology to determine how English words were deduced from foreign languages (p. 128) will be facilitated by the excellent "writers of our glossaries" (p. 129); Quintillian supports his notion that speech cannot be immutable (pp. 129–30); for aid in definitions he will "consult the best writers" (p. 132); and he insists that "the credit of every part of this work must depend" upon "citing authorities" for illustrative quotations (p. 137). Finally, he attempts to silence criticism by telling us on "what authority the authorities are selected." Again, the source is external to Johnson: "many of the writers whose testimonies will be alleged, were selected by Mr. Pope, of whom I may be justified in affirming, that were he still alive, solicitous as he was for the success of this work, he would not be displeased, that I have undertaken it" (p. 137).

We might also notice the *Plan*'s conception of the *Dictionary*'s audience: it is composed largely of purchasers. The first paragraph, for instance, begins by mentioning Johnson's "prospect" of the "price of [his] labor" (p. 121). Part of this price will come from the sale of the *Dictionary*, and Johnson is therefore careful to include what the reader hopes to find: some foreign words "seem necessary to be retained," because the purchaser who looks into his dictionary for such a word "will have reason to complain if he does not find it" (p. 124). Similarly, "the terms of war and navigation should be inserted so far as they can be required by readers of travels, and of history" (p. 124). A few pages later we hear that "common readers" should find the definitions sufficient for their use, "since without some attention to such demands the dictionary cannot become generally valuable" (p. 132).

Of course the desire to increase the sale and approbation of his book is hardly unnatural; but the importance of Chesterfield and the combined attention to external authority and the needs of the purchaser suggest that in the *Plan* Johnson is "other-directed." There is nothing morally culpable about such a state; but in the case of Samuel Johnson it is out of character and affects the speaker's ability to convince us of the high level of lexicographical competence and emotional maturity necessary for his job. Indeed, as I have already suggested, this negative view of the speaker in the *Plan* would probably have been shared by Johnson as portrayed in the Preface to the *Dictionary*. I should now like to show how the later character of Johnson approaches the rhetorical aspects discussed above: the roles of patronage and authority; fixing of the language; the nature of the audience; and how, along the way, these suggest a speaker who is both far more convincing and, finally, capable of a terrifying insight into the nature of his own achievements and those of mankind.

§ 3

The attempt to acquire a patron is a social act, one in which, if successful, the gentleman and scholar combine efforts. Such patronage probably appealed to Johnson's ego, purse, and sense of community between the intellectual and fashionable worlds. In spite of its appearance at the head of the *Dictionary*, however, the Preface is essentially a private essay and, paradoxically, portrays Johnson as the lexicographer whose work will touch thousands but who is himself cut off from all human contact. This is made clear in the first five paragraphs, which establish both the Preface's dominant tone and its place as one of the most moving of English prose pieces. The *Plan* announces that it "appeared" that the province of lexicography was "the least delightful" and fruitful "of all the regions of learning" (p. 121); but, as we have seen, Johnson later reverses that judgment and elevates lexicography, so that "all who desire the praise of elegance or discernment must contend in the promotion" (p. 122) of his dictionary. In the Preface Johnson insists that the *Plan's* first description was reality not appearance, and that he must look at his literary province through his own eyes rather than through those of a noble lord's. The first paragraph thus portrays members of the class of "those who toil at the lower employments of life," as passive, driven by fear and exposed to censure, disgrace, or punishment. Johnson then introduces and repeats the word *without:* such a person is not only "exposed to censure," but exposed "without hope of praise," and is "punished for neglect, where success would have been without applause, and diligence without reward" (p. 301).

He then moves from general to particular, places the writer of dictionaries among the class of "unhappy mortals," and continues the paradoxical premise of the actively engaged passive scholar. He is the "slave of science, the pionier of literature, doomed only to remove rubbish and clear obstructions from the paths through which Learning and Genius press forward to conquest and glory, without bestowing a smile on the humble drudge that facilitates their progress" (p. 301). The lexicographer is thus acted upon by cosmic forces of fate and doom, while he himself acts on rubbish and obstruction; he is a slave who helps to make others free, a mere pioneer who makes a path for the conqueror. The martial image highlights an important difference from the *Plan.* There Johnson was one of the soldiers of the invading Caesar, and took pleasure and pride in his modest share of the imperial, civilizing, role; in the Preface he is merely a foot soldier, the pioneer "whose business is to level the road, throw up works, or sink mines in military operations" (*Dictionary*). The first two paragraphs of the Preface thus reverse the dominant tone of the *Plan.* The view of the lexicographer as drudge dealing with rubbish was suggested in the *Plan* and then dismissed as clearly wrong, since Chesterfield would not trouble himself with such unimportant and gross matters. But reality has now replaced appearance, and the image of a lonely yet brave, heroic, and selfless man has replaced what is, for Johnson, the inappropriate social pose of client of Chesterfield.

The concept of a heroic task to be performed and a pioneer drudge to do it is consistent with the paradox of the active lexicographer acted upon by fate, fear, censure, disgrace, and punishment. We are thus aware of the immensity of the task, the paucity of reward, and the necessarily inadequate abilities of the lexicographer. Hence in the third paragraph we respond positively to the speaker's honesty, courage, and selflessness, as he says: "I have, notwithstanding this discouragement, attempted a dictionary of the *English* language." Once more we see a paradoxical inversion, as the gardener acquires the traits of an untended garden. The English language was "employed in the cultivation of every species of literature," but in the process "has itself been . . . neglected; suffered to spread, under the direction of chance, into wild exuberance; resigned to the tyranny of time and fashion; and exposed to the corruptions and ignorance, and caprices of innovation" (p. 301). Both the extent of the task and the courage and isolation of the lexicographer are made clearer still upon repetition of the term *without* and the words or phrases it modifies:

> When I took the first survey of my undertaking, I found our speech copious without order, and energetic without rules: wherever I turned my view, there was perplexity to be disentangled, and confusion to be regulated; choice was to be made out of boundless variety, without any established principle of selection; adulterations were to be detected, without a settled test of purity; and modes of expression to be rejected or received, without the suffrages of any writers of classical reputation or acknowledged authority. (P. 301)

In the process of creating order from disorder, Johnson comments obliquely on his former patron and former attitude toward authority. He now has "*no assistance* but from general grammar," and so depends upon his own lights, examines writers, notes what might best illustrate a word and "accumulated in time the materials of a dictionary, which, by degrees, *I* reduced to method, *establishing to myself*, in the progress of the work, such rules as *experience* and *analogy* suggested *to me*" (p. 302; italics added). He has begun to prune the unhealthy luxuriance of the garden; and he is doing so through his own efforts rather than through those of Chesterfield or Pope.

His earned independence impresses us favorably, as does his healthy respect both for the work of others and for the intelligence of his readers. He says of disputed areas like orthography: "I have left, in the examples, to every author his own practice unmolested, that the reader may balance suffrages, and judge between us" (p. 304). Moreover, he will not change orthography to suit ephemeral pronunciation, mere fashion, or pedantic idiosyncrasies. Instead, he has proceeded "with a scholar's reverence for antiquity, and a grammarian's regard to the genius of our tongue" (p. 304). As such a scholar he establishes his right to correct authorities if he believes them wrong. In matters of pronunciation, for instance, the reader will sometimes find that the author in the illustrative quotation has placed the emphasis differently from Johnson's: "it is then to be understood that custom has varied, or that the author has, *in my opinion,* pronounced wrong" (p. 305; italics added). Similarly, when discussing his word-list, Johnson mentions the "deficiency of [previous] dictionaries" and stresses the difficulty of finding new words in his "unguided excursions into books" or in "the boundless chaos of a living speech." Nevertheless, he adds, his search "has been either skillful or lucky; for I have much augmented the vocabulary" (p. 307). The evidence for that augmentation is in front of the reader in two substantial folio volumes; upon examining the evidence and finding the remark likely to be true, one believes all the more in the integrity of the speaker. Johnson's balanced evaluation of Skinner and Junius as etymologists, and Bailey, Ainsworth, and Philips as compilers of word-lists, again enhances our confidence in him, as he clearly states their strengths and weaknesses, and insists that he alone is responsible for inclusion of specific words: other words not in dictionaries, he says, "which *I* considered as useful, or know to be proper, though *I* could not at present support them by authorities, *I* have suffered to stand upon *my own* attestation" (p. 309; italics added). Authority is both respected and limited by the governing mind of Samuel Johnson.

However, Johnson never forgets that he is still the drudge faced with giving order to chaos; and so, paradoxically again, he buttresses his character by admitting his weaknesses. Hostility will be directed to his definitions, he predicts, not only by the malign, but, because of the supreme difficulty of the task, by Johnson himself: "I have not always been able to satisfy myself" (p. 309), he confesses, since many words do not admit of easy definition, and others, like particles, which "are not easily reducible under any regular scheme of explication," can only be defined with as much success "as can be expected in a task, which no man, however learned or sagacious, has yet been able to perform" (pp. 310–11). He is bound by his own intelligence, and admits: "Some words there are which I cannot explain, because I do not understand them" (p. 311). Significantly, Johnson inverts the use of authority in the *Plan*, by using the authority of ignorance not knowledge: Cicero and Aristotle confessed their ignorance, and so "I may surely, without shame, leave some obscurities to happier industry, or future information" (p. 311). Johnson's rhetorical stance, then, includes both awareness of an impossible task and his knowledge of his own great abilities, authority, and intelligence: the latter operate in a selfless way for the glory of learning, genius, and the English language and nation rather than for his own pride or material gain. Johnson's depth of perception is made clear in the three passionate and beautiful concluding paragraphs of the essay. They include acceptance of the human situation, of the subservient but necessary role of lexicography, and finally, of his own personal and terrible isolation.

The *Dictionary* is devoted to "the honour of my country, that we may no longer yield the palm of philology, without a contest, to the nations of the continent." Since the "chief glory of every people arises from its authors," and since Johnson cannot yet know whether his own writings will enhance English literature, he regards his employment as neither "useless nor ignoble if by [his] assistance foreign nations, and distant ages, gain access to the propagators of knowledge, and understand the teachers of truth; if [his] labours afford light to the repositories of science, and add celebrity to *Bacon*, to *Hooker*, to *Milton*, and to *Boyle*" (p. 322). This generous wish to propagate the work of greater men both animates and gives him pleasure; not the prideful pleasure of the *Plan,* but the pleasure of having endeavored well and achieved much, though imperfectly. He has learned "that no dictionary of a living tongue ever can be perfect," since words live and die while the book is being published (pp. 322–23), and that the weaknesses of the flesh, the intellect, and the spirit, will prevail in many instances. He has, then, accepted the role of the pioneer of literature, and passed the fruits of his labors to an enriched science and posterity, rather than to the reputation of Samuel Johnson or the Earl of Chesterfield.

But the Preface does more than discuss personal matters in abstract terminology; it discusses them in personal terminology as well. Hence Johnson again rejects the *Plan's* plea for patronage, and discusses his discomforts during the process of writing. We recall that in the *Plan* Chesterfield was characterized as a prodigy whose attentions would induce the emulation of "those who desire the praise of elegance or discernment." But the *Dictionary* actually "was written with little assistance of the learned, and without any patronage of the great; . . . amidst inconvenience and distraction, in sickness and in sorrow" (p. 323). Moreover, Johnson concludes, even the praise which one normally and fairly seeks is irrelevant to him; the social act of praise is valuable only for one active in a social world, not for one so wholly alone. The final paragraph of the Preface thus takes many of the terms of the opening paragraphs and moves them from a broadly intellectual to a personally emotional level. *Fear, hope, censure,* and *praise* now reappear in a grim context; earlier Johnson is alone, ahead of the army, but still aware of his human reactions, since he is "driven by the fear of evil," and a few lines later, admits that he can "only *hope* to escape reproach" (p. 301). One may read the *Plan* and Preface as signposts in the growth of the lexicographer's mind, as the records of intellectual and personal discovery; it is almost as if during the process of writing Johnson had reviewed the emotional trauma of his dictionary years, found himself now suffering not only an understandable postpartum depression, but found that depression heightened by the loss of many of those whom the completed *Dictionary* was designed to please. Hence, to be "psychological" for a moment, the *Dictionary* leaving his hands evokes memories of his wife leaving this world almost three years earlier. During the final summation of his seven years of work on the *Dictionary*, intellectual isolation is transmuted into personal isolation. Considering the difficulty of his task, Johnson says,

> I may surely be contented without the praise of perfection, which, if I could obtain, in this gloom of solitude, what would it avail me? I have protracted my work till most of those whom I wished to please have sunk into the grave, and success and miscarriage are empty sounds. I therefore dismiss it with frigid tranquility, having little to fear or hope from censure or from praise. (P. 322)

All readers of Johnson know the frequency with which the terms *hope* and *fear* appear in his work; they are generally part of the usual passions of mankind which the moralist must direct toward proper concerns.[40] "Where then shall Hope and Fear their objects find?" (l. 343) Johnson asks in *The Vanity of Human Wishes*. But in the conclusion of the Preface he virtually divorces himself from hope and fear, associates himself with those who have already "sunk into the grave," and declares that some of the words which he has been defining for the last seven years, are merely "empty sounds." The Preface concludes with rejection not only of public honor and Chesterfield, but of the ordinary pleasures of life. It is against these somber tones, against the ability to view the major achievement of his life as personally irrelevant, that the genteel obsequiousness of the *Plan* must be judged.

The changed attitude toward fixing the language is also a sign of Johnson's maturity. We recall the *Plan*'s brash confidence in the possibility of making at least a handsome start in that direction; and we will also see the Preface's embarrassed reaction toward and clear rejection of that earlier stance. Johnson now only hopes that he can slow down the speed with which the language changes, since a living language is "variable by the caprice of every one that speaks it," and words are "hourly shifting their relations" (p. 310). Hence he admits that though he has "laboured" at "settling the orthography," he has "not always executed [his] own scheme, or satisfied [his] own expectations" (p. 316). We are, therefore, not surprised when we hear Johnson say what would have been impossible in the *Plan*; the overlapping meanings of

words in some illustrative quotations are "not to be imputed to
me, who do not form, but register the language; who do not teach
men how they should think, but relate how they have hitherto
expressed their thoughts" (pp. 317–18). Johnson then repeats some
of the terminology of the *Plan,* alludes to it, and clearly rejects its
concept of a potentially static language.

> Those who have been persuaded to think well of my design,
> will require that it should fix our language, and put a stop to those
> alterations which time and change have hitherto been suffered to
> make in it without opposition. With this consequence I will confess
> that I flattered myself for a while; but now begin to fear that I have
> indulged expectation which neither reason nor experience can justify.
> (P. 319)

Indeed, a lexicographer who wishes to separate language from the
human condition of growth and decay uses foolish imagination,
proudly overrates his own powers, and misunderstands the nature
of language. The man who fancies "that his dictionary can em-
balm his language, and secure it from corruption and decay, that
it is in his power to change sublunary nature, and clear the world
at once from folly, vanity, and affectation," is not only "vain," but
morally dangerous: "sounds are too volatile and subtle for legal
restraints; to enchain syllables, and to lash the wind, are equally
the undertakings of pride, unwilling to measure its desires by its
strength" (pp. 319–20). Johnson here is telescoping two facts about
Xerxes—the enchaining and lashing—which, in *The Vanity of
Human Wishes,* he used to show the madness and pride which led
to the death of thousands at Salamis:

> Attendant Flatt'ry counts his myriads o'er,
> Till counted Myriads sooth his pride no more;
> Fresh Praise is try'd till madness fires his mind,
> The waves he lashes, and enchains the wind.
> (*Ll. 229–32*)

"Causes of change," Johnson insists, ". . . are perhaps as much
superior to human resistance, as the revolutions of the sky, or

intumescence of the tide" (p. 320). Attempting to enchain syllables is thus also an affront to the healthy processes of human thought.

> Those who have much leisure to think, will always be enlarging the stock of ideas, and every increase of knowledge, whether real or fancied, will produce new words, or combinations of words. When the mind is unchained from necessity, it will range after convenience; when it is left at large in the fields of speculation, it will shift opinions. (P. 320)

On the *Plan's* side of the ledger, then, we see self-flattery, irrationality, inexperience, concepts worthy of derision, vanity, false imagination, unnatural and impossible restraint, and pride. On the Preface's side, we see proper modesty, experience, freedom, thought, and growth. Johnson now hopes only "to acquiesce with silence, as in the other insurmountable distresses of humanity"; he hopes to "retard what we cannot repel," and give longevity to the language which finally must decay (p. 322). The nature of language and the nature of man are intimately related in their pattern of growth and decline.

But man and language are different in an important way as well; and here too we see an advance over the thinking of the *Plan*. One of the reasons Johnson no longer attempts to fix the language is that he realizes that the demands of "civilization" and its written language are at variance with the "wild and barbarous jargon" of oral speech. Thus the earliest attempts to record speech induce great diversity of spelling, and this "perplexes or destroys analogy, and produces anomalous formations, that, . . . can never be afterward dismissed or reformed" (p. 302). Language is not only the purveyor of noble truths; as the martial image with which the Preface opens suggests, it is also an intransigent enemy of the lexicographer. He hopes to normalize and make analogies, whereas language hopes to destroy analogy. It will baffle the finest lexicographer, since there are "spots of barbarity impressed so deep in the *English* language, that criticism can never wash them away" (p. 303). Language is wanton and capricious (p. 301); the lexicographer seeks uniformity and system (p. 305, et passim). Language will borrow its words from other languages; the lexicographer warns against "the folly of naturalizing useless foreigners to the injury of the natives" (p. 307). Language is "variable by the caprice of every one that speaks it" (p. 310); the lexicographer hopes "to circumscribe . . . by . . . limitations" (p. 310). "Words are seldom exactly synonymous"; yet "the rigour of interpretive lexicography requires that the *explanation, and the word explained should be always reciprocal*" (p. 311). Language has an "exuberance of signification"; the lexicographer trying to record such exuberance finds it "scarcely possible to collect" words' many senses (p. 312). Language's "sounds are too volatile and subtile for legal restraints" (p. 319), yet the lexicographer puts sounds on paper and hopes they will be properly retranslated into the same sound. Language as an intransigent and ultimately triumphant enemy is thus quite different from language as discussed in the *Plan*. There Johnson believes that he can make "the harmony of the moderns . . . more permanent" than that of former ages (p. 127), and that the adjustment of orthography and pronunciation is an easy step toward "the attainment of our language" (p. 128). The *Plan* emphasizes facility and attainment; the Preface insists on what criticism can never wash away.

Johnson's different attitude toward his present audience is consistent with his growth and change from the *Plan*. In the latter work, we recall, he discussed the purchaser and, though addressing himself to Chesterfield, could not escape an occasionally commercial remark. In the Preface the members of the audience are not regarded as an adjunct to Johnson's purse; instead, he hopes to help their minds and guide them toward improved understanding of their language. He has, for instance, sometimes inserted different spellings of the same word, so "that those who search for them under either form, may not search in vain" (p. 303). In order to aid the foreigner, he has clarified anomalies which "interrupt and embarrass the learners of our language" (p. 305). Similarly, he has inserted many verbs with a particle subjoined ("as to *come off*"), because foreigners have "the greatest difficulty" with these, and no longer need find this difficulty "insuperable" (p. 309). And, he admits that he will not regard his work as "useless or ignoble if by [his] assistance foreign nations, and distant ages, gain access to the propagators of knowledge, and understand the teachers of truth" (p. 322).

We have seen several significant changes between the *Plan* and the Preface of Johnson's *Dictionary*: he has abjured Chesterfield and the notions of external authority and a clearly fixable language; he has reconsidered the role of the lexicographer and placed it in its proper necessary but subservient place; he has stopped regarding the audience as purchaser and turned, instead, to the audience as composed of those in need of a reasonably clear path through the boundless chaos of language, so that they may more easily arrive at truth; he convinces us of his wisdom, maturity, and skill necessary for the task; and he makes several allusions to the general puerility of the *Plan*. In sum, he overtly and covertly rejects the *Plan,* many of his own earlier notions regarding language, and much of the rhetorical stance of the brash young man flexing his muscles, convinced of his own omnipotence, but incapable of so convincing us. He becomes the mature and weary man, with a huge effort behind him, and a realization of the failings of the human situation within him. In the process of watching this change we see some of the steps in the making of a great mind and a great English dictionary; the growing intellectual and emotional sophistication of its maker; and his awareness of a central paradox regarding man's nature: the infinite importance and infinite irrelevance of human achievement.

Redefinitions of Style, *1600–1800*

DAVID A. HANSEN

ABOUT TWENTY-FIVE YEARS AGO Frederick W. Haberman gave an account of the changes in meaning and usage which *elocution* and *style* experienced during the eighteenth century.[1] In this account, *elocution*, the seventeenth-century rhetorician's term for *style*, eventually became in the eighteenth century a term which referred mainly to the art of delivery with its twofold interest in voice and gesture in public speaking. In consequence of this change in meaning, eighteenth-century rhetoricians were likely to use the term *style* rather than *elocution*. "The meaning of style," Haberman suggests, "did not change, though it did gain more philosophical depth. What changed was the 'status' of the word. Its status changed from that of a synonym or sub-topic of elocution to that of a title designating a whole area of expression."[2] *Style*, it is true, tended to replace *elocution* in the latter half of the eighteenth century, but it is not also true that the meaning of *style* remained invariable or that it failed to undergo any change in meaning during the eighteenth century. Haberman's account, then, is not wholly satisfactory. Moreover, it overlooks lexical and encyclopedic definitions and the oblique relation of some of them to two dominant trends in the criticism of prose style: the antirhetorical trend and the opposition to it.[3]

The main purposes of this essay are to establish the variable meanings of *style* in the eighteenth century, to determine the extent to which the term did undergo a change in meaning, and to suggest some of the possible relations between the dominant trends in the criticism of prose style and some definitions of *style* in dictionaries and encyclopedias of the century. The close association between *elocution* and *style* makes it impossible to attempt any one of these purposes without first giving an account of seventeenth-century definitions of *elocution.*

§ 1

The earliest lexical definitions of *elocution* in the seventeenth century are etymological. John Bullokar's *An English Expositor* (1616) and Henry Cockeram's *The English Dictionarie* (1623) agree in giving "utterance" as the meaning of *elocution,* though Bullokar also gives "eloquence." [4] Both definitions are etymological since they derive, as does *elocution* itself, from *eloquor,* which means, of course, "to speak out." Bullokar and Cockeram wholly ignore rhetorical definitions of *elocution,* which tend to be Ciceronian or Ramian and which help to explain the close association between *elocution* and *style.* Ciceronian rhetoricians define *elocution* in terms of several distinguishing characteristics. For example, Thomas Wilson in *The Arte of Rhetorique* (1560) gives two definitions of *elocution:* "an applying of apt wordes and sentences to the matter" and an *"apt chusing and framing of words and sentences together."* [5] *Elocution,* it is clear, refers not to utterance, to speaking out, but to diction and composition. When Wilson enlarges upon his meaning of *elocution,* he reveals that it pertains to several distinguishing characteristics which are at once the marks of excellence in the expression of ideas and the chief requirements of expression. Elocution, according to Wilson, has four parts: 1] "Plainnesse" or the use of English words instead of "straunge ynkehorne termes";   2] "Aptnesse" or perspicuity, since aptness dictates using only those words which express clearly the thing they signify;   3] "Composition" or a pleasant arrangement of words and sentences that produces harmony; and   4] "Exornation" or a "gorgious beautifying" of expression principally by means of ornament or the tropes and figures. [6] The example of Wilson illustrates how the rhetorician in clarifying one set of his defining terms for *elocution* converts them into the principles and criteria of expression. Thomas Farnaby in his *Index rhetoricus* (1625) illustrates how a seventeenth-century Ciceronian rhetorician can use a set of defining terms slightly different from Wilson's, but in clarifying them can arrive at principles and criteria of expression that are similar to his. "Elocution," Farnaby says, "consists in elegance, composition, and dignity." And elegance, he explains, requires clarity and purity of expression; composition, a harmonious order of words; and dignity, appropriateness and ornament or the proper use of tropes and figures.[7]

By contrast to Ciceronian rhetoricians, the Ramians define *elocution* solely in terms of the tropes and figures. Dudley Fenner, for example, says in *The Artes of Logike and Rethorike* (1584) that "Garnishing of speech [is] called Eloquution" and that "It is eyther The fine maner of wordes, called a Trope [or] The fine shape and frame of speech called a Figure." He explains also that elocution provides the means "whereby the speach it selfe is beautified and made fine."[8] Another Ramian, Charles Butler in *Rhetoricae Libri Duo* (1598), says that "elocution consists in either the tropes or the figures."[9] Ramian definitions reduce *elocution* to mere ornament and are prescriptive as well as normative since they require the use of the tropes and figures to attain a fine manner of expression.

In general, then, definitions of *elocution* in the seventeenth century are etymological and rhetorical, and the latter are either Ciceronian or Ramian. With this frame of reference, it is possible to make several categorical observations about the treatment of the term in dictionaries and encyclopedias of the seventeenth and eighteenth centuries.

The first categorical observation is that the etymological and rhetorical definitions appear separately in some dictionaries and jointly in others. After Bullokar and Cockeram, no seventeenth-century lexicographer confines *elocution* to the etymological definition, except Edward Cocker in his *English Dictionary* (1704). Thomas Blount, the author of a Ciceronian handbook of rhetoric, *The Academie of Eloquence* (1654), owns the distinction of being the first lexicographer—so far as I can tell—to give *elocution* a rhetorical definition. In his *Glossographia* (1656) he defines *elocution* to mean "a fit and proper order of words and sentences." [10] Several eighteenth-century dictionaries give this definition of the term.[11] Another definition of it combines a truncated version of the rhetorical definition with the etymological: "proper speech, handsome utterance" as in Edward Phillips's *The New World of English Words* (1658) or "*a fit and proper order of speech, or good utterance*" as in John Kersey's *A New English Dictionary* (1702).[12] In general, the evidence suggests that *elocution* begins with an etymological definition and eventually acquires a rhetorical sense.

The second categorical observation is that no seventeenth- or eighteenth-century dictionary offers a Ramian definition of *elocution*. It does, however, appear in one eighteenth-century encyclopedia, *The Universal Library: Or, Compleat Summary of Science* (1712), where elocution means "an Elegant Order of Words and Sentences used in the Utterance, and is performed by the fine manner of Words, called a Trope, or by the fine Frame of Speech called a Figure." The first part of this definition is at once rhetorical and etymological while the second part is Ramian to the extent that it may well have been borrowed from Fenner's rhetoric.

All other encyclopedic definitions of *elocution* tend to be Ciceronian. Ephraim Chambers, the compiler of the popular *Cyclopaedia* (1728) defines *elocution* in terms of proper words in their proper places, ascribes this definition to Cicero, and explains that "the beauties of elocution" consist chiefly in the use of tropes and figures. Benjamin Martin, the compiler of *Bibliotheca Technologia: or, A Philological Library of Literary Arts and Sciences* (1737), says that elocution "provides a *Diction* enrich'd and embellish'd with all the Ornament of proper *Tropes* and *Figures;* and in which chosen words are adapted to express the things invented with *Force* and *Energy.*" This definition, somewhat Ramian in its emphasis on the proper use of Ornament, is in the end Ciceronian in its ascription of force and energy to tropes and figures. A wholly Ciceronian definition of *elocution* appears in Temple Henry Croker's encyclopedia, *The Complete Dictionary of Arts and Sciences* (1764):

> **Elocution,** in rhetoric, the adapting words and sentences to the
> thing or sentiments to be expressed. It consists in elegance,
> composition and dignity. The first, comprehending the purity
> and perspicuity of a language, is the foundation of elocution.
> The second ranges the words in proper order; and the last adds
> the ornaments of tropes and figures to give strength and dignity
> to the whole.

This definition, one may observe in passing, appears without any
changes in the first edition of the *Encyclopaedia Britannica* (1771),
and also in the second and third editions (1778–83, 1797). When
one considers that the Ciceronian definition of elocution appears in
four eighteenth-century encyclopedias and a half dozen or more
dictionaries, one might be tempted to conclude that encyclopedists
and lexicographers of the period must have been wholly unrespon-
sive to any change in meaning happening to the term. This conclusion, however, applies only to encyclopedists.

The third categorical observation is that a good number of
eighteenth-century lexicographers define *elocution* to mean "delivery." In an article on the elocutionary movement in England,
Wilbur S. Howell recounts an episode that marks an attempt to
reject this definition of *elocution.* John "Orator" Henley used the
term in the sense of delivery when in 1727 he claimed that he was
"*'the restorer of ancient elocution.'*" Ephraim Chambers, in the
second edition of his *Cyclopaedia* (1738), censured Henley for
confusing the meaning of *elocution* and pointed out that he
should have called himself the restorer of ancient pronunciation or
delivery. Professor Howell also observes that the first writer to
defend his use of *elocution* in the sense of delivery was John Mason
in his *Essay on Elocution, or Pronunciation* (1748).[13] Henley, it
should be emphasized, was hardly the first to use the term in an
"objectionable" way. The *Glossographia Anglicana Nova* in 1707
defined *elocution* to mean "Utterance, Delivery; as a Man of good
Elocution is a man of good and handsome Delivery." Moreover,
three later dictionaries between 1721 and 1738 define *elocution* as
delivery, and so, too, do a half dozen more in the years between
1741 and 1765.[14] The acceptance of *elocution* in the sense of de-

livery among lexicographers especially in the years between 1737 and 1765 may be an index of the growing strength of the elocutionary movement during these several decades, a movement which endeavored to confine rhetoric to the art of delivery or to the proper use of voice and gesture in public speaking.

The last categorical observation is that some eighteenth-century lexicographers combine several definitions of the term. Benjamin Martin, as prodigious a lexicographer as compiler of an encyclopedia, defines *elocution* in *Lingua Britannica Reformata* to mean "a fit and proper order of words and sentences, utterance, delivery." Similarly, Samuel Johnson in *A Dictionary of the English Language* (1755) gives these several meanings of *elocution:* 1] "the power of fluent speech"; 2] "Eloquence; flow of language"; and 3] "The power of expression or diction." To clarify this last meaning Johnson quotes Dryden's remark: "The third happiness of [the] poet's imagination is *elocution,* or the art of cloathing or adorning that thought so found, and varied, in apt, significant, and sounding words." The last meaning in Johnson's *Dictionary* alludes ultimately to the art of ornamentation.

The example of Dryden may serve as a reminder that during the last several decades of the seventeenth century, critics often took away the art of elocution from prose writers and gave it to poets. Dryden himself, for example, defended the poet's license to express his fictions by means of the tropes and figures, but not without first declaring that the severity of prose does not admit them.[15] Joseph Addison made a similar distinction in his first published critical essay (1697) when he allowed that the prose writer and poet may express the same truth but in a different manner: whereas the prose writer expresses it as directly, fully, and plainly as possible, the poet conveys it indirectly by means of figurative language. More specifically, the poet takes a part of the truth and conveys it by means of metaphor, circumlocution, or illustration, and the reader, apprehending the part, discovers the whole truth for himself in a way that pleases his imagination.[16] John Locke may have been using figurative language to mark the difference between poetry and prose when in the *Essay Concerning Human Understanding* (1690) he reiterated a commonplace of the day: the tropes and figures may have their place in discourse that seeks only to delight the reader, but they are wholly inappropriate in discourse that pretends to instruct, inform, and improve him.[17] The antirhetorical trend evident in this distinction is clearly manifest in *Some Thoughts Concerning Education* (1693) where Locke censures schoolmasters for teaching their students how to use all the tropes and figures in Farnaby's *Index rhetoricus* instead of how to write plain English.[18]

Somewhat like these schoolmasters, lexicographers in the last several decades of the seventeenth century appeared to have paid scant attention to the repeated attacks on rhetoric and all of its tropes and figures, for the dictionaries in this period included the names and definitions of some tropes and figures, such as "aenigma," "allegory," "anaphora," "antiphrasis," "metaphor," and "simile." As if totally heedless of the attacks on rhetoric, a reviser of Bullokar's *Expositor* in 1707, Robert Browne, pronounced it deficient in the terms of art, particularly the terms of rhetoric, and added a number of tropes and figures which Bullokar had not entered in the first edition.[19] In short, the antirhetorical trend, encouraged as it might have been even by the highly influential Locke, did not have any immediate impact on lexicographers. Indeed, their dictionaries fostered a knowledge of *elocution* in the rhetorical sense of the term and provided, in effect, a handbook of tropes and figures.

§ 2

By way of transition from *elocution* to *style,* there lies conveniently at hand Swift's *Letter to a Young Gentleman Lately Enter'd into Holy Orders* (1721) with its "true Definition of Stile": "proper Words in proper Places." [20] The wittiest observation on this definition appears in a late eighteenth-century essay on Shakespeare by William Belsham. He uses the observation to point up the inadequacy of Swift's definition and says: "it has been observed with no less justice than wit, that this definition conveys in it as little real information, as if a telescope were described, as an instrument consisting of proper glasses in proper places." [21] The same observation, one may say, applies as well to Ciceronian definitions of *elocution* which make it consist solely in a "fit and proper order of words and sentences."

Swift's definition of *style* bears a superficial resemblance to a Ciceronian definition of *elocution*. The two are alike in defining their terms with reference to a proper diction and a proper arrangement of words. The similarity, however, is superficial and even misleading. For Swift's sense of what is proper in each case is anti-Ciceronian. Proper words, it becomes clear in his *Letter*, are always plain and simple English words, and the proper arrangement of them in his view should make their meaning clear and understandable. Unlike the Ciceronian definition of *elocution*, Swift's definition of *style* does not lead to any demand for the use of tropes and figures. Indeed, the *Letter*, in opposing that demand, helped to perpetuate the antirhetorical trend in the criticism of prose style.

"What the Greeks call φράσις, we in Latin call *elocutio*," Quintilian remarks in that part of the *Institutes* where he addresses himself to matters of style.[22] It is tempting to paraphrase his remark in the following manner: what the seventeenth century called *elocution*, we in the eighteenth century call *style*. Swift could be cited as an example of the eighteenth-century writer's tendency to retain one meaning of *elocution* while giving up the term itself in favor of *style*. The difficulty with the example of Swift lies less in the anti-Ciceronian context of his definition than in its remarkable uniqueness. Lexicographers before 1724 defined *style* in other terms than his. So, too, did later lexicographers until Johnson cited Swift's use of the term to illustrate one of its several possible meanings. This is as much as to say that perhaps one of the most memorable definitions of *style* in the eighteenth century was at odds with the several meanings which lexicographers gave the term prior to 1755.

Robert Cawdrey's *A Table Alphabeticall* (1604) and Bullokar's *Expositor* have the distinction of being the only seventeenth-century dictionaries which in their first editions include a definition of *style*. Other dictionaries, such as Cockeram's *English Dictionary*, admit the term in some later edition than the first. In Cawdrey and Bullokar, the term means "a manner or forme of writing, or speaking." This definition, at one with the meaning given to *style* in the first edition of the *Dictionnaire de l'académie françoise* (1694), also appears in thirteen English dictionaries published between 1702 and 1791. In these dictionaries the term sometimes means "a manner of writing, a way of expression" or simply a "Character, or manner of Writing." [23] In other dictionaries of the eighteenth century, yet another and different definition appears: "the manner of a Person's speaking or writing on any Subject." [24] The difference is slight but important. The common definition makes *style* a manner of expression in general while the other definition particularizes the manner by referring it to the individual speaker or writer. For the purpose of convenience, the first definition can be called "broad" and the second "narrow."

Sir Richard Blackmore, in "An Essay upon Epick Poetry" (1716), explains how *style* acquired several meanings in such a way as to make use of the broad and narrow meanings of the term:

> By degrees the Term Stile came figuratively to express the Way or Character of Writing in general, and was divided into several sorts that arose from the various Modes of Diction, in Discourses on various Subjects. It was likewise us'd to signify the Manner of Expression peculiar to this or that Author: So we say *Virgil's* or *Livy's* Stile. So *Cicero,* in his Book on Famous Orators, describes a wonderful Variety of Eloquence in the *Romans,* whose different Stile he delineates with admirable Distinction.[25]

In addition to illustrating the difference between the broad and narrow meanings of *style,* the example of Blackmore shows how the term lent itself to a generic definition. When he speaks of the several sorts of style that arose from the various modes of diction in discourses on various subjects, he has in mind principally the low style and the lofty or sublime style, and especially this last in relation to epic poetry and its lofty or sublime subject.[26]

The generic definition has a tendency to become prescriptive. For an example of this tendency, one may turn to a popular rhetoric of the day, *The Art of Speaking,* the so-called Port-Royal rhetoric by Bernard Lamy, which was published in England three times between 1676 and 1708. Lamy defines *style* to mean "a manner of expression" characteristic of an individual and goes on to say that he will eventually determine "what ought to be the Style of the Orator, the Historian, or the Poet." [27] When he attempts this determination, he actually prescribes a copious and eloquent style for the orator, a clear and compact style for the historian, and a highly figurative style for the poet. Along the way, he prescribes for the pulpit orator an ardent, impassioned, and lofty style that is in keeping with the divine truths of religion and also with the majestic style in which they are expressed by the holy Fathers in Scripture. Lamy, in short, passes from a narrow definition of *style* to a loose generic concept of the term and eventually to prescriptions. Among the latter, the style that he prescribes for the sermon is precisely the style which Swift in his *Letter to a Young Gentleman* derogated and represented as unsuitable to the pulpit.

The generic definition of *style,* as the example of Lamy may suggest, reveals its tendency to become prescriptive in any clarification of the term which seeks to establish what manner of expression ought to be appropriate to a particular kind of writing. The generic definition was perhaps actually no more prescriptive than the broad definition, for this kind of definition, as we shall see, left open the possibility of prescribing for all prose, irrespective of its kind or subject, a manner of expression that reconciled plainness with ornament or simplicity of expression with figurative language. For the moment, it is perhaps sufficient to say that *style* in the eighteenth century had variable meanings, received different kinds of definitions, and at times lent itself to prescriptive definitions that betray the influence of the antirhetorical trend and the opposition to it.

§ 3

The common lexical definitions of *style* in the eighteenth century are broad or narrow, sometimes both, and occasionally also generic. Another lexical definition begins its career in Chambers's *Cyclopaedia:*

> [A] **Style,** in matters of language, is a particular manner of delivering a man's thoughts in writing, agreeably to the rules of

syntax; [B] or, as F. Buffier more accurately defines it, the manner wherein the words constructed according to the laws of syntax, are arranged among themselves, suitably to the genius of the language.

The source of these definitions is the *Grammaire françoise, sur un plan nouveau* (1709) by the Jesuit philosopher Claude Buffier who offers the first definition [A] in the quotation above in order to correct it, though not in the way Chambers's collocation of the two definitions would suggest.

In the *Grammaire* Buffier remarks upon the tendency to confuse syntax with style, and he offers his own definition [B], as he says, "pour définir donc le stile en tant qu'il est distingué de la sintaxe." [28] Although his own definition appears to perpetuate the confusion by including a reference to the laws of syntax, it does mark the essential difference between syntax and style. In his view, syntax sets forth the rules for the inflection of words and for the functional relation between them while style, presupposing an observance of these rules, goes beyond them by consigning the arrangement of words to what Buffier calls the taste and usage of a language. Although his definition of *style* does include a reference to the laws of syntax, his clarification of his meaning subordinates the observance of them to the principle that idiosyncratic patterns of usage in a language should govern the arrangement of words. Consequently, Buffier believes that the manner of arranging them is too diverse to reduce to a single rule. Chambers, who paraphrases Buffier's discussion of these matters, succeeds in making clear his distinction between style and syntax.

Chambers fails, however, to indicate that Buffier refers to *style* in his sense of the term as the *grammatical style*. In addition, Chambers further confuses Buffier by saying that *grammatical style* is "that directed by the rules of grammar" and vaguely ascribing this definition to grammarians. As a result, Chambers misrepresents Buffier and does not make clear at all his distinction between the *grammatical* and the *personal styles*. To make this distinction, he turns to the *Dictionnaire universel* (1690) by Antoine Furetière, the seventeenth-century novelist and satirist. Furetière, according to Buffier, defines "stile en général" when he tells us that it means " *'la façon particuliére d'expliquer ses pensées ou d'écrire, qui est diférente selon les auteurs & les matieres.'* " [29] Chambers, it should be noted, uses Furetière's definition as the first definition of *style* [A] for the article in the *Cyclopaedia* but radically changes Furetière's meaning: he omits his statement that the particular manner of expression varies according to the author and the subject in order to make room for his own remark that the particular manner should be agreeable to the rules of syntax. The reference to these rules has the effect of making Buffier's more accurate definition, as Chambers calls it, a puzzle. To Buffier's way of thinking, Furetière defines not *style* in general but the *personal style*. Unlike the *grammatical style,* which always remains within the province of grammar and its rules, the *personal style* is less dependent upon them and may often transgress them. For Buffier, the essential difference between the two styles lies in their manner of arranging words. Their arrangement in the *grammatical style* is limited by the laws of syntax. By contrast, the arrangement of words in the *personal style* is capable of an infinite variety since their arrangement here is governed by the writer's individual imagination which in turn is under the direction of rhetoric and relies upon its tropes and figures to express the same thought in any number of ways. Although Chambers is far less clear than Buffier about these matters, he does manage in his paraphrase to establish the characteristics of the *personal style* and its inseparable relation to rhetoric.

Buffier, Chambers claims, "fixes the notion of *style,* to something determinate, which before was very vague and arbitrary." A preposterous claim to be sure, it suggests that Chambers must have seen in Buffier's more accurate definition an important redefinition of *style*. Ironically, it is Chambers's adaptation of Furetière's definition—"a particular manner of delivering a man's thoughts in writing, agreeable to the rules of syntax"—that appears in Benjamin Defoe's *A Compleat English Dictionary,* Benjamin Martin's *Lingua Britannica Reformata,* and James Barclay's *Universal Dictionary* (1774). Perhaps none of these lexicographers could see any difference between that definition and Buffier's. William Smellie, the compiler of the first edition of the *Encyclopaedia Britannica* (1771), however, borrowed both definitions and used them without making any changes in them. In the next century, Abraham Rees went further. In *The Cyclopaedia: or Universal Dictionary of Arts, Sciences, and Literature* (1819), he paraphrases Chambers's entire article on *style* and as silently borrows a briefer article on the *philosophical style* from *A Supplement to Mr. Chambers' Cyclopaedia* (1743), an article which brings us to the subject of prescriptive definitions.

To what extent are the definitions of style in Chambers's *Cyclopaedia* prescriptive? Furetière's definition, in referring the particular manner of expressing thoughts to the writer or to his subject, is at once narrow and generic, but Chambers, changing this definition, removes the twofold reference, introduces the principle that the manner ought to agree with the laws of syntax, and thereby clouds the definition and makes it prescriptive. By contrast, Buffier's is wholly prescriptive since it presupposes an observance of those laws and confines the arrangement of words to the taste and the usage peculiar to the language. Although neither of these definitions standing alone makes much sense, Buffier's does amount to a redefinition of *style* which excludes rhetoric. What he excludes from the *grammatical style*, however, he restores to the *personal style*. Indeed, he places this style under the governance of rhetoric. Given the popularity of Chambers's *Cyclopaedia*, one can say that it may have fostered the view that, however a writer might choose to arrange his words, his arrangement in the end could only be either grammatical or rhetorical.

§ 4

Outright prescriptive definitions of *style* are the exception rather than the rule in eighteenth-century dictionaries. Just the reverse of this is true in encyclopedias. Few though the total number of prescriptive definitions may be, they remain oblique testimony to one of the central issues in the criticism of prose style during the century: the proper place and use of rhetoric.

Defoe's *Compleat English Dictionary* has an encyclopedic rather than a lexical treatment of *style*. Not content to enter several possible meanings of the term, Defoe offers a lengthy article that

falls into three parts: 1] a definition and further clarification of
it,   2] a generic definition in terms of the sublime, middle, and
low styles, and   3] several prescriptive definitions, two of which
oppose the antirhetorical trend. Defoe's article is on *stile*. Later he
also defines *style* and for the definition of that term he borrows
from Chambers's article but omits its distinctions between the
grammatical and personal styles. Perhaps Defoe regarded these
distinctions as idle and therefore left them out.

His own definition of *stile*—"the manner of an author's expressing himself"—is narrow rather than broad. His clarification
of this meaning brings to mind Ben Jonson's memorable statement: *"Language* most shewes a man: speake that I may see thee.
It springs out of the most retired, and inmost parts of us, and is
the Image of the Parent of it, the mind. No glasse renders a mans
forme, or likenesse, so true as his speech." [30] Somewhat similarly,
Defoe says: "Discourse is the character of the soul; men's words
paint out their humours, and every one follows that stile to which
his natural disposition leads him; and thence proceeds the difference in stile among them that write in the same language and
there is as much difference in stile as in complexion." *Style* in the
sense that it is a manner of expression which reflects man's soul
or mind is, of course, at least as old as Seneca. Defoe blends this
sense of the term with the commonplace view that a man's individual manner of expression is the result of his unique disposition.

Defoe abandons the narrow sense of the term when he prescribes the styles appropriate to oratory, history, theology, and
other subjects, such as mathematics, physics, and ethics. The *oratorical style*, he says, "should be rich and abounding" since its
design is "to enlighten obscure or doubtful truths." This style is
rich with tropes and figures, and it abounds with a multitude of
epithets and synonymous expressions. Defoe does not explain how
any of these devices enlighten obscure or doubtful truths, but he
does indicate that tropes which are not too dazzling can make
"reasons more valuable" than they would otherwise be. In any
event, contrary to advocates of plainness who had attacked rhetoric
because its figurative language obscures the truth, Defoe suggests
that this language can reveal it. He may have had in mind the

commonplace view in his day that figurative language, especially
the metaphor, can convey abstractions sensibly to the mind of man.

The *historical style,* Defoe says, "requires eloquence as much
as any other subject whatsoever." By admitting eloquence to this
style, he runs directly counter to the view that most advocates of
plainness maintained, namely, that the chief characteristics of the
historical style are clarity and simplicity. His opposition to the
antirhetorical trend is as evident in his view that the *theological
style* "should be clear and solemn, harmonious and majestical," a
style which in the context of his discussion depends on the use of
tropes and figures. Defoe denies, in effect, that plainness alone
is appropriate to this style. In this respect he is at one with earlier
writers, such as Henry Felton in *A Dissertation on Reading the
Classics and Forming a Just Style* (1713), Sir Richard Blackmore
in *The Accomplished Preacher* (1731), and Father John Constable
in *Reflections upon Accuracy of Style* (1734).[31] Defoe's opposition
to the antirhetorical trend, however, terminates when he avers
that rhetoric has no place in the style suitable to discourses on
mathematics, physics, and ethics. In these discourses, only the
plain style is appropriate.

The article on the *philosophical style* in the *Supplement to
Mr. Chambers' Cyclopaedia* offers a prescriptive definition by
virtue of stating the sole end of this style and laying down its rules:

In a philosophical *stile,* the only end is accurately to explain
our thoughts to others; thence the particular rules to be observed by a philosopher, in delivering his doctrines, naturally
follow: such as,

1. Not to deviate from the received signification of terms.

2. That the same terms be always taken in the same sense.

3. To fix the meaning of such words as have only a vague
sense.

4. To signify objects, essentially different, by different names.
From these rules, the use and necessity of the terms of art [phi-
losophy in particular] appear, and shews with how little reason
they are vulgarly condemned.

5. The philosopher ought always to make use of proper ex-

pressions, and use no more words than what are precisely
necessary to establish the truth of his doctrines. *Wolf* Disc.
Praelim. Logic. Cap. 5.

The source of these rules, as the reference indicates, is Christian
Wolff's chapter on the style of philosophy in his *Discursus prae-
liminaris de philosophia in genere* (1728). There Wolff, the con-
troversial and highly influential German philosopher, actually sets
forth seven principles rather than six and in addition to elabo-
rating on each principle, makes a number of pertinent observations
of tangential relation to a principle. The article in the *Supplement*
leaves out all of Wolff's discussions of a principle and omits one
of them. (The article contains six of Wolff's principles, for the un-
numbered statement about the use of philosophical terms is also
one of his principles.) The omission is perhaps significant.

Wolff's principles are akin to those which Hobbes and Locke
had set forth in their endeavors to assure clarity in the communication of philosophical knowledge or perspicuity in the philosophical style. Like the British philosophers, Wolff prohibits the
use of rhetoric in philosophy, saying: "Things which are foreign
to philosophy should be banished from the philosophical world.
However, such things should not be condemned, nor excluded
from the world of literature." Though he does not condemn rhetoric, he casts some doubt upon its usefulness when he goes on to
say: "From this it follows that the philosopher should avoid the
verbal flourishes used by orators. For such expressions are based
upon either improper or ambiguous words, both of which are
contrary to the simplicity of philosophical style." [32]

Whoever omitted this principle while composing the article
for the *Supplement,* Chambers himself before his death or John
Hill the compiler of the *Supplement,* may have been indifferent
to the philosopher's prohibition against the use of rhetoric or bent
upon removing that prohibition. As to this last possibility, Chambers or Hill may have concluded that rhetoric does have a place
in philosophy. It is this conclusion which another anonymous author reached in an "Enquiry whether Philosophy is not capable of
receiving the Ornaments of Poetry," an article which appeared in
an issue of the *Gentleman's Magazine* in 1735.[33] In the same maga-

zine four years later, Samuel Johnson, writing about the Dutch physician Hermann Boerhaave, who gave the first half of the eighteenth century its standard text on physiology, praised him "for recommending the truth by elegance, and embellishing the philosopher with polite literature," or for using the art of rhetoric in scientific discourse.[34] The *Supplement's* omission of Wolff's prohibition against the use of rhetoric in philosophy may, then, be a reflection of a tendency in the day either to remove the prohibition or disregard it in scientific as well as philosophical discourse.

Although Johnson the critic and the writer opposed the antirhetorical trend in theory as well as practice, he did not as a lexicographer use his *Dictionary of the English Language* as an opportunity to define *style* in such a way as to encourage the use of rhetoric in prose. In other words, his *Dictionary* does not offer a prescriptive definition of the term. One meaning, however, is possibly ambiguous and warrants attention.

Of the eight meanings which Johnson gives to *style* two pertain to a manner of writing or expression. In one sense, *style* means a "Manner of speaking appropriate to particular characters." This sense of *style* goes back to Aristotle and appears frequently in literary, especially dramatic, criticism from classical antiquity down to the eighteenth century. The primary meaning of *style,* or the first given by Johnson, is a "Manner of writing with regard to language." A broad sense of the term, it may have had a more particular meaning for Johnson since one of his illustrative quotations is Swift's observation: "Proper words in proper places, make the true definition of a *stile.*" Swift's remark in the context of *A Letter to a Young Gentleman,* as I suggested earlier, is antirhetorical. For Johnson, however, the remark might have meant something different from plain words so arranged as to make their meanings clear and understandable. In his theory of prose style he was the rhetorician who could praise the labored ornaments of composition, doubt that composition and conversation have anything in common, encourage the use of ornaments to recommend known truths, and admire harmony and cadence.[35] In short, for Johnson, "proper words in proper places" perhaps implied a use of rhetoric in the choice of words and in the arrangement of them.

As an illustrative quotation in Johnson's *Dictionary*, Swift's remark is, in effect, a prescriptive definition that is vague enough to suggest some sanction of rhetoric.

John Walker in the Preface to his *Critical Pronouncing Dictionary* (1791) averred that he "scrupulously followed Dr. Johnson" and added that "his Dictionary has been deemed lawful plunder by every subsequent lexicographer." [36] Thomas Sheridan, John Ash, and Walker himself were content to copy Johnson's definition of *style*. To my knowledge, the only lexicographer who ignored Johnson for Chambers's definition was John Barclay. Borrowing a phrase from Chambers, one could say that Johnson fixed the notion of style to something determinate for most lexicographers in the latter half of the eighteenth century.

As one might expect, Johnson's manner of treating *style* did not gain any acceptance among encyclopedists in the same period. Ambitious to be compendious, most of them continued to enlarge upon the meaning of the term and, more pertinently, usually in such a way as to encourage the use of rhetoric in prose.

Encouragement of this kind is evident in Croker's *Complete Dictionary of Arts and Sciences*. His definition of *style*—"the manner of expressing ourselves, or of cloathing our thoughts in words" —is hardly prescriptive. When he goes on to lay down the principle that "the matter ought to direct us in the choice of the style," he turns from a broad definition of the term to prescription, for he confines the writer's choice to one of three styles, the sublime, plain, and intermediate. After discussing each of these styles briefly, he alludes to the commonplace that there are different styles for history, poetry, and oratory in order to determine how variety is possible within any of these styles. Variety, he explains, enters into a style as a result of certain "qualities" of expression that are dissimilar to one another. Ease and clarity of expression derive from ample exposition of ideas and a fluency rather than a roughness in the arrangement and cadence of words. By contrast, strength and boldness depend, as he says, on the use of "short and nervous expressions, of great and comprehensive meaning and such as excite many ideas." Another quality, floridness, uses tropes to convey abstractions and figures to animate the expression of ideas and to awaken the attention of the reader. By contrast, "the

last quality is severe," Croker says, "it retrenches everything that
is not absolutely necessary; it allows nothing to pleasure, admitting
no ornaments or decorations." Presumably, the historical as well as
the poetical or oratorical style admits all of these qualities in order
to lend it variety. Croker's article may finally reflect a tendency
in eighteenth-century criticism of prose style to regard variety as
the mark of a writer's great talent and consummate skill in
adapting his manner of expression to one kind of discourse and its
diverse subject matter.

The two great encyclopedias of the eighteenth century are
strikingly different in their articles on *style.* Louis de Jaucourt,
the author of the article in Diderot's *Encyclopédie* (1765), is as
comprehensive as possible. He defines *style* narrowly to mean
"maniere d'exprimer ses pensées de vive voix, ou par écrit" and
explains that style is the result of choosing and arranging words
according to the laws of harmony and number which are relative
to the elevation or simplicity of the subject. After arguing that
even the individual's manner of expression must conform to these
laws, he goes on to discuss a variety of matters. He marks the
differences between the several kinds of style and explains that
all of them—the sublime, the simple, and the middle styles—may
appear in the same work because its subject matter ranges from
the simple to the sublime. Subsequently, he marks the principal
differences between prose style and poetic style (only the latter,
for example, admits inversions and epithets); reviews the characteristics of a variety of styles, such as the comic, lyric, and
bucolic; and identifies and explains the distinguishing features of
the oratorical style, the historical, and the epistolary. For his discussion of the philosophical style, he borrows the brief article of
this style from the *Supplement to Mr. Chambers' Cyclopaedia.*
Lastly, he describes the great faults of style: obscurity, lowness,
inflation, coldness, and constant uniformity. By contrast to this
compendious discussion of *style* which everywhere encourages the
proper use of rhetoric in prose, the article on *style* in the first
edition of the *Encyclopaedia Britannica* merely reproduces the two
definitions of the term which appeared first in Chambers's *Cyclopaedia.*

As if to rectify matters, one of the compilers of the third

edition of the *Encyclopaedia Britannica* (1797), probably George Gleig, who took charge at the letter *M*, discarded Chambers in order to make room for a lengthy article which draws liberally and randomly upon two parts of Hugh Blair's discussion of style in his *Lectures on Rhetoric and Belles Lettres* (1783), the part on style itself and the part on directions for forming a style.[37] The statements culled from these two parts do not sit well together, and the article as a result lacks coherence in moving from a definition of *style* to a paragraph on the qualities of a good style and thence to an assessment of the prose styles of Swift, Addison, and Johnson. Definition, in short, gives way to prescription and evaluation. The incoherence stems largely from the absence of any common set of terms for the several procedures. Incoherent and unrepresentative of Blair's view as the article is, it reveals, I shall risk saying, several tendencies in literary criticism.

First the definition and the clarification of it: "Style, in language is the peculiar manner in which a man expresses his conceptions. It is a picture of the ideas which rise in his mind, and of the order in which they are there produced." A narrow definition of *style,* it gives way in the clarification to a psychological interest in the formation and arrangement of ideas in the imagination. In doing so, the clarification reveals the concern of the Scottish associationist with the natural movement of thought and the natural mode of expression. Blair's attempt to bend the meaning of *style* toward a natural mode of expression is evident in his statement: "Style is nothing else, than that sort of expression which our thoughts most readily assume." [38] I go beyond the article to his *Lectures* for this statement in order to make the commonplace point that he, like other Scottish critics and rhetoricians, may discuss the natural manner of thought and natural mode of expression, but their discussion brings them to art, the principles of rhetoric, and skills in composition.

The second paragraph in this article on *style* begins with the statement that "All qualities of a good style may be ranked under two heads, Perspicuity and Ornament." In the brief discussion that follows, perspicuity emerges as the principal quality, virtue, or standard of style, and ornament as the dress of thought which makes it pleasing, interesting, and impressive. This discussion grossly misrepresents Blair on two accounts. First, like some other rhetoricians and critics in his day, he tries to establish the view that ornament is not the dress of thought but something inseparable from thought. "It is," he says in his *Lectures,* "a very erroneous idea, which many have of the ornaments of Style, as if they were things detached from the subject, and that could be stuck to it, like lace upon a coat. . . . the real and proper ornaments of Style are wrought into the substance of it. They flow in the same stream with the current of thought." [39] In this statement and others, Blair reveals his concern to remove the stigma from the ornaments of style that had been placed upon them by advocates of plainness who perpetuated the antirhetorical tradition. In making perspicuity and ornament the chief standards of style, Blair may have been concerned to reconcile the differences between two qualities which the advocates of plainness had pronounced antithetical and inimical to one another. The highest achievement in writing for Blair is to unite the two, and his parting caveat to the advocates in remarks on precision in style is that "We must study never to sacrifice, totally, any of these qualities to the other," that is Copiousness and Ornament to Precision and Accuracy.[40]

The third paragraph of the article in the *Encyclopaedia,* includes praise of Swift for his simple and unadorned style, of Addison for his elegance, and of Johnson for the impetuosity of his style and its effectiveness in fixing our attention on the truth. This concern to appraise their styles reveals one of the main tendencies in the criticism of prose style during the eighteenth century, the tendency to determine the relative merits of major English writers and, along this line, to resolve the issue of Addison's elegance versus Johnson's energy.[41] The article in the *Encyclopaedia* appears to resolve this issue by allowing the individual merit of each style and by omitting Blair's remarks on the faults of each. The effect of the article, as indeed the effect of Blair's entire discussion of style, amounts to an effort to cultivate a catholicity of taste. The article does not fail to make Blair's case for diversity of styles or for variety within a single style. The article in the *Encyclopaedia,* different as it is from those in Croker's *Complete Dictionary of the Arts and Sciences* and Diderot's *Encyclopédie,* agrees with them on the necessity of variety in style. In this respect, all of them oppose the antirhetorical tradition and its demand for the plain style.

§ 5

In retrospect, perhaps the most surprising fact is that lexicographers in the century did not find any use for Swift's memorable definition until Johnson used it as an illustrative quotation in his *Dictionary*. Equally surprising, I think, is that Swift's definition, while akin to a rhetorical definition of *elocution,* is wholly at odds with the broad and narrow meanings which lexicographers were wont to give to *style*. The term, variable in meaning throughout the century, received different meanings in Chambers's *Cyclopaedia* and the third edition of the *Encyclopaedia Britannica,* and in each case the meaning given amounts to a redefinition of the term. The emergence of prescriptive definitions may testify obliquely, as do the definitions themselves, to the influence of eighteenth-century criticism of prose style and particularly the opposition to the antirhetorical trend. Generally, encyclopedists seem to have been more susceptible to this influence than lexicographers. Lastly, de Jaucourt's compendious article may represent the tendency in French criticism to assume the usefulness of rhetoric in prose as well as in poetry while the *Encyclopaedia Britannica,* based though it is on Blair's *Lectures,* may stand as an epitome of the tendency in English criticism of prose style to oppose the antirhetorical trend by reconciling its demands for plainness and perspicuity with the growing demand for elegance and force.

The Nineteenth and Twentieth Centuries — and Beyond

Dollars and Dictionaries
The Limits of Commercial Lexicography

> "Great noise and little wool!" the Devil said as he was shearing a pig. — *Irish proverb*

§ 1

"61 MILLION DICTIONARIES will go out of date in 1969," the latest advertisement of our newest American desk dictionary announces —but begins the sentence with the figures and thus outrages all well-bred conservatives. "The American Heritage Dictionary," the boast goes on, "the new authority on the English language" for everyone, "will date them all the day it's published"; for it will be "the first dictionary on the market to provide contemporary guidance on usage," the first "that adequately records the histories" of English words, the first "to base its definitions on the analytical method of defining and the Brown University Corpus of Present-Day English." It will even have "computer set type . . . and a contemporary format"—virtues which Dr. Johnson and Sir James Murray never dreamed of.

But Johnson and Murray, though they would not have known the word, would still have found nothing strange in the chutzpa[1] of Houghton Mifflin's advertising. Like any student of dictionaries

for the past two hundred years or more, they would have recognized it immediately as the sort of stuff that got into the papers
during the competition between Johnson's *Dictionary* (1755) and
its contemporary, the Scott–Bailey *New Universal*, or during the
rapid publication of the four posthumous editions of the Johnson
some thirty years later,[2] or during the nineteenth-century wars of
Webster and Worcester;[3] and they would have known from experience that puffs for new wordbooks must be read figuratively,
like medieval allegories, "so that the exterior shell of falseness
having been cast away, the reader may discover within secretly
the . . . kernel of truth."[4] Indeed, a severe judge might find the
Houghton Mifflin chutzpa rather unexciting. Mr. Jess Stein did
better in 1966 when he said that he and his colleagues of the
Random House Dictionary "have endeavored to preserve all that
is worthy in the great lexicographic traditions of Samuel Johnson,
Noah Webster, James A. H. Murray, William Craigie, William
Dwight Whitney, and others"[5]—though perhaps the charitably
inquisitive might justify Stein's claim by showing how often his
"completely new" dictionary shows verbal identities with Whitney's
old *Century*, which C. L. Barnhart frankly acknowledges as a
source of much "scholarly information" for the commercial lexicographer.[6]

Ironically, if the responsibility had to be placed on just one
man, Dr. Johnson himself would be the culprit who kept descriptive English dictionaries in the hands of businessmen and thus
guaranteed a continuous display of cupidinous prevarication.
Everybody remembers how Johnson beat the forty Frenchmen[7]—
how Voltaire urged the Academy to imitate him,[8] how the Accademia della Crusca thanked and praised him,[9] how Klopstock
praised him in Germany and Adelung copied him,[10] how his influence lived on to affect the historical dictionaries of the nineteenth
century;[11] but if Johnson's success in doing the work of an academy
helped to prevent the establishment of one in England, it did not
make money any the less necessary for the support of lexicography. His *Dictionary* has been followed by many others which
scholars have made so that businessmen could make a profit. Sometimes entrepreneurs have made both dictionary and profit too.

In nineteenth-century America, the most familiar commercial

dictionaries were those of Noah Webster and Joseph Worcester.[12] Viewed from the later twentieth century, with a century of historical lexicography in between, Webster can be made to look strangely contradictory. The Connecticut farm boy who "marched with his father against Burgoyne" [13] has been reprehended for his etymologies by the Sanskrit scholar Franklin Edgerton;[14] for Webster scorned Sir William Jones and devoted himself to searching out the words which survive by common descent from "the primitive language of man," the Chaldee spoken by "the descendants of Noah . . . on the plain of Shinar." [15] Yet the provincial was also the patriot. Though the believing etymologist mythologized about Chaldee, the patriotic lexicographer insisted on making a new dictionary for a new world, a dictionary for a society that was moving into the age of science and technology without a closed, established ruling class; and as the maker of an *American Dictionary,* Webster might be considered as partly anticipating the "period dictionaries," the latest offshoots of the *OED.*[16] The man who did not keep up with Jacob Grimm prefigured Sir William Craigie—or so one might say.

A less distorted view would likely be that Webster hoped to make a dictionary which his countrymen would buy and use, to their profit and his. To a considerable extent he succeeded, notably in his definitions and in his extension of the vocabulary to include scientific and technical terms and a good many Americanisms; and more than one of the principal obstacles to his achievement—like Chaldee etymologies and reformed spellings—were of his own making, the results of his firm conviction that he knew better than they did what his countrymen would find useful. Joseph Worcester, in the dictionary war, took advantage of just those eccentricities. Scholarly, restrained, conservative, New Hampshire's farm boy had cultivated all the virtues which qualify a man to be the son-in-law of the Boylston Professor of Rhetoric. He saw Webster's strength, acknowledged it, and matched it fairly by writing sensibly about Americanisms, by extending the wordlist and the encyclopedic features of the dictionary even further than Webster had done, and by introducing "the discriminative synonymy with cross references." [17] He also saw Webster's weakness and alluded to it politely and accurately. Webster, he said, had less "taste and judgment" than "industry and erudition";[18] and Worcester made it his own task to give fresh utility to the utility dictionary by avoiding ill-judged flights of etymology and the tasteless exaltation of his own preferences over good usage in spelling and pronunciation. He died while his *Dictionary of the English Language* still rivaled the Webster–Mahn of 1864 as the world's best.

Commercial competition, with the competitors learning from one another, was in this instance to the good of a readership still relatively small, homogeneous, and literate—at least by present standards; and the joint accomplishment of Worcester and Webster was recognized in Britain as well as in the United States. In 1850, for example, Blackie & Son published John Ogilvie's encyclopedic two-volume *Imperial Dictionary* at Glasgow and Edinburgh, "on the basis of Webster's English dictionary [*sic*]";[19] in 1853 Henry Bohn in London audaciously reissued Worcester's *Universal*, with both Webster's name and Worcester's on the title page and on the back;[20] and some twenty years later, Harper's and Macmillan's proposals of "a new dictionary . . . to rival those of Webster and Worcester" helped to revive the Philological Society's dictionary project and to make Murray the editor of what would become the *OED*.[21] Ogilvie's *Imperial* as revised by Charles Annandale in turn provided a basis for the *Century Dictionary*, Whitney's encyclopedic work, which appeared in six volumes between 1889 and 1891 (New York: The Century Company). The *Century* was highly and deservedly successful and reappeared many times in various formats—in 8 volumes, 10 volumes, 12 volumes, sometimes with and sometimes without an added "cyclopaedia of names" and atlas. The reviewer of an advance copy of section 1 called it "an apotheosis of Webster." [22]

As the literate public widened, a new competitor for the Merriam Company appeared in 1893 and 1894. Its editor, in a day when lexicography engaged the attention of the best linguists, was virtually an amateur, and the emphasis of its planners was on ease of use. Lutheran minister, religious publisher, and prohibitionist, Isaac Kauffman Funk was determined to inform and edify the common reader—which he did by such undertakings as the founding of the publishing house of Funk & Wagnalls, the launching of the

Literary Digest (1893), and the publication of the familiar *Standard Dictionary* (1894). By meeting the needs of readers who wanted a one-volume reference library in which they could easily find miscellaneous encyclopedic matter as well as the spelling, meaning, and pronunciation of English words, the *Standard* gained a considerable market. It became the *New Standard* in 1913, and in various guises it is still issued almost every year.[23]

The contrast between the scholarly *Century* and the popular *Standard* marked a problem for future lexicographers. With the population always increasing, literacy spreading, and the costs of dictionary-making rising, the publisher of a big dictionary had to have big money; and if he could not get it from sales of his other books or from a subsidy of some kind, he had to reach a mass market. The traditional device was to keep the "unabridged" on the highest possible level and to use it as the source for smaller books which more people could buy and use. The *Standard* emphasized another possibility—to make the unabridged itself more widely marketable. Since the derivation of words meant little to most readers, etymologies should follow the definitions in an entry, not precede them; and since more readers were concerned with current meanings than with the archaic or the obsolete, in the definitions themselves "the order of usage" should "supersede the old-time chronological order." The ambition was that everything should "be of the handiest, and the best" [24]—but could it? One gets nothing from even the best dictionary unless he brings a good deal to it, and if the best dictionaries were to be easy for everybody to consult, goodness by scholarly standards might have to be sacrificed to the handiness that would bring big sales. The ideal of a good popular unabridged would be hard to realize.

If literate middle-aged or aging sentimentalists are fit judges, the second edition of *Webster's New International* came closer to that ideal than any of its competitors—or W3. At any rate, for twenty years or more W2 was pretty much unchallenged as the best unabridged one-volume utility dictionary, a book which scholars had made and scholars respected but which students and intelligent laymen also consulted, safely granting it the kind of authority it did not claim because it had the kind of authority that learning gives. Even the new generation of American structural linguists, if their concern for Bella Coola and Potawatomi left them time to think about the English vocabulary at all, were generally happy with the respected Merriam–Webster. It was a cozy situation for everybody except the Merriam Company's editors and rivals.

The editors' problem in making a *Third International* was even more formidable than the revision of a standard work must always be. The rate of social change, and hence of lexical change, had increased sharply, and at the same time more people were reading than ever before, and reading more varied matter; yet not even the best educated guess at usefulness would make everybody happy about the choice of new words and senses for inclusion or about the old ones that would have to go to make the needed room. On this and other matters, the widened audience was too varied to make any one judgment generally acceptable. The structuralists, for example, had not given much help in making the new dictionary new, since in lexicography they had few new ideas to give; yet they would write reviews, and they would be angry if the dictionary did not embody their notions of correctness— which were guaranteed to enrage the journalists and editors and pundits-at-large who would review *W3* for the newspapers and the popular magazines. Besides, in the background there was always usury. The dictionary would cost almost as much as the Merriam Company took in in a single year, and the only way to appease the usurers was to sell more copies. In the words of President Gordon J. Gallan, "as costs go up the answer is volume." [25] Sound scholarship would have to be made pleasing to the unscholarly.

Now that the uproar has died down,[26] perhaps most people will at least agree that *W3 is* a dictionary—and hence a generally traditional book. The omission of encyclopedic matter, for example, was a departure from Websterian tradition but had behind it the authority of Murray, who had said in the Preface to the first volume of the *OED* "that a Dictionary of the English Language is not a Cyclopaedia";[27] and the new style of "completely analytical one-phrase definitions" [28] was just what Dr. Gove has called it— a matter of style, not basic theory. Reviewers who knew where to look could have found a much more radical kind of definition in the dictionary of William Lloyd, which had been printed three hundred years earlier, in 1668, with Bishop Wilkins's *Essay towards a Real Character*. Following Wilkins, Lloyd gave all his definitions in a system of categories, a universal scheme of concepts, which catalogued man's world; but W3 in 1961 held aloof from the world-views of conceptual dictionaries, from notions about fields of meaning and the conceptual world between the ego and reality, from the structural semantics of the anthropologists, and—since the editors were not prophets—from the now-proliferating speculations of the M.I.T. group and of their chief opponents.[29] Precisely because the *Third International* does not embody a significant semantic theory, one of its few serious reviewers felt constrained to label it (or libel it) as "an anecdotal dictionary on a dinosauric scale." [30]

But serious discussion of fundamentals made no great part of the controversy over W3. Most of the foofaraw was about standards of goodness and correctioness in language and its use—standards which Dr. Gove's critics said he had abnegated, while he accused them of trafficking in "artificial notions of correctness and superiority." [31] In this accusation he echoed the linguistic gurus of the NCTE.

The theoretical arguments of these sages generally involve the assumption that the insistence on standards other than their own resulted from the new ascendancy of the middle class in eighteenth-century England—a partial explanation only, since English prescriptivism is much older than the eighteenth century and since its eighteenth-century variety was much influenced by ideas emanating from the very different societies of France and Italy. In their practice, on the other hand, the NCTE's linguists have been surprisingly like the middle-class schoolteachers whom they have despised for teaching "It is I" and "Whom did you see?" The "linguistic engineers" have tried to impose an interdental spirant and a postvocalic /r/ on the children of the black ghetto, pretending that if little blacks will add these incongruous embellishments to their native speech, they will be masters of "Standard English as a second dialect" and so will get jobs which they have not been trained to hold and which white employers and white labor unions are determined not to let them have if they can help it. What emerges from such tragic fooling is that convictions about goodness and badness in language are little understood but are anything but "artificial." They run so deep in the mind of our society that most of us do not inwardly realize how relentlessly speech operates to establish our social identities and to maintain the harsh distinctions that we take for granted.

The disaster to the Merriam Company was a disaster to descriptive English lexicography in the United States; for the chance of a quick profit now lay in taking advantage of Merriam's bad luck, not in the long, hard, expensive job of providing, for the second half of the twentieth century, a truly international dictionary of the world's most popular language. The attacks on W_3 had created a demand for an easily read alternative with a more pious approach to usage. The alternative duly appeared in 1966.

The treatment of usage is the obvious basis for comparison between the *Random House Dictionary* and the *Third International*, and some levity will be necessary in the discussion to mitigate the painfulness of the subject. Walking carefully on thin ice, Jess Stein of the *RHD* says quite rightly in his Preface that judgments *concerning* usage are as much a part of the lexicographic record as the facts of use itself;[32] but the middle course that he announces is so very middle that one can't be quite sure what it is. On the one hand, presumably the left, there is the "special panel of linguists under Professor Raven I. McDavid, Jr." The linguistic panel "reviewed and, where necessary, amended the usage *labels* [italics added] throughout the *RHD*." [33] On the other hand, among the literary, there is "Mr. Theodore M. Bernstein of *The New York Times*." The dexterous Mr. Bernstein directed the preparation of the usage *notes*, which unlike the labels were not reviewed by linguists but "by a group of editors and teachers." [34]

The two names of Bernstein and McDavid are thus duly dropped, one on each side of the unabridgeable abyss; and the imaginative reader, though he knows that he really cannot tell who is responsible for saying what, fancies that he can hear linguists and editors shouting their dialogue-at-a-distance. So, in his prefatory essay on "Usage, Dialects, and Functional Varieties," McDavid announces that "essentially, in the usage of native speakers, whatever is, is right"—but qualifies his subversion by acknowledging that "some usages may be more appropriate than others, at least socially." [35] To that egregious understatement, the voice of the Bernstein is heard replying, in the entry for *ain't*, that "the well-advised person" who shuns the imputation of illiteracy "will avoid any use" of that foul word; but the panel of linguists are neatly ambiguous again in labeling *ain't* for *am not* nonstandard in the United States "*except in some dialects,*" whose identity they do not betray.

Even the reviewers got into the game and shouted *'tain't* and *'tis.* Mario Pei in the *Nation* said that *RHD's* "linguistic philosophy" would not grieve so many tender spirits as the *Third International's* "doctrine of usage" had done. "In most disputed cases," Pei declared approvingly, "Random House minces no words and makes few concessions to substandard and confusing usages." [36] At almost the same time, however, J. M. Edelstein in the *New Republic* called Pei's "excellent buy" only "the latest event in the long history of the corruption of the language." The "norm" of the *RHD,* he complained, "is the lowest common denominator," for its editors have abdicated "their responsibility to the language" and have made their appeal "to the broadest possible market." [37] Joseph Wood Krutch got in the last word for the tongue that Shakespeare twisted with his accusation that though *RHD* is fairly sound, Editor Stein had written a grievously permissive article in *TV Guide.*[38]

Krutch should be slower to discover dangerous principles where none may be entertained. As Stein said, "the officers and directors of Random House" gave him no instructions except "to produce the best dictionary [he] possibly could," [39] and the proof that he understood his orders is the jingling of the cash registers. With the help of four computers, the *Random House Dictionary* was quickly made, its actual compilation taking only some seven years, and substantial economies must have been effected in the production of this new and completely independent work by copying from the *ACD.*[40] Packaging and advertising were equally skillful. Its editorial tendency to face both ways still left the *Random* dictionary profitably to the right of *W3* in matters of usage, an advantage which Stein multiplied by covert sneers at his competitor; his book is handsomely bound and legibly printed on excellent paper; though distinguished scholars were invited to contribute, their contributions were not allowed to make the work look hard for common men to use; and it contains enough irrelevant miscellaneous information to place it squarely in the tradition of the respectable homeowner's one-volume reference library. It was such advantages, presumably, which led Mr. Bennett Cerf to express the hope that as Johnson's was the dictionary of the eighteenth century and Webster's that of the nineteenth, so *RHD* will be that of the twentieth.[41] No one need hesitate to call it a characteristic product of our times.[42]

The desk dictionary announced by American Heritage and Houghton Mifflin will not alleviate the crisis of descriptive English lexicography in the United States. The dictionary may be well done, though its advertising has been disgraceful; but one more desk dictionary will hardly reconcile private profit with public good, even if it should represent a substantial advance in method beyond its predecessors of similar scope. The future of the Merriam–Webster, under the new ownership of Encyclopaedia Britannica, Inc., is also unpredictable without private information.

What is clear is that the commercial competition which served the public in the nineteenth century has ceased to do so in the twentieth. Our best unabridged descriptive dictionary, the *Third International*, was badly received on the common market; the *Random House Dictionary*, a decidedly inferior "unabridged" which is not much more than an oversized desk dictionary, has been enormously profitable because it was skilfully engineered and advertised. No publisher, however, who wants an immediate profit can attempt the kind of dictionary that we need today; for as the good and bad example of the Merriam Company has showed, really useful things in lexicography can now be done only by large, permanent staffs, operating under the direction of scholarly editors with plenty of money at their disposal and under no pressure to recover what they spend. But profit is what commercial publishing is all about.

§ 2

Not much learning or intelligence is needed to show the elements of the present crisis or one precedent for dealing with them.

One problem is certainly the gap between linguistic theory and lexicographic practice. Practical men have been the heroes of our lexicographical tradition, and by comparison they dwarf the less numerous scholars whose work has been more fully permeated by distinctive ideas. Yet there is another side to these judgments of theoretical ingenuity and practical effectiveness. The man who mistakes a new set of diacritics for a new analysis of pronunciation, or a new style of defining for a new theory of definition, is the most impractical of all. In spite of himself the least theoretical lexicographer must assume a phonology, a syntax, a semantics; and he might as well examine his commitment.

Today he has plenty of theories to examine—more theories, in fact, than grammars and dictionaries built on them. After the structural hiatus, when *meaning* was almost a dirty word, semantics and the lexicon are hot subjects once again; and it is not only the erudite practitioners who will suffer if the men who make dictionaries and the men who talk about them never talk to one another. Restatement linguistics is almost inevitably *bad* linguistics; for restatement is hardly necessary unless theory has changed significantly, and if theory has significantly changed, new questions will be asked and new data will be needed, while the old data become at best inadequate and at worst irrelevant.

But what most impresses the amateur of lexicography (and keeps him moderately honest) is not the fact that our lexicographers are unlikely to be theorists and our theorists are unlikely to make dictionaries. The amateur is simply overwhelmed by the huge mass of information which lexicographers of English are expected to make accessible and which users of English dictionaries find it so impossible to get at. The whole vocabulary of the world's most popular language, in all its local and national varieties, from the beginnings to the present day—that is the enormous object of our lexicographers' collective studies; and the student who wants to know what has been said about it must be prepared to paw through piles of notes and articles, stacks of books, and to shuttle from dictionary to dictionary—all with no assurance of finding what he wants in collections to which the alphabet is the only clue. With the twentieth century three-fourths gone, the hand-making of even one more big alphabetical printed dictionary must seem like masochism to its makers and sadism to its users.

Dictionaries which take a century to make, or even a quarter century, cannot keep up with a living language anyway. The exploding technical vocabulary alone, posing as it does a whole new set of questions, should warn the lexicographer of English against the prevailing disorganization, duplication of effort, and (in some quarters) unconsidered traditionalism. At a time when the making of a good dictionary demands the efficient collection, storage, and retrieval of enormous and constantly growing masses of material, lexicographers at Oxford and Edinburgh and Ann Arbor and Madison and Victoria and Sydney continue to work separately; and scholars elsewhere must still content themselves with expensive lexicons which record only a fragment of the available evidence and which can never be economically or efficiently revised. The very fact that the individual mind is inescapably limited should make us impatient with practices which multiply its limitations unnecessarily.

The precedent for dealing with our crisis in descriptive lexicography is of course the precedent of the historical dictionaries, which marked the next great advance, in the central tradition of European lexicography, after the standard and standardizing dictionaries of the academies and Dr. Johnson. The historical dictionaries of English are all related, in one way or another, to the *OED*; but the principal antecedents of the *OED* itself were not English at all, but Continental. Only one dictionary of English before the *Oxford* deserves particular mention in this connection.

The separate publication of Charles Richardson's *New Dictionary* (which began to appear in 1818 as part of the *Encyclopaedia Metropolitana*) was complete by the spring of 1837.[43] It was generally well received and has since been repeatedly described as a precursor of the *OED*. Richardson's purpose and accomplishment are better understood, however, if it is remembered that he was a disciple of the Philosopher of Purley, John Horne Tooke, whose theory of language taught Richardson, among other things, "that words have only one meaning, which is immutable," and that the only words which are necessary for communication are verbs and nouns, "the names of the mind's impressions." All other words, as well as the various affixes, are merely abbreviations which in the progress of language have been introduced for brevity and speed.[44]

Accepting those beliefs as principles, Richardson made etymology as he understood it the means of finding in abbreviations the necessary words they stand for and of discovering the unique, literal meanings by which metaphorical and consequential applications could be explained. His definitions were not elaborately divided but relatively brief, and the burden of exhibiting the different applications of each word's underlying meaning fell on a series of chronologically ordered illustrative citations. It is these citations that partially justify the description of the *New Dictionary* as historical.

When the Philological Society set out, however, to remedy the deficiencies of existing English dictionaries (including Richardson's),[45] its leaders turned for models to the Continent, and especially to Germany, where the Grimms had begun the publication of their *Wörterbuch* in 1852. Their example had already stirred up similar activity in the Netherlands,[46] so that Trench was only expressing a general European interest when he referred, in his famous paper, to "the new German dictionary now in course of publication by the two Grimms." [47] Though Henry Sweet some fifteen years later spoke disparagingly both of the Dutch *Woordenboek* and of the Grimms' "huge dictionary," [48] his judgment was characteristically his own; Henry Bradley told the *Philologenversammlung* at Hamburg in 1905 that "the great German dictionary associated with the illustrious name of Grimm" ought in his view "to be the constant companion of every lexicographer of a modern European (especially, of course, a Germanic) language; . . . in my own labours," he said, "I have been greatly indebted to the learning, acumen, and diligence of its editors." [49]

But Dean Trench, Herbert Coleridge, and the other first movers of the Philological Society's undertaking were not so much indebted to the Grimms as to another, earlier German lexicographer, Franz Passow. Passow's dictionary of Greek had first appeared in 1819–23, and by 1843 it had been made the basis of Liddell and Scott's *Greek-English Lexicon,* the immediately famous work whose compilers were both original members of the Society.[50] Like Liddell and Scott, Herbert Coleridge announced his allegiance to Passow's theories. In his "Letter to the Dean of Westminster" in 1860, Coleridge wrote of himself and his colleagues that "the theory of lexicography we profess is that which Passow was the first to enunciate clearly and put in practice successfully—viz., 'that every word should be made to tell its own story.' " [51] In 1888, when Murray stated "the aim of this Dictionary," [52] his words were strikingly reminiscent of Passow and Liddell and Scott.[53]

Other influences naturally operated, just as the *OED,* in its turn, became a model for dictionaries on the Continent; for West European lexicography has always been an international and interlingual undertaking. When in 1873, after some thirty years of labor, Émile Littré completed the historically based *Dictionnaire* that made him a member of the French Academy, the *OED* was still projected only, and the Grimms' *Wörterbuch* would not be finished for almost another century.[54] The Philological Society had recognized Littré's achievement by electing him as an honorary member in June 1869;[55] the Society's president, A. J. Ellis, praised the completed *Dictionnaire* in his address in May of 1874;[56] and the always-generous Murray paid his respects in his Preface when his own first volume had appeared. "Since the original scheme of the Philological Society was projected," Murray wrote, "the great French Dictionary of M. Littré has been given to the world, and has been made use of in determining some of the features of the present work." [57]

Murray's reciprocal contribution to Continental lexicography can only be exemplified, perhaps most strikingly today in the volume *Lexicologie et lexicographie françaises et romanes,* the account of a conference held at Strasbourg in November 1957, just a hundred years after Trench wrote the "Deficiencies." In 1957, Littré's *Dictionnaire* had entered the public domain, and the question arose whether it should be reedited or whether a new French dictionary should be begun. Since Littré's time, the *OED* and the Danish *Ordbog* had been completed; the Grimms' *Wörter-buch* was nearing completion; the Dutch and Swedish historical dictionaries had run through many volumes; and after some disasters, a historical dictionary of Spanish was well under way, and an Italian one was being vigorously discussed. French scholars gathered at Strasbourg, then, to discuss what should be done for French, and the *OED* was prominent in their conversations. The spokesmen for the Spanish and Italian undertakings referred to it as a model, and the Anglicist Paul Bacquet said pointedly, "Son histoire commence en mai 1857. Cent ans plus tard, ce dictionnaire va-t-il en inspirer un autre?" [58]

It had already inspired a considerable number, including several for English. Long before the *OED* was finished, its editors had seen the necessity of a supplement, which appeared in 1933; and since in the 1960s "there is no early prospect of a revision of the main dictionary," [59] a new supplement has now been brought almost to publication. The supplements, however, are much less ambitious than the "period dictionaries" which are most commonly associated with the name of Sir William Craigie.

As early as 1905, Bradley had remarked that the *OED* does not supersede Mätzner for Middle English or Schmidt for Shakespeare; and "it leaves room, also," he said, "for future dictionaries, if they should ever be written, of the various successive stages of Modern English." [60] In a series of papers for the Philological Society, Craigie developed such ideas considerably further. Between 1919 and 1925, he argued that by its nature the *OED* was unable to do justice to particular periods in the development of the language or to its distinctive national varieties; and so he proposed dictionaries for American English and for Scottish, as well as a chronological series which would include a Middle English dictionary, a Tudor-Stuart dictionary, perhaps a dictionary for the period from 1675 to 1800, and (notably) a dictionary for "the modern period," 1800 to the present, with its vast accession of technical terms. By 1925 he could report that steps had been taken toward the actual production of several of these works.[61]

Craigie's activity was so vigorous and so successful that the period dictionaries have been the principal undertakings in English lexicography since the *OED*. He himself shared the editing of the *Dictionary of American English* (published by the University of Chicago Press between 1938 and 1944), which was followed in 1951 by Mitford M. Mathews's *Dictionary of Americanisms,* also a Chicago book. Universities have likewise been instrumental in the publication of the two Scottish dictionaries, one of them formerly located in Oxford and the other in Aberdeen, but both now in Edinburgh, along with the survey of Scottish dialects and the place-name survey.[62] Craigie and J. A. Aitken have served as editors of the *Dictionary of the Older Scottish Tongue from the Twelfth Century to the End of the Seventeenth* (Chicago, 1931–); and the *Scottish National Dictionary,* which deals with all Scottish words since 1700, has been in the hands of William Grant and David Murison (Edinburgh, 1931–).

Of the chronologically ordered dictionaries which Craigie proposed, only one has begun publication, the *Middle English Dictionary* of Hans Kurath, Sherman Kuhn, and John Reidy (Ann Arbor, 1952–); but work has been resumed—again at Ann Arbor —on the dictionary of the Early Modern English of the Tudor-Stuart periods. A new Old English dictionary to replace that of Bosworth and Toller is under discussion by scholars in the United States, England, and Canada, where the University of Waterloo has "massive computer facilities";[63] but editing and publication must wait for the prior editing of a number of prose texts and for the completion of concordances for both prose and poetry.[64]

Meanwhile, the vocabularies of other local and national varieties of English have been recorded. The most notable accomplishment of the kind so far has been the six-volume *English Dialect Dictionary* of Joseph Wright (London, 1898–1905). For the United States, the American Dialect Society is sponsoring a *Dictionary of American Regional English,* which is being prepared by F. G. Cassidy at the University of Wisconsin, with support from the U.S. Office of Education. With R. B. Le Page, Cassidy has also done a *Dictionary of Jamaican English* (London, 1967). A less exotic national variety is the subject of the *Dictionary of Canadianisms on Historical Principles,* edited by Walter S. Avis of the Lexicographical Centre for Canadian English at the University of Victoria (Toronto, 1967); and a historical dictionary of Australian

English has been projected by the Australian Language Research Centre at the University of Sydney.

The length and distinction of this list make the one main item which is missing all the more striking by its absence. Governments, universities, and learned societies have cooperated across national boundaries to produce our historical dictionaries; but they have not attempted the dictionary of the modern period which Craigie also proposed. Descriptive English lexicography remains essentially commercial. William Benton and Bennett Cerf have more power to direct its future than our lexicographers and linguists have.

A last glance at the European scene heightens the incongruity of our situation. On the Continent, interest in the scientific study of the vocabulary is widespread among the international community of scholars. There are a number of well-organized groups and centers for lexical work, equipped with modern machines; and in many, if not most nations, academies are active in the recording and cultivation of the national languages. The conference at Strasbourg brought together scholars from Belgium, England, Germany, Holland, Italy, Poland, Spain, and Switzerland; and its proceedings were published by the Centre National de la Recherche Scientifique, whose representative declared that for a major work like a French thesaurus private resources would be inadequate and the assistance of the state would be necessary. Such a meeting has never taken place in the United States, where there is no academy to make a dictionary and where the present generation of linguists, until very recently, has had little interest in lexicography or lexicology. But the same year that produced the volume on the Strasbourg conference began the foolish argument over W3.

§ 3

An amateur of lexicography does not propose a National Center for Lexical Research. He must mainly content himself, if he is not to be laughed at for his vanity, with the arrangement of facts in patterns that speak for themselves. Where the patterns seem clear, however, and the authority of experts can be cited, perhaps a simple conclusion can be drawn without false pretenses.

The scholarly importance of the *Random House Dictionary* and the brawl about W3 is that they have no importance for scholars. The average man and the average reviewer cannot demand the best in a big dictionary, because they have no idea what the best might be; and even if they did demand the best, the businessmen who run commercial publishing houses would not give it to them unless they saw a direct relation between quality and profits. A farsighted entrepreneur might conceivably be able and willing to give his editors the resources which would protect them from the pervasive corruption of a pecuniary society which does not value learning; but probably no single corporation, no single institution of any kind, can do now what needs to be done in English lexicography. In the eighteenth century, Englishmen rejected an academy as the maker of their authoritative descriptive dictionary; in the nineteenth and earlier twentieth centuries, speakers of English were given historical dictionaries by cooperation among governments, universities, and learned societies; in the later twentieth century, someone must choose whether descriptive English lexicography should still be left to the Cerfs and Bentons, or whether private enterprise should be supplemented, in that field too, by uncommercial cooperative effort. Johnson's choice must be made all over again.

There is no reason to reject the uncommercial cooperative effort if it is directed by genuine scholars and not by amateurs or manipulators. Such effort, in any event, will continue in many areas. Though another *OED* will not be attempted in this century, dictionaries for limited periods and for national and regional varieties of English will continue to be made. In their making, duplication and waste of effort should be avoided; and from many separate collections of material, the greatest good should be derived. Craigie's scheme for the period dictionaries, moreover, will not be complete until a dictionary for the nineteenth and twentieth centuries—a really international dictionary—has been prepared. Von Wartburg in 1957 argued convincingly for a similar work for French, no matter what different or larger schemes might be attempted in the unknown future.[65]

Precedents for more extensive cooperation already exist. The Australian Language Research Centre, for example, corresponds with the makers of the new supplement to the *OED*, with the Institute for Dialect and Folklore Studies at Leeds, the Lexicographical Centre for Canadian English, the Center for Applied Linguistics, Random House and the Merriam Company, and so on.[66] Such precedents, and examples from the Continent, do suggest the establishment of international centers for research on the English vocabulary.

Proposals for those centers must be made, if they are made at all, by those who are competent to make them; and if the centers should be established, the experts will also have to decide what they should do. The French example suggests that one function of the centers, in the imagined best of possible worlds, might be to duplicate materials from the files of major English dictionaries everywhere, so that more extensive collections than any now available might be established and kept up to date. For this and other purposes, machines would be necessary (the Accademia della Crusca, whose name itself embodies the conservative ideal, has already gone in for international collaboration and electronic storage);[67] but the most important equipment would be the good brains which might find common ground for grammarians and lexicographers, practitioners and theorists. In the United States, a serious attempt to describe and judge the vocabularies of different dialects and styles—different "varieties of usage"—could have immediate social consequences; and complete and current information about technical terminologies would delight industrialists and the military.

The feeblest vision can foresee other functions for the imagined centers: the publication of bibliographies and reports on work in progress, the coordination of research, the devising of uniform methods of collecting and recording so that materials would be interchangeable, the provision of relevant materials for private use by qualified applicants, a variety of publications in a variety of forms for a variety of users.

But the centers do not exist. What exists is the necessity for a choice. At some future conference on lexicography, another amateur may presume to say what choice was made, and why.

The Sociology of Dictionaries
and
the Sociology of Words

SHERIDAN BAKER

MODERN DICTIONARIES, I believe, have faltered before the complex sociology of the word. And that sociology is bound up not merely in our daily dealings with one another, but in our deepest meditative moments, with thought itself, and our valuing of thought. The controversy over *Webster's Third New International Dictionary* (1961) revealed the sociological dissonances in our attitudes toward language, with linguistic theoreticians assuming one thing and a vocal segment of the literate public assuming another. The linguistic assumptions are perfectly representative of the general assumptions of modernity—assumptions that would seem to render modern man incapable of making a dictionary of his language, assumptions that make the very idea of a dictionary impossible, or obsolete.

Modern man believes in social equality, but words seem to insist on sociological and evaluative hierarchies. Modern man believes in scientific objectivity, but words seem to incorporate subjective values beyond the reach of empirical observation. Modern man believes in change, and dictionaries, like all books, represent permanence. The modern belief in Progress militates strongly against the permanence of the recorded past and even against the

permanence of present description. Thus dictionaries, the repositories of the past, the describers of what *is*, are out of tune with
the keynote of modernity, which values change and cancels yester-
day's record with today's new observation.

Marshall McLuhan and Father Ong have declared the printed
word obsolete,[1] welcoming man's release from the dark ages and
metal racks of typography, and now McLuhan is not so sure even
about speech:

> The computer abolishes the human past by making it entirely
> present. It makes natural and necessary a dialogue among cultures
> which is as intimate as private speech, yet dispensing entirely with
> speech. While bemoaning the decline of literacy and the obsolescence
> of the book, the literati have typically ignored the imminence of the
> decline of speech itself.[2]

But society continues to buy books, and continues to buy dictionaries, presumably to understand the printed words it reads,
those unfamiliar in daily speech.[3] The market in dictionaries suggests that modern man, in spite of his typical philosophical assumptions, still does look for the fixity and authority that dictionaries inevitably represent, the permanence of the written word,
to which they are the key, and the sorting out of social ratings of
better and worse, high and low, which they reflect. Modern lexicographers, who have grown up with the linguistic thinking of
the past forty years, have been faced with a paradox: disclaiming
authority but claiming scientific authoritativeness, praising change
but making permanent records, exalting speech but writing books
distilled from writing, believing in equality but finding hierarchies,
believing in relativism but finding the absolutely persistent concept of "better" and "worse," assuming determinism but hoping
to encourage the "patterns of tendencies that have shown themselves in the drift of the English language." [4]

The modern lexicographer, schooled in linguistics, has been
disposed to describe language synchronically, that is, to slice it
horizontally across a moment of the present, which would be
largely to describe speech, but his material has forced him as well
to consider language historically, since he must also deal with
language as it appears in written documents that stretch back at

least as far as Shakespeare. The claims for, and defenses of, W3
lead one to expect a synchronic dictionary, a dictionary of present
speech; the pages of W3 reveal a historical dictionary, with history slightly muted by the omission of dates and the preponderance
of modern quotations.[5] Caught between the written past and the
spoken present, between subjective evaluations and objective observations, between inner depths and apparent surfaces, the modern lexicographer has held to the empirical surface and has shown
himself at a loss to handle the sociology of language: he has disliked levels of usage; he has described them only partially and
with apparent reluctance, as the controversy over W3 has indicated in detail and at length. The modern lexicographer has been
inhibited, I believe, by the prevailing scientism of the modern
world. And the solution to this inhibition, I shall suggest, is, first, a
deeper philosophical adjustment to epistemology and to the reality
of man's linguistic consciousness—indeed to reality itself—and,
then, simply a deeper sociological approach to language.

Let me speculate, first, about the school of thought that culminated, after a span of some forty years, in W3. We could well
trace it back to Bacon's induction, if we liked, and follow it forward through the empiricism of the eighteenth century and the
whole of scientism, historicism, and logical positivism that arose
in the nineteenth and persists in the twentieth. The observed empirical fact became the only truth and the whole of reality. The
assumptions and beliefs of the past—that is to say, tradition, the
belief that the past had already discovered essential validities and
values—was set aside for the new observation on the clean sheet
of the present. Clearly, de Saussure's synchronic linguistics—the
botanist's cross section of the linguistic stem—is part of this ide-
ational movement—and clearly this transverse slicing, whatever
de Saussure's hopes of eventually comparing historical slices,[6]
tended to cut off history as irrelevant. Present observation replaces
traditional belief, rendering tradition either unnecessary or invalid.
Clearly, Sapir's approach to American Indian languages both par-
took of the scientistic climate and established the scientistic approach to all language for some time to come.

Sapir's approach is that of the naturalist. Language must be
patiently stalked and observed in its native glade, with the ob-

server obscured as much as possible so as not to disturb its natural movements.[7] The scientific attitude immediately introduces the assumption that all languages, and all words, are equally good, just as all birds are equally good. These attitudes clearly remain basic to linguistic studies, before Chomsky began to open larger questions in the sixties. And inevitably we notice a third assumption lying, unnoticed, beneath the linguistic thinking that culminated in W3: namely, that civilization spoils language. The naturalist inevitably sees the Noble Savage.[8]

To the linguist, the spoken language is not only poorly represented but also distorted by book learning, by the schoolmarm, by "a pseudosophisticated aristocracy that resists change, that perpetuates artificial notions of correct English." [9] Lloyd and Warfel, for instance, tell their students that "all systems of writing are relatively modern and relatively crude. . . . In comparison, speech is sophisticated and mature," that compared to "the old, complex, and polished systems of spoken signals," writing is "new and crude": "instead of getting better, it has been getting constantly worse," that writing is "not only a crude and loose parallel . . . ; it is a limited and restricted system in comparison to the plenitude of speech." [10] Linguist Clyde T. Hankey indicates how typical of linguistic thought are these primitivistic glorifications of speech: "The fundamental observation that writing is not language but a partial and imperfect record of language regularly dismays our students, just as it frequently dismays their elders." [11] So speech is natural and perfect; writing unnatural and imperfect; and the scientist of the modern minute has taken the stance of Jean Jacques Rousseau, seeing the primitive Eden spoiled by civilization, education, and books. To the linguist, then, the language of the streets is as good as—indeed, better than—the language of the libraries, which in his eyes, is not language at all.

The program of *The Linguistic Atlas of New England* was clearly based on these naturalistic assumptions, and its admirable results doubtless strengthened those assumptions that went into W3. Professor Hans Kurath's interest was largely philological as distinguished from linguistic, historical as distinguished from scientific, a longitudinal look into the past as opposed to a horizontal slicing of the present. Nevertheless, Kurath wrote into his program the linguistic naturalist's prejudice against education, because education was covering up the evidence he most wanted to discover: the rural speech of the oldest inhabitants, which would reflect the dialects of their native England, so that he could "relate this regionalism in the speech of New England to the more tangible factors of population history . . . , the population shifts resulting from the rise of industries, the development of cultural and economic centers, of trade centers, of education, etc." [12] The oldest informants were to be without formal schooling, if possible: "an elderly descendant of an old local family . . . ; a simple but intelligent farmer or farmer's wife . . . , a workingman, tradesman or shopkeeper." Middle-aged informants were to have no education beyond high school. And "cultivated informants, with a college education," though not categorically specified as "young," were clearly to represent youth in Kurath's thinking and in subsequent work in linguistic geography.[13]

   This view of New England's history is quite different from that of historian Clifford K. Shipton:

> All of the American colonies contained men of education, often a good many. But only in New England, and specifically in Massachusetts and Connecticut, were they numerous enough to shape the society in which they lived. In Massachusetts, the immigrant generation contained a larger percentage of university-educated men than any other society that has ever existed. In Connecticut and Massachusetts, the American Revolution was made by Yale and Harvard graduates.[14]

Whatever kind of linguistic atlas Mr. Shipton might have produced (he is Director of the American Antiquarian Society), his sampling would have been different from Kurath's, who is clearly motivated by the primitivistic assumption that true language is a natural phenomenon, uncontaminated by books, and that the primitive evidence is precious because rare and easily damaged, presumably, by education. His early settler is an uneducated rustic, Shipton's an educated and learned collegian. Kurath instructs his fieldworkers to seek the "natural, unguarded response," to avoid the direct inquiry that "may put the informant on guard" (p. 45)

—the instructions of the naturalist stalking his quarry in the pristine wilds of nature.

Kurath's massive accomplishment—six huge folios of maps, 1939–43—obviously strengthened the naturalistic approach to language, the belief that limited sampling was statistically valid, that linguistics was at last becoming a precise science. Philip Gove well reflects the general attitude in 1961:

> Within the lifetime of nearly all who are teaching today—within the last three decades that is—the study of the English language has been deeply affected by the emergence of linguistics as a science. . . . Although some resistance remains, acceptance of the basic tenets of this new science is hardly any longer a matter of opinion. It is a matter of demonstrable fact now set forth in scores of reliable books and hundreds of articles in learned journals and repeatedly being orally dispersed in an increasing number of classrooms and meetings of linguistic groups.[15]

Mr. Gove goes on to cite Leonard Bloomfield's "charter" for descriptive linguistics (*Language* [New York: Henry Holt, 1933]; earlier versions, 1914, 1926). The "essential first step required by scientific method" in descriptive linguistics "is observing precisely what happens when native speakers speak." And this first step entails a radical change. "Instead of observing a language in terms of its past, specifically its relations to Latin grammar, the linguist must first observe only the relationships of its own elements to each other" (p. 3).

Now, the severe limitations of this "radical change in analytical method" should be evident. Observing "what happens when native speakers speak" cuts off the past and the whole phenomenon of the written word at a stroke. Mr. Gove goes on to say that linguistics has affected lexicography in little more than its management of pronunciation, that lexicography "is not yet a science" (p. 8). But Mr. Gove's essay of 1964 virtually glows with a sense of triumph: linguistic science has at last triumphed over error—only a few dark pockets of resistance remain—and W3 is somehow a culmination of that triumph.

The idea that linguistic science describes only the present

evidence, and that the lexicographer "should have no traffic with guesswork, prejudice, or bias or with artificial notions of correctness and superiority" explains why W_3 has been unable to handle the evidence that is not present on the surface of its citations—precisely those ideas of correctness and superiority that subjectively inhere in our perceptions of words, especially as the written word forces the writer to think about ideas of correctness, to make his choices, to seek his meanings, to seek his emotive effects. If we were to say, "observe precisely what happens when a native writer writes," we would see wherein linguistic science has limited itself, and how those limits have inhibited the lexicographers from accepting as evidence those things that do not show on the statistical surface. What happens when a native writer writes is an intensely subjective and cognitive linguistic activity that simply cannot be observed in the naturalistic exterior way. Empirical observation, which linguistics has taken as producing the only valid facts about language, will produce nothing at all.

What happens when a native writer writes is to take the pastness of language intensely into present consciousness. The writer meditates and searches among a vast vocabulary of written words that rarely enter his daily speech, his simple communications about changing the oil, his sociable chat about the Detroit Lions and Tigers—words he can find again and clarify only in the dictionary, as part of his inner cognition. Language comes to us from the past, and the pastness of language contains at its center a kind of timeless present. The individual word is not unlike the individual consciousness. At its center is a kind of timeless identity, which persists as long as it lives. Words like *mid-, bad, hut, city,* and *virtue,* for instance, have remained essentially unchanged through many centuries and across several languages. The individual word can indeed live a very long time, retaining its timeless identity. It responds to present circumstances, fitting its general identity to particular occasions, but its identity stretches from past to present very much as a person's consciousness of his own identity remains the same, as it expands and contracts and evolves around the edges, from cradle to grave. Modern linguistics, in looking only at present occasions, has tended to deny this durable pastness of words, especially those kept alive mostly on paper and in the mind, because empirical observation of what happens when native speakers speak will not detect them at all.

In short, lexicography needs to abandon the old empirical scientific faith that has cut it off from the whole vast subjectivity of language, so intimately connected with the silent printed word, with the conceptualizing power of letters and print. Linguist William Labov has recently deprecated the prevailing linguistic assumption, as epitomized by Bloch and Trager, who tell the linguistic apprentice that the "native speaker's feelings about sounds or about anything else is inaccessible to investigation by the techniques of linguistic science, and any appeal to it is a plain evasion of the linguist's proper function." [16] Labov also criticizes the linguist's characteristic emphasis on language as communication, thus excluding "the role of language in self-identification, an aspect of the expressive function of language" (p. 13).

Labov's work is indeed "a ground-breaking study, a milestone in the emerging field of sociolinguistics" [17]—even though Labov limits himself only to the vowel sounds of speech. Labov shows precisely what has been lacking in the naturalistic-empirical approach behind W3. Labov, too, is a naturalist. He, too, is interested only in speech. He, too, stalks his game and observes unobserved. But to these findings he adds what he learns from a series of direct inquiries about subjective feelings and evaluations. This is the sociologist's approach, the familiar opinion poll, based broadly enough to yield some statistical certainty. This is precisely what has been lacking in the older approach, accounting for that self-limiting denial of any knowledge not empirically observable, which James Sledd—the "generally admiring reviewer," as he calls himself—detected long ago in W3, an inadequate handling of "those opinions concerning speech and writing which properly enter into their own definitions of *standard* and of *Standard English*," revealing an odd "opposition between theory and practice . . . , as though some notion of scientific objectivity should require the scientist to deny that he knows what he knows because he may not know how he knows it." [18]

The problem is epistemological—how we know what we know—and the knowledge yielded by the naturalistic-empirical approach, which the modern world has characteristically considered the only valid source of knowledge, is often superficial compared to the intricate and vast subjectivity of language. The linguist, so as not to be blinded by any previous knowledge, has been operating something like a man from Mars observing human life for the first time. The linguistic man from Mars would notice dandelions even on the most spacious lawns, and would presume them standard. He now needs to go up and ring doorbells and ask the owners how they feel about them.

The new *American Heritage Dictionary* has taken precisely this approach, circulating questions to a panel of some fifty writers and editors, people who spend their days using and weighing words—Katherine Ann Porter is one, Louis Kronenberger another. And the responses of these men and women will assist the lexicographers in estimating levels of usage, in estimating how people feel about words. Here is a sample of their questionnaire:

> The following topics pose frequently encountered problems in usage. Please indicate your opinion in each case by checking the appropriate space. We realize that your preferences may not fit readily into a "yes" or "no" category, so we shall welcome your comments in the column provided for that purpose, or at the end of the ballot.
>
> By "would you accept?" in the examples stated here, we mean this: as a writer or speaker, as the case may be, would you use the word or phrase in this sense? As an editor, would you pass it willingly? As a listener, could you hear it without being vexed? By "acceptable in writing" we have in mind the large body of writing between the extremes of conscious formality (of a diplomatic paper, for example) and the deliberate informality and striving for effect characteristic of much fiction (as in dialogue designed to establish character) and humorous nonfiction (such as that which stresses dialect).
>
> In every case, we are primarily interested in determining standards of usage, not in the refinements of style, though obviously the two are related.
>
> FINALIZE. Is *finalize* acceptable to you in general speech and writing, as in "to finalize plans for a class reunion"? (This is distinct from governmental and military usage, where the term is said to have a technical sense.)   Yes _____ No _____
>
> IMPLY–INFER. The relationship between *imply* and *infer*, according to most modern sources, approximately parallels that between speaker and listener or between writer and reader. To *imply* is primarily to express indirectly, or hint, and thereby to give ground

for an inference: "the report implies that we were negligent." To *infer*, in careful usage, is to deduce or surmise: "I infer from the report that you think we were negligent." In earlier usage, *infer* was rather widely employed in the senses listed above for *imply*, and *infer* is still sometimes defined, secondarily, as "to imply." Is it acceptable to you in that sense, on the basis of the following example? "In your statement you inferred (hinted, said by indirection) that we were to blame." Yes _____ No _____

In short, these lexicographers are no longer embarrassed by evidence beyond that of empirical observation; they acknowledge the subjective sociology of language; they are not reluctant to give advisory weight to the thoughtful users of language, the group that Mr. Gove has rejected as a "pseudosophisticated aristocracy" whose opinions somehow warp the natural growth of language and yet whose practice is not significant because not numerically large. *W3* has, as I have said before, confused scientific objectivity with social equality. The *American Heritage* editors are acknowledging the aristocracy of words, their social hierarchies, which Mr. Gove's democratic empiricism cannot take into account. The hierarchies exist in our sociology and our language, as even *W3*'s reluctant labeling testifies.[19] And the hierarchies have to do both with social status and with intellect, with intellectual choices and values.

The whole logical-positivistic and empirical approach has militated vigorously against the mental and subjective side of knowledge. The physical observable fact is all, and values, which are inner and unobservable, are at best a kind of pragmatic illusion, which man should outgrow. But the climate seems to be changing. The year after *W3*, Karl R. Popper published his *Conjectures and Refutations: The Growth of Scientific Knowledge* (New York: Basic Books, 1962), suggesting that the whole epistemology of empiricism and induction, which stretches from Bacon to modern times, and which indeed misunderstands Bacon's induction, is wrong—as an explanation for knowledge. The basic empirical question asked for the *source* of knowledge presumes that only a physically observable fact is a valid source. The basic question is not, says Popper, "What is the source?" but "Is it true?"; not "How do you know?" but "Is it valid?" The source does not matter, he says; physicality does not matter; we are free to accept knowledge from tradition or instinct or innate ideas or wherever. His answer to the question about the sources of knowledge is simply this: "There are all kinds of sources of our knowledge; but *none has authority*" (p. 24). And the answer as to the validity of any proposed piece of knowledge is simply the most rigorous testing that reason, together with physical observation, can give it.

I bring in Popper to show how the theoretical grounds under what we have known as linguistics, the grounds under what we have taken as the ultimate in scientific validity, are shifting. And they are shifting in the direction of the inner and mental side of our linguistic experience. Jerrold J. Katz, for instance, has cut below the surface and clear back to the innate ideas that Locke's empiricism expelled once and for all, as we have supposed. Katz's "rationalist hypothesis" denies the empiricist's "contention that all our ideas come from sense experience, arguing instead that sense experience serves to activate . . . natural inclinations, dispositions, habits or powers, i.e., to transform the latent unperceived ideas with which men are innately equipped into clearly perceived, actual ideas." Katz argues that "*the language acquisition device contains, as innate structures, each of the principles stated within a theory of language,*" all the phonological, syntactic, and semantic components, all the grammarian's rules, all the structuralist's signals.[20] Man is programmed, in other words, to acquire and use language, to attach meanings to sounds, and by some rules common to all languages, just as the bird is programmed to acquire one cry, and only one, from all the possibilities surrounding him.

We empirical moderns may find Katz's ideas startling, and perhaps old-fashioned—he quotes a long passage from Leibnitz to support his conception of innate ideas—but I, for one, find them hard to refute. Owen Barfield has recently put forth another antiquated idea, one wholly unacceptable to the modern empirical linguist, wholly contrary to the basic modern assumptions about progress, namely, that language does indeed degenerate semantically, just as Dr. Johnson and his predecessors assumed: "Historically observed, the outstanding feature of language in its semantic aspect turns out to be the fact that words which were once figurative have ceased to be so and words that are still figurative are ceasing to be so." [21]

Naom Chomsky, whom Katz, in particular, is following, has similarly gone back to older ideas and found them good. He finds structural liguistics a regression (but with great contributions in methodology) from the universal grammarians of the seventeenth and eighteenth cenuries.[22] His *Cartesian Linguistics* (New York: Harper and Row, 1966) gets at the deep structures of language in the mind, at language as thought, which the mind then transforms into those outer structures and phonetic interpretations that the structuralist observes from the outside only. Chomsky makes a seminal point as he summarizes the Cartesian views: "human language is free from stimulus control and does not serve a merely communicative function, but is rather an instrument for the free expression of thought and for appropriate response to new situations" (p. 13). Modern linguistics, in other words, has limited itself not only by observing "what happens when native speakers speak," but by assuming that language is primarily communication. When you say "the spoken language is the language," you indeed presume that language is communication only. When you ask not what happens when native speakers speak, but what happens when native writers write, or when human thinkers think, your concept of language explodes to a new dimension. The language of animals, as Chomsky's Cartesians pointed out, is mere communication—specific signals for specific things. But for man, language is also "an instrument for the free expression of thought" (p. 13).

I am willing to suggest that for man language may be essentially conceptual, a means to knowing, and that the communicative function lies only around the edges of our primary communion with language—the primary murmuring dialogue in the mind we know as "thinking." We daydream in moving pictures, but we meditate in language, and these are both essentially noncommunicative, egocentric, self-satisfying activities. Their aim is not communication. We do communicate our simple animalistic needs and responses, of course; we do fill up our time with sociable communication that sometimes partakes of thought; we do clarify our ideas by talking them over; we do attempt to communicate, in papers written in agony and read aloud, the results of our thinking, which we ourselves have finally come to know only by working them out on paper. But at least our deepest and highest engagement with language is not in communicating but in knowing and thinking.

We know things by attaching names to them—name it and you can have it—and this is not communication at all. When a baby says "mama" or "dog" for the first time, he is not communicating but conceptualizing, pleasing himself with discovered knowledge. When the man attempts to get his thoughts straight, he writes them down on paper, reaching for the word to catch the idea he cannot grasp until he finds the word, distilling from the running debate, the silent oration, the insistent, silent questions and negations, the verbal discussions, a written statement of what he thinks, one to be revised and polished and straightened further, from a further round of silent debate and dramatization.

Linguistics, through Chomsky, is only beginning to reach the whole cognitive and cogitative side of language, represented not by speech but by reading and writing. The printed page is not merely a clumsy representation of speech, to be filed away as a record of the already irrelevant past; it is an active ingredient in man's deepest engagement with language, the product of man thinking, an activator and formulator of thought in other men. We find in the written words of others those thoughts we have not yet been able to put into words, to conceptualize, to grasp, that inchoate preverbal impulse of the mind toward understanding and knowledge. Labov has reached the subjective levels behind speech; he sees that speech is not only communicative but expressive, a means of self-identification. But he is still dealing only with reactions to the sounds of speech, to the way we react to Gomer Pyle. We now need some similar sociology of that vaster vocabulary of writing and thinking, and some study of the function of reading and writing in that most essential side of language—language as cognition, and recognition.

And here, I dare say, the sociology of the dictionary itself will prevail. For some time, linguistic lexicographers have been denying that the dictionary is prescriptive. Its authority lies only in its empirically accurate description, they say. You may take your pick, and use it as you like. But readers will continue to go to the dictionary primarily as a cognitive aid—to tell them what the words they read mean, and to tell them the social parameters of the words they are thinking of writing. This testifies to the need for permanence and certainty, even in modern man. It testifies to the essential permanence in words, which is in them just as memory and consciousness are in men, in spite of the pressures and potentials of change. Dictionaries are essentially of and for the written word. The synchronic dictionary, whose ideal is to record, across society, a moment of the present, immediately becomes little more than an historical document, for the curious specialist, as the next synchronic record displaces it—or reveals those permanencies in language that the total of man's word-hoard reveals, as he uses and applies it, bit by bit, to his present cognitive needs, formulating his thoughts in words as he reads and writes, communing with his deepest, cognitive self, in language.

Both Dwight Macdonald and Mr. Sledd agree, from opposite sides of the Websterian debate, that "laymen will misread [the dictionary's] declaratives as imperatives," in Mr. Sledd's words.[23] They do so because the dictionary represents the permanence and certainty in language. This is one of the sociological facts about language that future lexicographers will simply have to take into their total account of description and purpose. Accurate description is still what we want of any dictionary. But we want that dictionary to take into its account all the available evidence, from whatever direction, particularly from the subjectivity of language that has previously been excluded on theory and allowed back in only grudgingly and partially. We want a dictionary deeply aware of the cognitive function of language, aware that the thoughtful preferences of the writer have more cognitive, intellectual, and even more social weight than the thoughtless accidents of speech, which may yield a higher count. We want a dictionary sensitive to the thoughtful and cognitive preferences of language at its best —that is, to language as thought, which probably crystallizes at its best only in the crucible of writing.

English Dictionaries of the Future

PHILIP B. GOVE

MONOLINGUAL ENGLISH DICTIONARIES of the future—of the next century—will be much better than those of the twentieth century. All students of language observe without dispute that language is always changing. *Who's Who in America* recently announced that America's leading athletes will hereafter be included, Carl Yastrzemski and Denny McLain and Bob Gibson, for example. Think what that will do to a dictionary tradition that once thought the word *homer* and other baseball terms slang or cant. Some observers believe language is changing for the better. Although it may seem intemperate to call indisputable this opinion advanced by one lexicographer[1] over a century ago, I believe it. It follows that if dictionary makers continue to be competent observers of present-day English, their dictionaries will improve. But this is not a particularly strong reason for supporting hopes for the future.

My title may have led one to assume that I will discuss computers. It would be rash indeed not to consider briefly the role of the computer in the dictionary of the future. In brief, then, the role is principally fourfold. First, a dictionary can be printed by computer. The technique has already been used but generally not with perfection and not with economy. One huge problem, end-of-line hyphenation, has not, as far as I know, been satisfactorily solved. Some improvement in dictionary quality may come with more rapid production, which will close the gap between defining and publishing. A computer-printed dictionary will not necessarily be any better than a traditionally printed one. Second, a dictionary already in print can be put into a computer to be used for the making of its successor. No one who wishes to make a new unabridged dictionary today within his normal lifetime would think of doing so from scratch, that is, without a predecessor to serve as a starting place. Webster's fourth unabridged will be based on $W3$ (*Webster's Third New International Dictionary*, 1961), just as $W3$ was based on $W2$ (1934) no matter how extensive the changes.[2] At least three Webster dictionaries have been computerized. Other dictionaries have been put on magnetic tape. One cannot always be sure what the word *computerized* means. The *Seventh Collegiate* (upon which an *Eighth Collegiate* will someday probably be based) has been completely programmed so that most of the relationships seen by the eye on a printed page can be output by the computer, everything, that is, but the pictorial illustrations (and their captions), tables, guide words, folio numbers, and first and last lines. The chief reason for programming a dictionary into a computer is to facilitate getting out of it for study various desirable groupings. Before the computer there were two principal ways to study as a group words of similar morphology or relationships (words having the same suffix,[3] for example): 1] to go through the dictionary entry by entry and 2] to list them from memory. The first way is intolerably tedious; the second is hit-or-miss. Third, a computer can be connected with a universal scanner—one that can read typefaces of all sizes and kinds—to store citations. One research and development company predicts that such can be perfected in a few years. Scanners capable of reading a few typefaces are already in use. A computer at Brown University is now being used with a pilot corpus of one million words of running text published in 1961.[4] The students using it are interested both in the future role of the computer as a place to store words in context and in the kinds of language analysis that can be done with its help. It is easy to suppose that a way can be found to pass over the high-frequency words that fill up 90 percent of our reading matter—that is, pass over them after what they are is clearly established—but, as far as I know, the way has not yet been found simply because no one has wanted this kind of storage and retrieval. With it a dictionary could have thousands of millions of citations instead of ten million—to my knowledge the maximum number ever used for one English dictionary. Obviously if a dictionary maker has a hundred million citations instead of ten million, he needs a staff ten times as large or ten times as much time. The possibility of having either is flabbergasting. The fourth use of a computer is completely visionary: to write definitions. I have talked about this with several systems engineers and computational linguists and have so far found no one who says that a machine may someday be able in some way to define. I have read that "machines of the future will be designed in radically different ways. They will not be based on present design techniques which use formal logic. We will be able to communicate with future computers more effectively than is now possible. They will learn from experience and eventually, if we are ingenious and diligent enough, they will be able to handle natural language as we do." [5] It is a prophecy that is never going to give me a headache. If there is another unabridged in the twentieth century, it will be made mostly by editors. The twenty-first century is already promising to be rather different. So much for the jobs a computer might do for future dictionaries. I want to turn to software.

For about two centuries English lexicography received little or no help from students not concerned with the making of dictionaries. The first lexicographers were for the most part their own phoneticians, etymologists, and grammarians. Johnson had his harsh critics. Noah Webster was treated much more harshly than Johnson. But not until the leading grammarians of the early twentieth century, such as Curme, Jespersen, and Poutsma—not to overlook Henry Sweet in the nineteenth century—were there studies which helped the lexicographer substantially with the kind of language analysis he could rely on. It cannot be held now that either Fowler's *Modern English Usage* (1926) or Krapp's *Comprehensive Guide to Good English* (1927) helped much, although each exerted some influence. They were of more help to a long line of freshman and high school handbooks that have probably done as much harm as good. These handbooks can be held partly responsible for at least two generations of English teachers who have insidiously taught that there is only one kind of acceptable English. I remind you that Kemp Malone referred to Fowler's *Modern Eng-*

lish Usage as "that brilliant but vicious book." [6] I refrain from pointing at this time to some of the viciousnesses.

I do not particularly want to discuss the making of W3, but if I am to stay within reach of my title I must mention something of the help available to the editorial staff in the late 1940s. The editors had W2, of course, for a base and the *Oxford English Dictionary*. The beautifully full *OED* is indispensable for determining historical order and for attestations of usage, especially in early modern English. The W3 editors inherited two dozen thick notebooks which consisted of minutes and memoranda that had accumulated in the editing of W2. Most of them recorded decisions rather than reasons. Almost nothing in them could be called language analysis. The methodology that served as a guide to the making of W2 seems to have been buried in the pages of W1 of 1909. I suggest hesitantly and apologetically that the editors of W2 were not as aware of their ignorance of language behavior as were the editors of W3. Perhaps the W2 editors did not have as much compulsion as W3 editors did to keep looking at the evidence and to question over and over again the traditional evidence that the study of comparative philology had provided. In any case, from the late 1940s until the late 1950s the W3 editors were constantly paying attention analytically to problems of language behavior about which they felt they did not know enough. From these studies, done by individual editors or small committees, came hundreds of pages of directives to the whole staff.[7] A mere decade was not long enough to find solutions for more than a fraction of the problems needing investigation. If they all could have taken some time off to write books half as percipient as Martin Joos's *English Verb* (1964), a high ambition indeed, W3 might have been a better dictionary. But while an editor is making a study of such magnitude as that, he cannot be a practicing lexicographer. In addition to innumerable matters of defining technique, such as use of synonyms, formulas, getting rid of archaic wording (archaisms in office jargon became *Noahisms*), use of *a* or *the* with substantives, use of *to* with infinitives, editorializing vs. informing, treatment of variants, use of abbreviations, subject orientation; the editors studied functional change, objects of transitive verbs, logico-historical order, cardinal and ordinal numbers, interjections, attributive nouns, two-word verbs, reflexive verbs, and affixes of all types, which, incidentally, led *W3* to recognize that words like *basketful* and *cupful* have variant plurals: *cupfuls* also *cupsful* and *basketful* also *basketsful,* facts not recognized in either *W2* or *OED* at *cupful* and *basketful.* Some of the behavior studied did not produce the results hoped for. For example, a long time experimenting on grouping the senses of multisense verbs into transitive and intransitive failed to produce a better system. As far as I can recall, I had never heard then of middle verbs[8] (which have no passive, like *cost, weigh, resemble,* and *have*) nor of pseudopassives[9] (like *agreed on* in "the new course of action was agreed on" or *looked up to* in "he was looked up to"). Perhaps the *OED* system of ordering the senses without regard to transitivity or intransitivity is better than the separations in *W3.*

A small number of resulting improvements I mentioned in one paragraph of the preface to *W3:*

> A number of other features are   1] the recognition and separate entry (with part-of-speech label) of verb-plus-adverb compounds (as *run down*) that function like one-word verbs in every way except for having a separable suffix,   2] the recognition (by using the label *n* for noun) that substantive open compounds (as *clothes moth*) belong in the same class as nouns written solid or hyphened,   3] the recognition (by using the label *often attrib*) of nouns that often function as adjectives but otherwise do not behave like the class of adjectives,   4] the indication (by inserting suffix-symbols, as -s or -ES, -ED/-ING/-s or -ES, -ER/-EST) of the inflectional forms of nouns, verbs, adjectives, and adverbs at which the forms are not written out in full,   5] the recognition (by beginning entries with a lowercase letter and by inserting either the label *cap, usu cap, often cap,* or *sometimes cap*) that words vary considerably in capitalization according to circumstances and environment,   6] the recognition (by not using at all the status label *colloquial*) that it is impossible to know whether a word out of context is colloquial or not, and   7] the incorporation of abbreviations alphabetically in the main vocabulary.[10]

I do not now want to defend any of these. I know that some do not think all of them are improvements. I can admit (more or less confidentially) that some of them were experimental and that, therefore, all of them are open to deeper examination. Such examination is my current editorial assignment. I can say, no matter how inappropriate it may sound, that I know more than anyone else alive about what W_3 hoped to accomplish and wherein it fell short. And I have a long list of important and trivial lexical matters that should be looked at in preparation for W_4. Therefore, I will spend almost full time anticipating some of the problems that are sure to settle upon the editors of W_4. This is not an announcement of its imminent appearance, as anyone who can subtract 1934 from 1961 should perceive.

In 1960 I wrote an article for *Word Study* entitled "Linguistic Advances and Lexicography." Perhaps I could have gone out of my way to avoid use of the word *linguistic* and to avoid reference to the "emergence of linguistics as a science." It hardly seems possible, however, to think about the state of language study between W_2 in 1934 and W_3 in 1961 without such reference. Unfortunately, the article seemed to the uninformed, and even to some of the informed, to establish a relationship between W_3 and linguistics that invited critics to condemn the dictionary, the science, structural linguists, and me all in the same vituperative breath. It would have been fatuous to try to explain that the word *linguistic* in my title phrase "linguistic advances" was really broad and probably somewhat obsolescent. It became clear only after an unhappy year or two that W_3 had not unwittingly taken over the role of spokesman for linguistics or linguists. If only I had written "grammatical advances."

I find myself approaching thin ice in coming to the point concerning better dictionaries of the future. I do so in the face of some rather dismal statements about our knowledge today. I. A. Richards, for example, writes:

> We may reasonably hope that systematic study will in time permit us to compare, describe and explain these systematic ambiguity or transference patterns on a scale as much surpassing our best present-day Dictionary Technique as, say, our present competence in chemistry surpasses that of Bacon who foresaw it. Even now, if we could take *systematic* cognizance of even a small part of the shifts we fleetingly observe, the effect would be like that of introducing the multiplication table to calculators who just happened to know the working of a few sums and no others.[11]

And Mills F. Edgerton, Jr., writes:

> It is one thing to say that the problem of "listing" the elements
> of all sorts that are intrinsically and objectively present in a work of
> literature is so complex and complicated that it is impractical to
> undertake to solve it, given the utter inadequacy of the available
> tools with which to work, such as sociological, anthropological, lin-
> guistic, and other greatly detailed studies of the culture represented
> by a particular language (most of which remain to be undertaken),
> as well as the sophisticated lexicographical works which could be
> built from such data and which would be vastly different from the
> primitive and unsophisticated dictionaries with which we struggle
> to operate today. In fact, not only are most of the data necessary to
> such a listing lacking, but even if they were available there would
> not be enough people or time to manipulate them so as to achieve
> useful syntheses of them.[12]

These opinions about our language and our dictionaries are only
remotely hopeful. They are basically pessimistic as far as the
twentieth century is concerned. They reflect a recent statement by
Wallace L. Chafe: "It is truly remarkable that so many highly
intelligent scholars have pawed over [language] for so many
centuries, and that we still know little about it."[13] What we know
is little. "There are few scholars today who would claim that we
know everything about the way in which the English language
. . . really works."[14]

Nevertheless, a beginning has been made, although "much
time, probably centuries, has yet to pass before sufficiently exact
and detailed knowledge of language will be available to permit a
truly intelligent handling of literature."[15] I am not going to fob
off on you a prediction about better dictionaries centuries hence.
Karl Teeter observes that "there are more linguistic facts around
than we can make sense of without a guide."[16] When the plans
for setting up a center for applied linguistics were being drawn
up, one of the reasons was, according to Charles A. Ferguson,
"that not even nineteenth-century findings were being applied to
the solution of language problems, let alone the existing advances
of the current reseearch."[17] If the semantic properties of language
are not now systematically obtainable, it may be possible for a
traditional dictionary for the time being to fill the gap, to be a

guide to current linguistic facts. In saying "traditional dictionary" I am recognizing that alphabetization of words does not yield a useful system. Since the earliest English dictionaries only one new systematic approach to containing vocabulary has been conceived, and that is the thesaurus (Roget, 1852), which is based on philosophical principles. I can think of no other competitor. Perhaps the traditional dictionary can be made to carry more semantic information. If the editorial staff as usually constituted cannot take time for the semantic analysis necessary, where can the editors turn?

I come again to "linguistic advances." I now am *on* the thin ice. If I do not myself speak as a linguist, I can still read and quote what linguists write. In 1966 the American Council of Learned Societies sponsored a national meeting to look at the future. Those present tried to "picture linguistics as the pansemiotic science of verbal structure, the study of the word—man's unique species-specific biological endowment—in time, in space, and in its relations with the rest of the world." [18] That seems to take everything written and spoken (and then some) to be its province. W. R. Merrifield says: "Only when we understand the semantic component of a grammar can we be sure of our understanding of the other two [the syntactic and the phonological]." [19] "A full synchronic description of a natural language is a grammatical and semantic characterization of that language." [20] "Another reason," writes R. A. Waldron, "for the extreme caution shown by some modern semanticists over the relation between words and things is a new awareness of the complexity of language itself, both in form and use. Some aspects of this complexity . . . : the extent to which grammatical form contributes to meaning, the dependence of the individual word upon its context, and the pragmatic nature of language." [21] Recently Paul Garvin and two coauthors have said: "the greatest gap in the field of semantics today is the lack of sufficient knowledge regarding the precise relations (similarities, differences, presupposition relations, and the like) between the meaning-carrying elements of a language." [22]

These four quotations are not at all typical of pre-W3 days. [23] They clearly say that some modern linguists are becoming increasingly concerned about the role of meaning in linguistic analy-

sis. When Martin Joos, after some twenty parturient years, discovered an almost-ideal corpus containing nearly 10,000 verb occurrences and brought forth his book on the English verb, he gave
it the subtitle *Form and Meanings.*[24] W. F. Bolton points out that
the nuances of difference between Hamlet's use of *you* in addressing his mother and her use of *thou* in reply are "no longer
available within the grammar of English." [25] Although this may be
true of the masculine/feminine nuance, the mother/child relationship never was "within the grammar."

Consider the sentence "He is singing at the Met." [26] All that
traditional analysis or linear diagraming, or even structural linguistic analysis, can yield is that "is singing" is progressive. But
the sentence is a four-way ambiguity and can mean:

he is at the moment in the process of _____
he is _____ at intervals these days
he will be _____ once in the future
he will be _____ at intervals in the future.

One way to show that four terms are needed here is this branching
diagram

progressive

± repetitive   ± future

The progressive function of "is singing" can be further analyzed
only by a knowledge of meaning. A better-known and by now
perhaps somewhat worn-out pair is "John is easy to please" and
"John is eager to please." [27] Traditional analysis makes *John* the
subject of both sentences because they have identical structure.
They can be differentiated by showing that John in "John is easy
to please" is logically an object in some underlying sentence, perhaps "It is easy for us to please John."

Another more complicated set of isomorphic phrases consists
of five phrases in which a verb-form in *-ing* modifies a noun:

talking machine (machine which talks)
eating apple (apple for eating)
washing machine (machine for washing things)
boiling point (point of boiling)
laughing gas (gas which causes laughing).[28]

It is hopeless to try to differentiate these phrases by the formalistic grammar of tradition. A different approach must be found. I do not know what kind of grammar will be most successful, but I am sure that inherent lexical properties will be relied upon in some way.

Such properties are called lexical features. How many features words have I do not know. There are many different schemes for representing them. One of the simpler is illustrated by a diagram for the *New Collegiate Dictionary* definition of *bachelor:*[29]

bachelor

noun

(human)   (animal)

(male)   (male)

| [who has never married] | [young knight serving under the standard of another knight] | [who has the first or lowest academic degree] | [young fur seal when without a mate during the breeding time] |

The words in parentheses are features. Katz and Fodor call them "semantic markers" as distinguished from "grammatical markers" (in this case only one, the label noun), but some linguists say that "no formal distinction exists between the 'syntactic' and 'semantic' features." [30] Two other features would be, in a complete analysis, (physical object) and (living), but by what are called redundancy rules they have been omitted because they belong to all four bracketed senses (or "distinguishers"). The features in this illustration are simple and obvious. No one able to analyze an

English sentence needs them. But they can get much more specific and complicated. The more complicated the more useful, it seems, in disambiguation or differentiation (although the features sometimes appear to be chosen ad hoc). A feature of the verbs *break* and *bend* is (change of state) whereas *hit* and *slap* have the feature (surface contact).[31] A very useful feature is (± animate). The use of the arithmetic signs to mean "present" or "absent" seems preferable to (animate) vs. (inanimate) although (± male) could lead to confusion. If (− male) is written, it would probably be necessary to show (+ female). Others might be (± determinate), (± abstract) and (± concrete), (± momentary) and (± durative), (± additive) and (± privative), (± adult) and (± young), (± count) and (± mass), (± divisible), and adverbs would have the features (time), (place), (direction), (measure), (manner), etc., but differentials that apply to things rather than words, like *hot* vs. *cold*—one might be tempted to think that (+ cold) is a feature of the word *cryology*, but he would be somewhat confused if he felt that *hell* has both features (+ cold) and (+ hot)—*tight* vs. *loose, rich* vs. *poor* would not generally be useful features.

Another use for the indication of features occurs in matrixes. For example, in an analysis of the verbs *get, take, have,* and *keep:*

	get *take*	*have*	*keep*
primary denotation:	possession	possession	possession
secondary denotation:	incipiency	state	continuation

in which the features are capitalized in these sentences:

take and *get* represent the INCIPIENCY of POSSESSION
have represents the STATE of POSSESSION
keep represents the CONTINUATION of a STATE of POSSESSION[32]

Or in this modality matrix, in which the distinctive features are italicized:

	imminent	*biased*	*precarious*
objective marked:	muss	soll	darf
subjective unmarked:	will	mag	kann[33]

I am not implying that such features should be put into a dictionary. To do so would be extraordinarily clumsy and probably impossible. The information would certainly be useless to dictionary users generally. Such features do not easily or clearly apply to abstract definitions. They go better with discrete words in sentential context. It seems obvious, however, that a definer with a record before him of all the features found in the relationships of the word he is defining could set up his definitions more easily and more accurately. At least, an indication of the features with examples of their application would serve as reminder. He could not define on the basis of features alone, but he might discover a need for more citations. And he could be much helped in making sense divisions. For example, the definition of the noun *generation* in W3 starts off with this alphanumeric order: 1 a, b (1), (2), (3), (4), (5). All the definitions through 1 b (4) have the feature (+ animate) but 1 b (5) is (− animate): "a type or class of objects derived or developed from an earlier type (the first of the Air Force's new *generation* of powerful supersonic fighters—Kenneth Koyen)." I doubt that anyone is likely to consider the presence of this definition in sense 1 a serious error. But the definer should have seen that it belongs with another group. Had there been on file an analysis of *generation* that groups the (+ animate) separately from the (− animate) senses, he, acting under applicable instructions, which for W3 did not exist in terms of features, could have avoided this minor blunder.

Familiarity with this way of analyzing words in context could help the editor who reads and marks for citations. In the sentence "Burials were made in concentrated cemeteries, with the body wrapped in many layers of cloth and accompanied by elaborate grave goods" [34] the word *accompanied* should be marked. How explain this to someone being instructed on what to mark? Instead of saying that one should intuitively recognize something about *accompanied* in that sentence, the explainer can point out that a usual basic feature of *accompany* is (+ animate); so an acceptable use of it in a (− animate) relationship should be marked.

The frequent use of features as tools reflects, of course, only one of the linguistic interests that can help the dictionary maker. Carter Revard, after a study of English denominal verbs, concludes that for every sentence using one there is a corresponding or equivalent base sentence using the noun from which the verb came.[35] If so, then in a dictionary one of the sense definitions of the verb should contain the noun in its wording. Take, for example, the verb *father.* Its first sense in W3 reads "to make oneself the father of" and so it has read in all unabridged dictionaries back through *W1864.* Apparently neither Webster nor Johnson realized that the verb *father* came from the noun father, for they do not show any direct relationship in this way. Revard sets up different types and names them: "ornative" for the denominal verb *butter,* "instrumental" for the verb *brake,* "locative" for *land,* "privative" for *dust* ("to make free of dust"), "effected object" for *bud* ("to set buds"), and "affected object" for *breakfast* ("to eat breakfast"). I have checked all of these examples against W3 and several others like *elbow* ("to shove aside by jabbing with or as if with the elbow") and *hullabaloo* ("to make a hullabaloo"). W3 definitions, based on a combination of historical and intuitive analysis, come off pretty well. Sometimes it is a later sense of the verb that contains the corresponding noun but there is usually a sound explanation. For example, *dust* ("to make free of dust") is sense 3 instead of 1 because there is an earlier sense ("to reduce to dust") that must come first. My purpose is not, however, to show how W3 comes off. It is to point out how useful Revard's analysis can be to future definers. W3's relevant definition at the verb *land* is "to catch and bring to shore or into a boat." This looks, by Revard's findings, as if it were wrong. Probably there should be a primary sense "to bring to land" and a secondary sense separately lettered "to bring into a boat" and probably the notion of "to catch" should be dropped altogether from the definition. I say "probably" to imply that competent dictionary definers should never rely on the kind of linguistic analysis being discussed here without confirmation from genuine citations. For example, one linguist gives the feature (+ human) to the verb *murder* and then says it "is used appropriately only when both subject and object nouns are capable of denoting human beings."³⁶ On the contrary, W3 sense 3 of the verb *murder* reads: "a : to put an end to: DESTROY ⟨if ever he were in power would . . . *murder* truth, freedom, and art—*Saturday Rev.*⟩ b : to harass or depress grievously: TEASE, TORMENT ⟨*murdered* this poor heart of mine—Shak.⟩ c : to mutilate, spoil, or deform by wretched performance: MANGLE ⟨someone's difficult sonata was *murdered* on the piano—Anne Green⟩ ⟨the average British traveler leads the world in *murdering* the French tongue—*Times Lit. Supp.*⟩."

Here, sketchily, are a few other examples of linguistic analyses that are sure to yield information useful to a dictionary maker. Eugene V. Mohr has worked out some transformational rules applicable to a distinction between *should* and *must* in "He's absent; he *must* be sick" and "He left at five; he *should* be here soon," in which *must* and *should* are not interchangeable.³⁷ In the ambiguous sentence "He saw the window broken by the thieves" Robert L. Allen looks into whether the *-en* of *broken* signals an earlier time relationship as well as passive voice.³⁸ Allen, in making a very useful study of verbs, collected 4800 of which 25 percent are finite forms of the verb *be* and only 4 percent an expanded form. He found no occurrence of "will have ____n" and only six occurrences of *shall*. Paul M. Postal argues that the personal pronouns (*I, we, you, he, she, it, they*) are types of definite articles,³⁹ and Martin Joos shows that English has no future tense, that all the eight modals have a connotation of futurity, but that no modal, not even *will* or *shall*, denotes futurity.⁴⁰ This could bring about revision of W3 definitions at several places besides at *future tense*. It is interesting (to me) that the W3 definition is written as if in anticipation of Joos three years later: "a verb tense traditionally formed in English with *will* and *shall* and expressive of time yet to come." If by deletion *future tense* is defined simply as one "expressive of time yet to come," it will probably never become inaccurate, and the "traditionally formed in English" part of it will also be accurate historically as long as man can remember pre-Joosian grammar.

The English adverb, particularly its position and relation to the adjective, has been insufficiently analyzed. A 1956 directive to definers of *W3* entitled "Adv or Adj" begins:

> There is much inconsistency in the assignment of *adv* and *adj* labels in W2, and there will have to be nearly as much in W3. Inconsistency is inherent in the conventional systems of distinguishing adjectives and adverbs in English, and so long as we must describe these conventions we will be inconsistent. An adverb in terms of meaning signifies manner, quality, position, time, degree, number, cause, etc. An adverb in terms of function modifies a verb, an adjective, an adverb. But since these two statements are neither complementary nor individually exhaustive, we are left with many instances of words that are adjective by function and adverb by meaning. The inconsistency can be resolved, more than by any other way, simply by vacating the field.

I expect that the editors of *W4* will find helpful information ready for their use. The matter is increasingly being given attention. There is, among others, an Uppsala dissertation by Sven Jacobson, which I have not yet seen, but it has been reviewed in *Language*.[41] Other titles that are sure to be useful to future dictionaries are Bruce Fraser's M.I.T. dissertation "Examination of the Verb-Particle System," Lakoff's unpublished paper on *some–any* rules,[42] M. A. K. Halliday's "Notes on Transitivity and Theme in English," [43] and Franklin Southworth's "Model of Semantic Structure" forthcoming in *Language*. The possible list seems unending, so active and far-ranging are the interests of modern linguists, especially the younger ones just entering the profession.

The beauty of all this activity is that the dictionary maker does not have to accept any of the linguist's theories or any of his inapplicable operations or even try to understand his tree diagrams or his rules. Whenever the linguist becomes concerned with disambiguation, his concerns are those of the dictionary maker. Theirs is a common interest, just as both are grammarians regardless of what kind of grammar each professes to know or use. However one uncovers what lies beneath the parallel but ambiguous sentences "He was knocked down by the wall" and "She was comforted by the fire," [44] the dictionary maker will have more (and perhaps better) knowledge for defining the preposition *by*. Sometimes the attempt to disambiguate confirms what the dictionary says. In the sentence "The helicopter is over the hill" *over* can mean "above" or "on the other side of." Instead of conceding that *over* has two senses in that sentence, one linguist postulates the underlying features of (+ path) and (+ completion), disambiguates the sentence to read "The helicopter is at the end of a path leading over the hill," and concludes that the apparent double meaning of *over* in the original sentence is the same.[45] This seems to me unrealistic and fanciful, even if ingenious. He produces no evidence that such a sentence has ever been used. I would like to see him go to work on real sentences such as "If you can't count it, it doesn't count"[46] or one that the Hong Kong flu brought us: "If you're lying in bed with the *bug*, you need relief from the things *bugging* you."[47]

Making up sentences and imagining usages that might be acceptable can be a sure way to get out of touch with genuine usage. As Max Black puts it, "The uncritical use of fictitious language creates monsters."[48] No matter how many useful relationships the linguist is able to uncover, the dictionary maker must be cautious against being taken in. None of the sterile sentences that turn up in exercises in transformational-generative grammar should become citations in the dictionary maker's files, above all those preceded by an asterisk; e.g., *"My goldfish believes that I'm a fool" and *"Max claimed that his toothbrush was pregnant."[49] Take the sequence:

> John's dictionary was in the other room
> John had his dictionary in the other room
> John's wife was in the other room
> *John had his wife in the other room

by which we learn that a noun phrase whose head is animate does not behave like one whose head in inanimate. The validity behind the rejection of anomalous or bizarre sentences such as *"I just swallowed my nose"[50] and *"It smells itchy" has been severely tested in this age of Rowan and Martin's TV show "Laugh-In." "Blessed are the meek for they shall inherit the watermelons" and "If you cross a flamingo with a policeman, you get pink fuzz" are both meaningful. The first is bitingly satirical. A collection of asterisked sentences is just about the last thing a dictionary maker wants. He has enough trouble making sure that, when definers must invent sentences to illustrate usage in context, the sentences read as if taken from actual usage. Instead of judging grammaticality by whether a sentence is theoretically acceptable to a native speaker, the dictionary maker observes what people say and write in genuine rather than artificial contexts. In a different situation there is nothing wrong with the sentence, "John had his wife in the other room" even if one is not sure about the antecedent of *his*. Is "life lives us" an improbable sentence? In Thornton Wilder's *The Eighth Day* (1967) one of the characters says: "We keep saying that 'we live our lives.' Shucks, life lives us." [51] Should an asterisk be put before the sentence "You better had"? After the first 100 miles of a week-long automobile trip a woman said to her nine-year-old grandson, a bright boy thoroughly in command of standard English patterns: "I know I left the stove on. I'd better stop and phone Doris. No, I guess I won't. She's probably not home yet and she's sure to notice it when she does get home. It can't do any damage. No, I guess I won't bother to phone." The boy then said: "You better had." Remember the *'d* used in the phrase "I'd better stop and phone," because in that boy's idiolect *'d* is a zero element present in "You better had." The sentence needs no asterisk.

If the methodology of linguistics sometimes provides us unwittingly with a few amusingly distorted English sentences, it is inadvertently piling up a mass of information about linguistic behavior that must someday be a direct contribution to lexicography. At no time in the past have there been as many contributors—and most of them have half their careers still ahead of them—as are busy with linguistic analysis today. I have merely hinted at the numbers, as anyone who keeps up with the "Bulletin of the ERIC Clearinghouse for Linguistics" can see for himself. The lexicographer of the future who neglects to tap these valuable contributions will do so at his peril.

NOTES / INDEX

List of Abbreviations

ACD	*American College Dictionary*
CL	*Comparative Literature*
GM	*Gentleman's Magazine*
IJAL	*International Journal of American Linguistics*
MLN	*Modern Language Notes*
MLQ	*Modern Language Quarterly*
MLR	*Modern Language Review*
MP	*Modern Philology*
N&Q	*Notes and Queries*
PMLA	*Publications of the Modern Language Association of America*
PQ	*Philological Quarterly*
OED	*Oxford English Dictionary*
RES	*Review of English Studies*
RHD	*Random House Dictionary of the English Language*
SEL	*Studies in English Literature, 1500–1900*
SP	*Studies in Philology*
TEPS	*Teacher Education and Professional Standards*
W3	*Webster's Third New International Dictionary*

Notes

Lexicography and the Silence of the Past HOWARD

1. F. J. E. Raby, *A History of Secular Latin Poetry in the Middle Ages*, 2 vols. (Oxford: Oxford Univ. Press, 1934), 1:304–5.

2. The former conception is owing to Karl Breul, *The Cambridge Songs: A Goliard's Song Book of the XIth Century* (Cambridge: At the Univ. Press, 1915); the latter to Raby, 1:291–301. For a more skeptical view see Karl Strecker ed., *Die Cambridger Lieder*, Monumenta Germaniae Historica (Berlin: Weidmannsche, 1926), pp. xii, xx–xxi.

3. Peter Dronke, *The Medieval Lyric* (London: Hutchinson Univ. Library, 1968), pp. 29–31.

4. Strecker, No. 40, p. 95. Translations are mine unless noted otherwise. The title which often appears over the poem, "Verna feminae suspiria," is spurious. I am indebted to Mr. Richard Kerr of the Cambridge University Library for informing me that "there is absolutely no trace of any titles or headings in the manuscript." Mr. Kerr suggests that the titles were invented by the first editor of the poems, Philipp Jaffé ("Die Cambridger Lieder," *Zeitschrift für deutsches Alterthum* 14 [1869]: 449–95); they were taken over by Breul, who also printed them as headings but with medieval spellings; Strecker, using Jaffé's spelling, prints them in the apparatus criticus without stating their source.

5. Cf. for example Bernard F. Huppé and D. W. Robertson, Jr., *Fruyt and Chaf: Studies in Chaucer's Allegories* (Princeton: Princeton Univ. Press, 1963), p. 45; they cite Alanus, *Distinctiones, Patrologia Latina* 210:770.

6. Cf. for example D. W. Robertson, Jr., *A Preface to Chaucer: Studies in Medieval Perspectives* (Princeton: Princeton Univ. Press, 1962), p. 225 and n. 138.

7. Cf. Strecker's note on stanza 2, p. 95.

8. Contrariwise she might be a soul whose eyes and ears are closed to the temptations of the World and who languishes for Christ.

The last line would thus be taken as an echo of Song of Songs 2:5 and 5:8; the spring would still suggest the Resurrection which in this case would cause the figure's lapse into unworldliness. It seems to me one might support either interpretation by this method with equal ingenuity, or argue for both.

9. Poems on the coming of spring and spring's association with love are common, and such poems sometimes mention the passing of winter. But Winter's defeat in springtime or any sympathetic treatment of Winter personified seems rare. On the *topos* of perpetual spring see Ernst Robert Curtius, *European Literature and the Latin Middle Ages,* trans. Willard R. Trask, Bollingen Series 36 (New York: Harper & Bros., 1953), pp. 185–86. On folk customs about Summer defeating Winter, see Kenneth Jackson, *Studies in Early Celtic Nature Poetry* (Cambridge: At the Univ. Press. 1935), pp. 158–59.

10. Philip Schuyler Allen, "Medieval Latin Lyrics," *MP* 5 (1908): 431.

11. *Medieval Latin and the Rise of European Love-Lyric,* 2 vols. (Oxford: Oxford Univ. Press, 1965–66), 1:271–77. Cf. Dronke, *The Medieval Lyric,* pp. 92–94.

12. On the Mozarabic poems and the tradition of the *winileod* or *Frauenlied* see Theodor Frings, *Minnesinger und Troubadours,* Deutsche Akademie der Wissenschaften, Vorträge und Schriften 34 (Berlin: Akademie-Verlag, 1949), and Leo Spitzer, "The Mozarabic Lyric and Theodor Frings' Theories," *CL* 4 (1952):1–22. Spitzer believed that the songs were not written by women but were male fantasies about women. Dronke, *The Medieval Lyric,* pp. 86–108, examines such songs in various languages.

13. Dronke, *Medieval Latin and the Rise of European Love-Lyric,* 1:275–76.

14. Specifically those of Papias (1053), Hugutio (d. 1212), and Balbi (1286). See John Edwin Sandys, *A History of Classical Scholarship,* 3 vols. (New York: Hafner, 1958), 1:521, 666 f., and Samuel Berger, *De glossariis et compendiis exegeticis quibusdam medii aevi* (Paris, 1879).

15. See n. 13. Cf. Strecker, p. 42 n. (line 37).

16. Dronke, *Medieval Latin and the Rise of European Love-Lyric,* 1:274; Strecker, No. 49, pp. 107 f.

17. *Poésies populaires Latines du moyen age,* ed. Edélestand du Méril (Paris, 1847), pp. 235–36; the emendation of "lageo" is customary, but not du Méril's.

18. *Carmina burana,* ed. Alfons Hilka and Otto Schumann, vol. 1, pt. 2 (Heidelberg: Carl Winter, 1941), No. 108, p. 178.

19. Dronke, *The Medieval Lyric,* pp. 93–94.

20. L. S. Vigotsky, *Language and Thought,* reprinted in *Psycho-*

linguistics: A Book of Readings, ed. S. Saporta (New York: Holt, Rinehart and Winston, 1961), p. 535.

Renaissance Dictionaries and Manuals STEADMAN

1. *The Poems of John Marston,* ed. Arnold Davenport (Liverpool: Liverpool Univ. Press, 1961), pp. 72–73. Cf. Alvin Kernan, *The Cankered Muse: Satire of the English Renaissance* (New Haven: Yale Univ. Press), pp. 60–61, on Marston's attitude to obscurity in satire; see also Arnold Davenport ed., *The Collected Poems of Joseph Hall* (Liverpool: Liverpool Univ. Press, 1949), pp. xxv–xxxiv, on obscurity in Roman and Renaissance satire and on Hall's "quarrel" with Marston.

2. Jean Seznec, *The Survival of the Pagan Gods: The Mythological Tradition and Its Place in Renaissance Humanism and Art,* trans. Barbara F. Sessions (New York: Harper & Row, 1961), p. 314; DeWitt T. Starnes and Ernest William Talbert, *Classical Myth and Legend in Renaissance Dictionaries* (Chapel Hill: Univ. of North Carolina Press, 1955), p. 341. Douglas Bush, *Mythology and the Renaissance Tradition in English Poetry,* new revised edition (New York: W. W. Norton, 1963), p. 29, correctly describes the passage as a "satirical hint."

3. Seznec, p. 314.

4. Davenport, *Marston,* p. 230, observes that "there is no evidence . . . that Hall was indebted to any of these books in his satires; but M[arston] himself is certainly indebted to Comes for much of the mythology he uses." For Marston's attack on Hall, see pp. 30, 37, 81–82, 164–65, 229–30, 244–45, 355–56, et passim.

5. Davenport, *Hall,* p. 33.

6. Cf. Davenport, *Hall,* pp. 49, 192. Hall is referring to J. C. Scaliger's *Teretismata.*

7. Seznec, p. 314.

8. For the authorship of these works, see Seznec, pp. 170–79, 246–47. For Renaissance editions of the *Liber* and *Libellus,* see ibid., pp. 225–26.

9. Robert Burton, *The Anatomy of Melancholy,* 2 vols (London, 1837), 2:191, 272, 525.

10. Burton, 2:190–91, 217, 229, 282, 290, 525.

11. See i.a., the following studies: Don Cameron Allen, "Ben Jonson and the Hieroglyphics," *PQ* 18 (1939): 290–300; Rosemary Freeman, *English Emblem Books* (London: Chatto & Windus, 1948); Allen H. Gilbert, *The Symbolic Persons in the Masques of Ben Jonson* (Durham, N.C.: Duke Univ. Press,1948); D. J. Gordon, "Chapman's *Hero and Leander,*" *English Miscellany* 5 (1954): 41–94; id., "Chap-

man's Use of Cartari in the Fifth Sestiad of *Hero and Leander*," *MLR*
39 (1944): 280–85; id., "*Hymenaei: Ben Jonson's Masque of Union*,"
Journal of the Warburg and Courtauld Institutes 8 (1945): 107–45; id.,
"The Imagery of Ben Jonson's *The Masque of Blacknesse* and *The
Masque of Beautie*," ibid., 6 (1943): 122–41; Henry Green, *Shakespeare
and the Emblem Writers* (London, 1870); Arthur Henkel and Albrecht
Schöne, eds., *Emblemata: Handbuch der Sinnbildkunst des 16. und
17. Jahrhunderts* (Stuttgart: J. B. Metzler, 1967); C. H. Herford and
Percy and Evelyn Simpson, eds., *Ben Jonson*, 11 vols. (Oxford: Claren-
don Press, 1925–52), 10:421; Charles W. Lemmi, *The Classic Deities
in Bacon* (Baltimore: John Hopkins Press, 1933); id., "The Symbolism
of the Classical Episodes in *The Faerie Queene*," *PQ* 8 (1929): 270—87;
William Lansdown Goldsworthy, *Shakespeare's Heraldic Emblems, Their
Origin and Meaning* (London: H. F. & G. Witherby, 1928); Allardyce
Nicoll, "Court Hieroglyphics," in *Stuart Masques and the Renaissance
Stage* (London: George G. Harrap, 1937); Erwin Panofsky, *Studies in
Iconology* (New York: Oxford Univ. Press, 1939); Mario Praz, *Studies
in Seventeenth Century Imagery*, 2nd ed., (Rome: Edizioni di storia e
letteratura, 1964); Franck L. Schoell, *Études sur l'humanisme conti-
nental en Angleterre à la fin de la Renaissance* (Paris: Champion, 1926);
W. Schrickx, "George Chapman's Borrowing from Natali Conti," *Eng-
lish Studies* 32 (1951): 107–12; Ernest William Talbert, "New Light on
Ben Jonson's Workmanship," *SP* 40 (1943): 154–85; L. Volkmann,
Bilderschriften der Renaissance, Hieroglyphik und Emblematik (Leip-
zig: Niew Koop, B. de Graaf, 1923); Charles Francis Wheeler, *Classical
Mythology in the Plays, Masques and Poems of Ben Jonson* (Prince-
ton: Princeton Univ. Press, for the Univ. of Cincinnati, 1938); Edgar
Wind, *Pagan Mysteries in the Renaissance* (New Haven: Yale Univ.
Press, 1958). Professor Douglas Bush's recent study *Pagan Myth and
Christian Tradition in English Poetry* (Philadelphia: American Philo-
sophical Society, 1968) admirably complements his earlier volumes—
Classical Influence in Renaissance Literature (Cambridge: Harvard
Univ. Press, for Oberlin College, 1952); *Mythology and the Renais-
sance Tradition in English Poetry* (Minneapolis: Univ. of Minnesota
Press, 1932), new revised edition (New York: W. W. Norton, 1963);
Mythology and the Romantic Tradition in English Poetry (Cambridge:
Harvard Univ. Press, 1937).

12. Seznec, p. 280; Starnes and Talbert, p. 139.

13. Seznec, p. 280; Starnes and Talbert, pp. 44–45.

14. Several recent scholars have justly emphasized the role of the
mythographies, dictionaries, and similar reference works in Renaissance
education as aids to "imitation" of the ancients. See T. W. Baldwin,
William Shakespeare's Small Latine and Lesse Greeke (Urbana: Univ.
of Illinois Press, 1944) on the influence of Giraldi, Conti, and Textor

and the florilegia of Farnaby, Mirandula, and Palmer; Donald Lemon Clark, *John Milton at St. Paul's School* (New York: Columbia Univ. Press, 1948), pp. 205–7, on handbooks recommended by schoolmasters such as Brinsley and Hoole for "principal places for imitation," variety and copy of Poetical phrases," or "store of Epithetes"; and Davis P. Harding, *Milton and the Renaissance Ovid* (Urbana: Univ. of Illinois Press, 1946), pp. 30–33, 43–44, 50–53, on reference works recommended by Hoole and Brinsley as aids to "imitation," on Milton's observations on the "rules of imitation" recommended by schoolmasters, and on his synthesis of classical and post-classical sources. See also Starnes and Talbert, p. 341.

15. See Harding, pp. 31–32. Hoole's allusion to Smetius is a reference to Henrich Smet; Harding renders this name as Smith.

16. Cf. Starnes and Talbert, p. 101: "If Spencer were familiar with the dictionary entries on Urania, and we must assume that he was, as they were standard reference works, he would not have needed to consult L. Gyraldus *de Musis Syntagma*, cited by Renwick or Plutarch's *Quaest. Conv.* referred to by Lotspeich"; p. 80: "little need to cite Comes"; pp. 88–89: "Lotspeich suggests as a source N. Comes. . . . Spenser doubtless knew Comes' *Mythologiae*, but he could also have known the characterization from various other sources. . . . There was scarcely need for Spenser to go outside the dictionaries". By citing the dictionaries Starnes and Talbert sometimes succeed in casting doubt on the conclusions of previous scholarship which had attempted to identify specific sources either in the classics or in Renaissance manuals; but the evidence they adduce rarely permits us to identify the dictionaries themselves as the actual sources. Their references to the lexicons are, therefore, chiefly valuable as negative evidence, compelling us to downgrade some of the conclusions of earlier scholarship—from "certain" sources to "probable," or from "probable" to merely "possible."

17. Cf. DeWitt T. Starnes and Gertrude E. Noyes, *The English Dictionary from Cawdrey to Johnson, 1604–1755* (Chapel Hill: Univ. of North Carolina Press, 1946); Starnes, *Renaissance Dictionaries, English-Latin and Latin-English* (Austin: Univ. of Texas Press, 1954); id. *Robert Estienne's Influence on Lexicography* (Univ. of Texas Press, 1963).

18. Starnes and Talbert, pp. 60–61, 73, 109, 117, 126–28, 228. In these and other cases the evidence for identifying specific sources is dubious, because the parallels cited as proof of borrowing are actually commonplaces. Though it is true that "the lexicons contributed toward making commonplace certain passages or ideas in ancient literature" (p. 138), so did other means of transmission—study of the classical texts themselves in the Renaissance schoolroom, diffusion of the mythological manuals, the popularity of emblem-books, the utility of com-

mentaries. In many cases, perhaps the majority, these "passages or ideas" were already commonplaces, or could have become commonplace through other media than the lexicons.

19. Ibid., p. 228. Many of the more dubious parallels included in this book originated in claims made by earlier source-hunters—usually on the basis of analogues that were little more than commonplaces. Unfortunately, in challenging these claims, the authors have sometimes pressed their attack on to rather dangerous ground, arguing, for instance, that a commonplace in Spenser came directly from Cooper rather than from Ovid or Conti. There is little point in arguing the immediate source of a commonplace, and in doing so the authors merely weaken their case. They are more convincing when they cite these parallels as illustrations rather than as sources (as they do on p. 77): "Even if he did not actually consult the Calepine, it is sometimes the best illustration of allusions in his poems." The authors' case would have been stronger had they attempted not to "demonstrate indebtedness to the lexicons" (p. 139), but to cite them primarily as illustrations rather than as probable sources. To a certain extent, moreover, a tendency to stress quantitative rather than qualitative proofs—to rely on a multiplicity of dubious parallels rather than a few, more substantial analogues—is implicit in the authors' criterion of evidence: "when a considerable number of instances can be assembled of similarities between the literature of the period and the lexicons—even if the information and phrasing in any one passage may have such a variety of possible sources that it amounts to no more than a commonplace—the probability increases that the stimulus for some of the passages came from the one account common to all" (p. 138–39).

20. Seznec, pp. 288–90.

Thomas Wilson's Christian Dictionary *and the "Idea" of Marvell's "Garden"* STEWART

1. On the need for qualification, here, see E. D. Hirsch, Jr., *Validity in Interpretation* (New Haven: Yale Univ. Press, 1967), p. 209 et passim.

2. *The Poems and Letters of Andrew Marvell,* ed. H. M. Margoliouth, 2 vols. (Oxford: Clarendon Press, 1952), 1:48–50; all citations from Marvell in my text will be from this edition.

3. Harold Wendell Smith, "Cowley, Marvell, and the Second Temple," *Scrutiny* 19 (1953): 184–205.

4. "Marvell's 'Garden," *Scrutiny* 1 (1932): 236–40.

5. "Marvell and the New Critics," *RES.* n.s. 8 (1957): 382–89.

Hirsch discusses the problem of the psychologistic view in *Validity of Interpretation*, pp. 6–10 et passim.

6. Unless otherwise indicated, all citations from *A Christian Dictionary* will be from the 2nd ed. (London, 1616); but the present quotations are from *A Complete Christian Dictionary*, 8th ed. (London, [1678]), sig. A5ʳ. In the 8th ed., Edward Calamy makes this trenchant remark: "The Frantick and giddy-brained Libertines, who term themselves Spiritual, denying the Scriptures to be Divine or Authentic (which in contempt they call The Written Letter), fly unto the Private Revelation of the Spirit, whereon (say they) they are to rest, as being taught of God" (sig. A6 ʳ).

7. *Theologicall Rules* (London, 1615), sig. A2ᵛ.

8. *From a Logical Point of View* (Cambridge: Harvard Univ. Press, 1953), Ch. iii.

9. *Validity in Interpretation*, pp. 236–37.

10. "An Open and Plaine Paraphrase upon the Song of Songs, which is Salomon's," bound with *Salomon's Divine Arts* (London, 1609), p. 12.

11. (London), sig E7ʳ.

12. Tr. by [T. B.] (St. Omer, 1627), pp. 22, 23.

13. (London), p. 238.

14. See *The Complete Works of Saint Teresa of Jesus*, tr. and ed. by E. Allison Peers, from the critical ed. of P. Silvero de Santa Teresa, C.D. (London: Sheed & Ward, 1946), 1:87.

15. Walter J. Ong, S.J., *The Presence of the Word: Some Prolegomena for Cultural and Religious History* (New Haven: Yale Univ. Press, 1967), p. 8.

Illustrative Quotations in Johnson's Dictionary   KOLB

1. For a description and discussion of this copy of Duppa's work, see Lindsay Fleming's article on "Dr. Johnson's Use of Authorities in Compiling His Dictionary of the English Language," *N&Q* 199 (1954): 254–57, 294–97, 343–47, esp. 294–97, 343–47. Fleming also alludes, much more briefly, to the copies of Hale's *Primitive Origination of Mankind*, Burton's *Anatomy of Melancholy*, South's *Sermons*, *The Works of the Most Celebrated Minor Poets*, Warburton's edition of Shakespeare's plays, Bacon's *Works*, Norris's *Collection*, and Walton's *Life of Dr. Sanderson*.

2. For a description and discussion of this copy of South's *Sermons*, see John E. W. Wallis's address on "Doctor Johnson and His English Dictionary," *Johnson Society Addresses and Transactions* 4 (1939–53): 3–24, esp. 14–19.

3. For a description and discussion of this copy of Bacon's *Works,* see Gordon S. Haight's article on "Johnson's Copy of Bacon's *Works,*" *Yale University Library Gazette* 6 (1932): 67–73.

4. For a description and discussion of this copy of Warburton's edition of Shakespeare's plays, see these articles: A. Cuming, "A Copy of Shakespeare's Works Which Formerly Belonged to Dr. Johnson," *RES* n.s. 3 (1927): 208–12; Arthur Sherbo, "Dr. Johnson's *Dictionary* and Warburton's *Shakespeare,*" *PQ* 33 (1954): 94–96.

5. Duppa's *Holy Rules and Helps to Devotion* is presumably a part of the estate of the late Lindsay Fleming, of Bognor Regis, Sussex, whose benevolence, hospitality, and knowledge we remember with pleasure and gratitude. Burton's *Anatomy of Melancholy* and Hale's *Primitive Origination of Mankind,* the property of the Philological Society, are on permanent loan to the Bodleian Library. Walton's *Life of Dr. Sanderson* is in the National Library of Wales. South's *Sermons* is in the Lichfield Cathedral Library. Norris's *Collection of Miscellanies,* Bacon's *Works,* and Drayton's *Works* belong to the Yale University Library. Watts's *Logick* is in the British Museum. Warburton's edition of Shakespeare's plays is in the University College of Wales Library at Aberystwyth. *The Works of the Most Celebrated Minor Poets* is a part of the Donald and Mary Hyde Collection, Four Oaks Farm, Somerville, N.J. To these institutions and individuals we express our cordial thanks for the generous cooperation which enabled us to secure microfilms of the relevant portions of all of the books.

6. See Johnson's *Plan of a Dictionary* (London, 1947), par. 1, and his Preface to the *Dictionary,* par. 5. These two works are cited hereafter as Johnson, *Plan* and Johnson, Preface.

7. See, for example, Sir John Hawkins, *Life on Samuel Johnson* (London, 1787), p. 175; *Boswell's Life of Johnson,* ed. George Birkbeck Hill, and rev. L. F. Powell, 6 vols. (Oxford: Clarendon Press, 1934–50), 1:188, esp. n. 2. The Hill and Powell edition of Boswell's *Life* is cited hereafter as Boswell's *Life.*

8. Johnson, Preface, par. 72.

9. Ibid., par. 62.

10. He describes his practice thus: "when it happened that any authour gave a definition of a term, or such an explanation as is equivalent to a definition, I have placed his authority as a supplement to my own" (par. 63).

11. Johnson, Preface, par. 57.

12. Ibid.

13. Boswell's *Life,* 2:121.

14. Ed. George Birkbeck Hill, 3 vols. (Oxford: Clarendon Press), 1:308; 2:47, 63.

15. Ibid., 3:308–10; Boswell's *Life,* 4:311.

16. Boswell's *Life,* 2:158.

17. Ibid., 3:248; 2:104; 4:505, 530.

18. In Johnson, *Plan* (par. 71), the author states his intention "of selecting, when it can be conveniently done, such sentences, as, besides their immediate use, may give pleasure or instruction by conveying some elegance of language, or some precept of prudence, or piety." In Johnson, Preface (par. 57), the author, while announcing the abandonment of his initial desire that "every quotation should be useful to some other end than the illustration of a word," asserts, nonetheless, that he has still "spared" "some passages" "which may relieve the labour of verbal searches, and intersperse with verdure and flowers the dusty desarts of barren philology."

19. Par. 61.

20. For evidence of their preeminence as sources of passages, see Lewis M. Freed's dissertation on "The Sources of Johnson's *Dictionary*" (Ph.D. diss., Cornell Univ., 1939), pp. 57–58, 73, 79–80.

21. Johnson, Preface, par. 57.

22. Ibid., pars. 57, 65, 58.

23. Ibid., par. 58.

24. *Dr. Johnson's Dictionary: Essays in the Biography of a Book* (Chicago: Univ. of Chicago Press, 1955), p. 206.

Johnson's Plan *and* Preface *to the* Dictionary
WEINBROT

1. For extensive details concerning the composition, publication, and reception of the *Plan*, see James H. Sledd and Gwin J. Kolb, *Dr. Johnson's Dictionary: Essays in the Biography of a Book* (Chicago: Univ. of Chicago Press, 1955), pp. 46–84. For reconsideration of some aspects of Sledd and Kolb's view of the writing of the *Plan*, see Jacob Leed's essay—originally presented to the Johnson Society of the Central Region, the University of Wisconsin, 1970—"Johnson and Chesterfield: 1746–47," in *Studies in Burke and His Time* 12 (1970): 1677–90.

2. *The Museum: or, the Literary and Historical Register* (London, 1747), 3:385.

3. *Boswell's Life of Johnson*, ed. George Birkbeck Hill, and rev. L. F. Powell, 6 vols. (Oxford: Clarendon Press, 1934–50), 1:185. Subsequent references to Boswell's *Life* are to this edition.

4. Ibid., pp. 183–84.

5. Hardwicke Papers, vol. 49. Correspondence of the 2nd Lord Hardwicke with Dr. T. Birch 1746–1750; letter dated August 8, 1747, in British Museum Add. Ms. 35, 397. I am indebted to Sledd and Kolb pp. 99, 225 n. 55, for this and the following reference.

6. Hardwicke Papers, vol. 53. Correspondence of . . . Hardwicke

and D. Wray. 1740–67, letter dated August 8, 1747. British Museum Add. Ms. 35, 401.

7. Sir John Hawkins, *The Life of Samuel Johnson, LL.D.,* 2d ed., rev. (London, 1787), pp. 188–89.

8. Bonamy Dobrée, ed., *The Letters of Philip Dormer Stanhope, 4th Earl of Chesterfield,* 6 vols. (London: Eyre & Spottiswoode, 1932), 5:2169. Subsequent references to Chesterfield's *Letters* are to this edition. Chesterfield is referring to Sheridan's *British Education* (see n. 20, this essay) which, he says, "upon the whole . . . is both a very useful and entertaining book."

9. *The Triumph of Wisdom, A Poem: Inscribed to His Excellency The Earl of Chesterfield, Lord Lieutenant of Ireland* (Dublin), pp. 5–6.

10. *Boulter's Monument: A Panegyrical Poem, Sacred to the Memory of . . . the Most Rev. Dr. Hugh Boulter . . .* (Dublin, 1745), pp. 65, 67. In "A Postscript To The Reader" Madden observes that "some Hundred Lines have been prun'd from [the poem] in order to lessen the Tediousness of the panegyrical Part" (p. 92). These deletions, however, must have taken place for the first edition, and were not seen by Johnson, who read the printed copy, "blotted a great many lines, and might have blotted many more, without making the poem worse" (Boswell's *Life,* 1:318). See also Hawkins, p. 391, for a more precise account than Boswell offers. I am indebted to Donald J. Greene for advice on this matter.

11. Chesterfield's *Letters,* 4:1217.

12. *The History of the Rise, Progress, and Tendency of Patriotism, . . . Dedicated to the Rt. Hon. The Earl of CHESTERFIELD,* 3rd ed. (London, 1747), pp. iv–vi.

13. See *A Letter Humbly Addressed to the Right Honourable, The Earl of Chesterfield* (London, 1750). For comment regarding Mrs. Muilman and Fielding, see F. Homes Dudden, *Henry Fielding: His Life Works, and Times,* 2 vols. (Oxford: Clarendon Press, 1952) 2:799, n. 2.

14. *Remarks on Mrs. Muilman's Letter to the Right Honourable The Earl of Chesterfield. In a Letter to Mrs. Muilman, By a Lady* (London, 1750), p. 56.

15. Chesterfield's *Letters,* 3:1078. Warburton dedicated *The Alliance Between Church and State* (London, 1748) to Chesterfield. See *The Works of the Right Reverend William Warburton* 7 vols. (London, 1788), 4:8–10. Of course there were numerous other works dedicated to Chesterfield. For a few more of these see Willard Connely, *The True Chesterfield: Manners-Women-Education* (London: Cassell & Co., 1939), pp. 493–94. Dr. Matthew Maty, Chesterfield's first editor, observes that "it would be equally difficult to enumerate [the praises of Chesterfield while he was Lord Lieutenant], and to point out the best." The value of "common dedications," he suggests, ". . . is exactly in an

inverse ratio to what the authors receive or expect for their panegyric" (*Miscellaneous Works of the Late Philip Dormer Stanhope, Earl of Chesterfield*, 2 vols. [London, 1777], 1:165–66).

16. In 1784 Johnson told Boswell that, though Chesterfield "had more knowledge than I expected . . . in the conversation which I had with him I had the best right to superiority, for it was upon philology and literature" (Boswell's *Life*, 4:332–33) Paul J. Korshin argues that, as early as 1741, Johnson would have been opposed to Chesterfield's political positions: see "The Johnson-Chesterfield Relationship: A New Hypothesis," *PMLA* 85 (1970): 247–59. Leed, n. 1, this essay, takes a different view. These changes had solidified by the writing of the *Dictionary*. Maty, writing in the *Journal britannique* for July–August of 1755, criticizes Johnson's style, and adds:

> Quand on voit sous les noms de *Torys* et des *Whigs*, et dans quelques autres articles également délicats, des descriptions, qui certainement ne sauraient plaire à ceux qui s'interessent à l'Administration présente, n'est-on pas tenté de reprocher à l'Auteur, comme un second défaut, la foiblesse qu'il a eu de faire connoitre ses principes de politique et de religion?

See A. De Morgan, "Dr. Johnson and Dr. Maty," *N&Q*, 2nd Series, 96 (1857): 341. See n. 38, this essay, for further comment on Maty and Johnson.

17. Chesterfield's poems appeared both in "Volume IV" (1748) of the *Collection*, the volume containing poems added to the second edition, and in the first volume of the second edition (which appeared in January, 1749). See 4:67–72, and (2nd ed.) 1:334–39. The intricacies of Dodsley's *Collection* have been discussed by William Prideaux Courtney, *Dodsley's Collection of Poetry: Its Contents & Contributors* (London: Printed for private circulation, 1910 [rpt. New York: Burt Franklin, 1968]); Ralph Straus, *Robert Dodsley: Poet, Publisher & Playwright* (London: John Lane, 1910), pp. 101–52; R. W. Chapman, "Dodsley's *Collection of Poems* (Collations, Lists, and Indexes)," *Oxford Bibliographical Society, Proceedings and Papers* 3 (Oxford: Oxford Univ. Press, 1933): 269–316; Donald D. Eddy, "Dodsley's *Collection of Poems by Several Hands* (Six Volumes), 1758. Index of Authors," *Bibliographical Society of America. Papers* 60 (New York, 1966): 9–30.

18. See Sledd and Kolb, pp. 90–93. Most of Chesterfield's remarks concern propriety: he often says, for example, "can one properly say . . . ?"; or "should it not be . . . ?"; or "is it not . . . ?"; or "This is no French expression"; or "is Davis a sufficient Authority"?; or Rowe's "bad Rhyme . . . should not be quoted as an authority."

19. For some of these letters, see Chesterfield's *Letters*, 2:535–36; 4:1390, 1620–21; 5:1860, and J. H. Neumann, "Chesterfield and the Standard of Usage in English," *MLQ* 7 (1946): 468–69. See also the

World, no. 100, and no. 101 (1754). Both numbers stress the value of a dictionary for the fair sex and their suitors.

20. *British Education: or, The Source of the Disorders of Great Britain* (London, 1756), pp. xviii, vi. Compare Chesterfield, in the *World,* no. 100 (1754). Johnson's *Plan* and Preface, and their attitudes toward fixing the language, have been studied by Scott Elledge. "The Naked Science of Language, 1747–1786," in *Studies in Criticism and Aesthetics, 1660–1800: Essays in Honor of Samuel Holt Monk,* ed. Howard Anderson and John S. Shea (Minneapolis: Univ. of Minnesota Press, 1967), pp. 266–95, especially pp. 266–79. More recently, Leo Braudy has returned to the view, unwarranted I believe, that even in the Preface Johnson wished to fix the language. See "Lexicography and Biography in the *Preface* to Johnson's *Dictionary,*" *SEL* 10 (1970): 552–56.

21. For Walpole's attack on Chesterfield as a debater, see *Horace Walpole's Marginal Notes, Written in Dr. Maty's Miscellaneous Works and Memoirs of the Earl of Chesterfield,* ed. R. S. Turner (London, 186?), pp. 6–7; on March 28, 1772, Johnson called Chesterfield "the best speaker in the House of Lords" (Boswell's *Life,* 2:161). For relevant information concerning Johnson and the Parliamentary Debates, see Benjamin Beard Hoover, *Samuel Johnson's Parliamentary Reporting: Debates in the Senate of Lilliput,* Univ. of California Publications, English Studies 7 (Berkeley and Los Angeles: Univ. of California Press, 1953), 43–44, et passim, and Korshin, n. 16, this essay. Johnson's remark regarding the erroneous attribution to Chesterfield is in Boswell's *Life,* 3:351.

22. *Dr. Johnson's Dictionary,* p. 93.

23. Boswell's *Life,* 1:183. See also Sledd and Kolb: "Johnson went a long way in the composition of the 'Scheme' with no thought of dedication to Chesterfield. Very probably he did not entertain that thought until after he had signed his contract on June 18, 1746" (p. 96).

24. Hawkins, p. 189. The remark regarding "gilding a rotten post" is also reported in the *Gentleman's Magazine* 64 (1794): 18, and Straus, pp. 91–2. But it is clearly a commonplace: see also Thomas Tyers, "A Biographical Sketch of Dr. Samuel Johnson," *GM* 56 (1784): 903; Tyers' expanded pamphlet of the *Biographical Sketch* (London, 1785), p. 8; Rebecca Warner, *Original Letters . . . with Biographical Illustrations* (Bath and London, 1817), p. 204. Miss Warner's amplification is an interesting example of (probable?) mythologizing:

> One morning, on Mr. [Joseph] Fowke's calling on Dr. Johnson, he found the Sage somewhat agitated. On enquiring the cause, "I have just *dismissed* Lord Chesterfield," said he; "if you had come a few moments sooner, I could have shewn you my letter to him." Then musing a little, he added, "However, I believe I can recollect it

pretty well;" and immediately repeated a very long and very severe epistle; much longer, Mr. Fowke used to say, than that which is given by Boswell. Mr. Fowke further remarked, that, upon this occasion, Johnson told him, Lord Chesterfield sent a present of 100 £ to Johnson, to induce him to dedicate the Dictionary to him; "which I returned," said he, "to his Lordship with contempt:" and then added, "Sir, I found I must have gilded a rotten post! Lord Chesterfield Sir, is a wit among lords, but only a lord among wits."

25. *Dr. Johnson's Dictionary*, pp. 95–96.

26. *Samuel Johnson: The Rambler*, The Yale Edition of the Works of Samuel Johnson, vols. 3–5, ed. W. J. Bate and Albrecht B. Strauss, 8 vols. to date (New Haven: Yale Univ. Press, 1969), 5:100.

27. Ibid., p. 317.

28. The incident is reported by Hawkins—who says that he has seen the letter—in his *Life*, p. 329, and Courtney, *Dodsley's Collection*, p. 97. The fullest description of the event is in Edward Cave's letter to Samuel Richardson, August 29, 1750. Cave tells Richardson that, as he suspected, "Mr. *Johnson* is the Great Rambler," and then says:

> When the Author was to be kept private (which was the first scheme) two gentlemen, belonging to the Prince's Court, came to me to enquire his name, in order to do him service; and also brought a list of seven gentlemen to be served with the Rambler. As I was not at liberty, an inference was drawn, that I was desirous to keep to myself so excellent a Writer. Soon after, Mr. Doddington sent a letter directed to the Rambler, inviting him to his house, when he should be disposed to enlarge his acquaintance. In a subsequent number a kind of excuse was made, with a hint that a good Writer might not appear to advantage in conversation.

See John Nichols, *Literary Anecdotes of the Eighteenth Century*, 9 vols. (London, 1812–15), 5:38–9. The first *Rambler* appeared on March 20, 1750, and *Rambler* no. 14, to which Cave is apparently referring, above, appeared on May 5, 1750. Lloyd Sanders, *Patron and Place-Hunter: A Study of George Bubb Dodington, Lord Melcombe* (London: John Lane 1919), pp. 89–90, accepts Cave's version. It is thus unlikely that the editors of Dodington's *Political Journal* are correct in their conjecture regarding Johnson and Dodington. On Sunday, January 7, 1750, the latter records: "At Leicester Fields. Din'd at Lord Poulet's, with Messrs Breton, Mildmay, Johnson, Williams, Ellison." The editors believe that this is "Not improbably Samuel Johnson, then launching *The Rambler*," since Dodington was known to have made contact with him. But it is quite unlikely that, more than three months before the fact, Dodington would have known anything about the launching; in-

deed, we do not really know when the *Rambler's* conception would
have been public knowledge. Even if it were known, there is little reason to think that Johnson's achievement to date would have merited an
invitation to such an exalted board. And, of course, Johnson is a perfectly common name. See *The Political Journal of George Bubb Dodington*, ed. John Carswell and Lewis Arnold Dralle (Oxford: Clarendon
Press, 1965), p. 35, and 35 n. 2.

29. Straus, *Dodsley*, p. 118. Unfortunately, one cannot determine
exactly when Johnson made his corrections, particularly since the correspondence of Shenstone and Dodsley concerning the former's contributions makes clear that poems were being sent to Dodsly as late as
December of 1754 and January of 1755 (*Letters of William Shenstone*,
ed. Duncan Mallam [Minneapolis: Univ. of Minnesota Press, 1939],
pp. 308–9). On January 22, 1755, Shenstone states that he expects
proof "before the close of this week"; the volume was published in
March 1755. Shenstone's packet of his own and his friends' poems was
initially sent in December, 1753, and January, 1754 (Mallam, pp.
307–8; 309–10), though on January 10, 1755, he insists that "The
Autumn Verses have been in Dodsley's hands this twelvemonth" (Mallam, pp. 309–10, 283). These works comprised the final section (pp.
302–63) of the volume. If Dodsley (or his printer, John Hughes)
consistently set the works in the order received, the placement of Johnson's poem on pages 156–70 may suggest that Dodsley received Johnson's revised *Vanity of Human Wishes* well before January of 1755.
Sledd and Kolb suggest that Johnson made the corrections "at about
the same time" as he wrote his letter to Chesterfield in February, 1755
(p. 225, n. 62); this is probably several months too late. Of course
Johnson might have changed one word at the last minute, but it seems
just as likely that he wrote the definition of *patron* (May, 1753?) and
changed *garret* to *patron* within a few months of one another. The
latter may then have come late in the autumn or early in the winter
of 1753–54.

30. *Samuel Johnson: Poems*, The Yale Edition of the Works of
Samuel Johnson, vol. 6, ed. E. L. McAdam, Jr., with George Milne,
8 vols to date (New Haven: Yale Univ. Press, 1964), p. 99.

31. Both definitions are taken from the first edition of the *Dictionary* (London,1755). The definition of "A flatterer" is also interesting: "a fawner; a wheedler; one who endeavours to gain favour by
pleasing falsities."

Again, one can only offer conjecture regarding the dates of composition of specific definitions. On Thomas Birch's authority, Sledd and
Kolb report that "by August, 1748, . . . Johnson's amanuenses had
almost finished transcribing his authorities; by September, 1749, some
part of the *Dictionary* was 'almost ready for the press'; and by October
20, 1750, . . . the first three letters of the alphabet" had been printed

(p. 107). Johnson started volume 2 (L–Z) in April, 1753, and finished most of it "by July or August, 1754" (ibid. pp. 108–9).

32. Boswell's *Life*, 1:265.

33. *Johnson: Prose and Poetry,* ed. Mona Wilson (Cambridge: Harvard Univ. Press, 1957), p. 122. All quotations from the *Plan* and Preface are from this edition: subsequent page references are cited in the text.

34. *The Letters of Samuel Johnson,* ed. R. W. Chapman, 3 vols. (Oxford: Clarendon Press, 1952), 1: 64–65.

35. See the conclusion of the *Plan* (Wilson, p. 139). For a very different letter to a nobleman, see Johnson's letter of thanks to Bute upon receiving notice of his pension (Chapman, *The Letters of Samuel Johnson,* 1:140–41). Johnson also wrote the Dedication (to Orrery) for Charlotte Lennox's *Shakespear Illustrated* (1753).

36. See Sledd and Kolb, pp. 100–104, for relevant comment. See also Maty's remark in the *Journal britannique* (n. 16, this essay).

37. *The World. . . . By Adam Fitz-Adam* (London, 1756), 1:600. Sledd and Kolb observe that Chesterfield's papers were widely reprinted, and in at least two instances writers assumed that Chesterfield was Johnson's active patron and guide (p. 103). I have discussed Johnson's possible reactions to these papers in "Johnson's *Dictionary* and the *World:* The Papers of Lord Chesterfield and Richard Owen Cambridge," *PQ* 50(1971):663–69.

38. As quoted in A. De Morgan, "Dr. Johnson and Dr. Maty," p. 341. I have not been able to determine when Maty first met Chesterfield, though it was probably early in the 1750s, when Maty's *Journal* began to flourish, and he met several eminent men of the literary and fashionable worlds. In any event, he knew Chesterfield well before writing this review, since he records having "a conversation . . . with his lordship, soon after his election into the French academy of *inscriptions and belles lettres,*" and offered to write Chesterfield's life to celebrate the occasion (*Miscellaneous Works,* 1:265 n. 3). The academy's offer was made in June of 1755, "which he communicated to me in English, and for the translation of which he did me the honor to borrow my pen" (ibid., p. 207).

39. Sledd and Kolb, p. 89.

40. For *hope,* see this example, among many: "Hope is itself a species of happiness & perhaps the chief happiness which the World affords" (Chapman, *The Letters of Samuel Johnson,* 1:137, June 8, 1762, to "A Lady"). And for *fear,* see the *Rambler,* no. 110 (1751): "Sorrow, and fear, and anxiety, are properly not parts, but adjuncts of repentance" (Johnson's *Works,* Yale ed., 4:223). Some of the roles of hope and fear in Johnson's moral thought have been discussed by Paul K. Alkon, *Samuel Johnson and Moral Discipline* (Evanston; Northwestern Univ. Press, 1967), pp. 170–72.

Johnson's (or his persona's) retreat from hope and fear was short-lived: see his letters to Thomas Warton, February 1, March 20, March 25; Thomas Birch on March 29; Charles Burney on April 8; Edmund Hector on April 15; and Bennet Langton on May 6, all in 1755 (Chapman, *The Letters of Samuel Johnson*, 1:61, 66–71). The independent tones of the Preface were noted by the Wartons. On April 19, 1755, Thomas wrote to Joseph informing him that "the Dictionary is arrived," and that "the preface is noble." He then quotes Johnson's lines regarding his rejection of *"patronage"* and his later *"frigid tranquility"* (italics are Warton's), and adds: "I fear his preface will disgust, by the expressions of his consciousness of superiority, and his contempt of patronage": John Wooll, *Biographical Memoirs of the Late Revd. Joseph Warton, D.D.* (London, 1806), pp. 230–31.

Redefinitions of Style, *1600–1800* HANSEN

1. "The Elocutionary Movement in England" (Ph.D. diss., Cornell Univ., 1947), pp. 68–90.
2. Ibid., pp. 74–75.
3. The most useful accounts of the antirhetorical trend in the seventeenth century are: Joel E. Spingarn, Introduction, *Critical Essays of the Seventeenth Century*, 3 vols. (Oxford: Clarendon Press, 1908), 1:xxxvi–xlviii; R. F. Jones, "Science and English Prose Style in the Third Quarter of the Seventeenth Century" and "The Attack on Pulpit Eloquence: An Episode in the Development of the Neo-Classical Standard for Prose," in *The Seventeenth Century: Studies in the History of English Thought and Literature from Bacon to Pope by Richard Foster Jones and Others Writing in His Honor* (Stanford: Stanford Univ. Press, 1951), pp. 75–142; W. Fraser Mitchell, *English Pulpit Oratory from Andrewes to Tillotson: A Study of its Literary Aspects* (New York: Russell and Russell, 1962); Robert Adolph, *The Rise of Modern Prose Style* (Cambridge: The M.I.T. Press, 1968), pp. 10–25. Although each of these studies touches such opposition to the antirhetorical tradition as arose in the seventeenth century, none gives an account of the two trends in the eighteenth century. For an account of them in the first half of the century, see David A. Hansen, "English Theories of Prose Style: 1698–1752" (Ph.D. diss., Univ. of Minnesota, 1966).
4. Unless otherwise indicated in the text, all lexical and encyclopedic definitions quoted in this paper are drawn from the first edition of a dictionary or encyclopedia.
5. Ed. G. H. Mair (Oxford: Clarendon Press, 1909), pp. 6, 160 (hereafter cited as Wilson, *Arte*). The most useful survey of Ciceronian

and Ramian rhetoricians is Wilbur Samuel Howell, *Logic and Rhetoric in England, 1500–1700* (New York: Russell and Russell, 1961).

6. Wilson, *Arte*, pp. 162–69.

7. 3d ed. (London, 1640), pp. 29–36 (my translation).

8. (Middleburg), sig. D1ᵛ.

9. (Oxford), sig. A1ʳ (my translation).

10. In the *Glossographia* Blount gives an illustrative quotation that suggests an etymological definition of the term, "*Elocution* (saith Judge Doddridge) consists of three things. 1. Of the voyce, as the instrument. 2. The words, that are the subject. 3. The manner of doing, which is the form of delivery, etc."

11. A similar definition appears in Benjamin N. Defoe's *A Compleat English Dictionary* (London, 1735), Benjamin Martin's *Lingua Britannica Reformata* (London, 1749), and Joseph N. Scott's revision of Nathan Bailey's *A New Universal Etymological Dictionary* (London, 1755).

12. A definition similar to Phillips's appears in Elisha Coles's *An English Dictionary* (London, 1676) and John Kersey's *Dictionarium Anglo-Britannicum: Or, A General English Dictionary* (London, 1708).

13. "Sources of the Elocutionary Movement in England: 1700–1748," in *Historical Studies of Rhetoric and Rhetoricians*, ed. Raymond F. Howe (Ithaca, N.Y.: Cornell Univ. Press, 1961), pp. 145, 139.

14. Nathan Bailey, *An Universal Etymological Dictionary* (London, 1721); Thomas Dyche and William Pardon, *A New General English Dictionary* (London, 1735); [John Kersey], *A New English Dictionary* (1737); James Manlove, *A New Dictionary* (London, 1741); Martin, *Lingua Britannica Reformata*; [John Wesley], *The Complete English Dictionary* (1753); *A Pocket Dictionary or Complete English Expositor* (1751); *A Vocabulary or Pocket Dictionary* (1765).

15. "The Author's Apology for Heroic Poetry and Poetic Licence," *Essays of John Dryden*, ed. W. P. Ker, 2 vols. (New York: Russell and Russell, 1961), 1:188–89.

16. "An Essay on Virgil's *Georgics*," *Eighteenth-Century Critical Essays*, ed. Scott Elledge, 2 vols. (Ithaca, N.Y.: Cornell Univ. Press, 1961), 1:2–3.

17. Ed. Alexander Campbell Fraser, 2 vols. (Oxford: Clarendon Press, 1894), 2:146–47.

18. *The Educational Writings of John Locke*, ed. John W. Adamson (Cambridge: Cambridge Univ. Press, 1927), pp. 156–57.

19. For example, aenigma, anacoenosis, anadiplosis, anaphora, anastrophe, antanaclasis, anthropopatheia, antimetabole, antiphrasis, antanomasis, catachresis, and ploce.

20. *Irish Tracts 1720–1723 and Sermons*, ed. Louis Landa (Oxford: Basil Blackwell, 1948), p. 65.

21. *Essays Philosophical and Moral, Historical and Literary,* 2 vols. (London, 1799), 2:484.

22. Trans. H. E. Butler, Loeb Classical Library, 4 vols. (London: Heinemann, 1959), 3:195.

23. The definitions quoted are from [Kersey], *A New English Dictionary* (1737), and Kersey, *Dictionarium Anglo-Britannicum.* Broad definitions of *style* appear in the following dictionaries: [Kersey], *A New English Dictionary* (London, 1702), where he is content to define *style* simply as "a manner of expression"; [Edward Cocker], *Cocker's English Dictionary* (London, 1704); Bailey, *An Universal Etymological English Dictionary;* Manlove, *A New Dictionary;* Martin, *Lingua Britannica Reformata;* [Wesley], *The Complete English Dictionary;* Johnson, *A Dictionary of the English Language;* John Ash, *The New and Complete Dictionary of the English Language* (London, 1775); Thomas Sheridan, *A General Dictionary of the English Language* (London, 1780); and John Walker, *A Critical Pronouncing Dictionary* (New York, 1810), which appeared first in London, 1791.

24. The quotation is from Dyche and Pardon, *A New General English Dictionary.* Narrow definitions of *style* appear also in Defoe, *The Compleat English Dictionary; A Pocket Dictionary;* and Scott–Bailey, *A New Universal Etymological Dictionary.*

25. *Essays upon Several Subjects* (London, 1716), p. 91.

26. Joseph Trapp, in his *Lectures on Poetry* (London, 1742), p. 37, says: "By Style I understand a Method of Writing peculiar to every Writing, every Writer, Art, or Science; or that which distinguishes Writings and Writers from one another." Trapp, I suggest, mixes narrow and generic definitions of *style* and illustrates the tendency in the century to give the term different meanings without enlarging on the differences. Trapp himself goes on to explain the difference between poetry and prose and, generally, to adopt a generic approach to the various poetical styles. The *Lectures* appeared first, in Latin, in 1711, and again in 1715 and 1736.

27. For accounts of Lamy, see Douglas Ehninger, "Bernard Lami's *L'art de parler*: A Critical Analysis," *Quarterly Journal of Speech* 32 (1946): 429–34 and Howell, pp. 378–82.

28. Nouvelle edition (Paris, 1732), p. 80.

29. Ibid., p. 84.

30. "Timber: or, Discoveries," *Ben Jonson,* ed. C. H. Herford and Percy and Evelyn Simpson, 11 vols. (Oxford: Clarendon Press, 1925–52), 8:625.

31. For an account of these writers and their opposition to the antirhetorical trend, see Hansen, "English Theories of Prose Style," pp. 122–74.

32. Christian Wolff, *Preliminary Discourse on Philosophy in Gen-*

eral, trans. Richard J. Blackwell (New York: Bobbs-Merrill, Library of Liberal Arts, 1963), p. 87.

33. 5 (1735): 252–53.

34. *The Works of Samuel Johnson, LL.D.,* 9 vols. (Oxford, 1825), 6:289.

35. On Johnson as a rhetorician, see W. Vaughan Reynolds, "Johnson's Opinions on Prose Style," *RES,* n.s. 9 (1939): 433–46.

36. (New York, 1810), p. 6.

37. Gleig, or another compiler, chooses as much or as little as he wishes. For example, Blair says: "It is not easy to give a precise idea of what is meant by Style. The best definition I can give of it is, *the peculiar manner in which a man expresses his conceptions,* by means of language. It is different from mere Language or words. The words, which an author employs, may be proper and faultless; and his style may, nevertheless, have great faults; it may be dry, or stiff, or feeble, or affected. Style has always some reference to an author's manner of thinking. *It is a picture of the ideas in which they rise there.*": *Lectures on Rhetoric and Belles Lettres,* ed. Harold F. Harding, 2 vols. (Carbondale and Edwardsville: Southern Illinois Univ. Press, 1965), 1:183 (hereafter cited as *Lectures*). I have italicized the statements which the compiler has culled from Blair. Other statements which appear in the third edition may be found in *Lectures,* 1:183, 184, 186, 209, 225, 247, 402–7.

38. Ibid., 1:184.

39. Ibid., 1:364.

40. Ibid., 1:203.

41. For an account of this issue, see William Kenney, "Addison, Johnson, and the 'Energetick' Style," *Studia neophilogica* 33 (1961): 103–19. For another account of the criticism in this period, see Morley J. Mays, "Johnson and Blair on Addison's Prose Style," *SP* 39 (1942): 638–49.

Dollars and Dictionaries   SLEDD

1. "chutzpa . . . , *n. Slang.* unmitigated effrontery or impudence." (*Random House Dictionary*).

2. James H. Sledd and Gwin J. Kolb, *Dr. Johnson's Dictionary: Essays in the Biography of a Book* (Chicago: Univ. of Chicago Press, 1955), pp. 127–31, 147–49.

3. Joseph H. Friend, *The Development of American Lexicography 1798–1864* (The Hague: Mouton, 1967), pp. 82–88.

4. Bernard F. Huppé and D. W. Robertson, Jr., *Fruyt and Chaf: Studies in Chaucer's Allegories* (Princeton: Princeton Univ. Press, 1963), p. 5, quoting Alanus de Insulis, *De planctu naturae.*

5. Jess Stein, Preface, *The Random House Dictionary of the English Language* (New York: Random House, 1966), p. v.

6. C. L. Barnhart, "Problems in Editing Commercial Monolingual Dictionaries," in Fred W. Householder and Sol Saporta, eds., *Problems in Lexicography,* 2d ed. (Bloomington: Indiana Univ. Press, 1967), pp. 164–65.

7. Sledd and Kolb, p. 238, n. 43.

8. Ibid., p. 161.

9. Ibid., p. 147.

10. Ibid., pp. 158–59.

11. Cf. Murray's long quotation from Johnson's Preface (*OED,* 1:xi) and his acknowledgment (1:xxi) that "the explanations of Dr. Johnson and of his editor Archdeacon Todd have often been adopted unchanged"; also P. J. Wexler, "Le fonds Pougens," *Cahiers de lexicologie* 1 (1959): 77–98, esp. p. 95. Wexler shows how Littré used the vast collection of some 300,000 citations which Charles Pougens had collected for a French dictionary in emulation of Johnson's.

12. Most recently discussed by Friend. Webster's great work was *An American Dictionary of the English Language,* in two volumes quarto (New York, 1828). "Webster's own revision and enlargement," also in two volumes, was published at New York in 1841; and after the remaining unbound sheets had found their way into the hands of G. & C. Merriam, "the first Merriam-Webster" was published at Springfield, Mass., in 1847, "under the editorship of Professor Chauncey A. Goodrich of Yale and a corps of associate editors and helpers." Meanwhile Worcester had established himself as a dangerous rival, notably by his *Comprehensive Pronouncing and Explanatory Dictionary* (Boston, 1830) and by his *Universal and Critical Dictionary* (Boston, 1846). Worcester's masterpiece, *A Dictionary of the English Language,* was published at Boston five years before his death in 1865. Though it almost immediately faced the competition of the 1864 revision of Webster by C. A. Goodrich and Noah Porter, with new etymologies by the German scholar C. A. F. Mahn, still Worcester's last work continued to enjoy some popularity. Its last edition appeared in 1886 and was reissued, according to Kennedy, as late as 1908. The *Universal and Critical* was reprinted as late as 1881. Webster's *American Dictionary* became *Webster's International Dictionary* in 1890, the *New International* in 1909 (2d ed., 1934), and the *Third New International* in 1961. (Details from Friend and from Arthur G. Kennedy, *A Bibliography of Writings on the English Language* [Cambridge: Harvard Univ. Press; New Haven: Yale Univ. Press, 1927]; quotations from Friend, pp. 82, n. 2; 107.)

13. "Noah Webster," in *Webster's Third New International Dictionary* (Springfield: G. & C. Merriam, 1961).

14. Sledd and Kolb, p. 197, with n. 236.

15. "Noah Webster," in *W3*.

16. W. A. Craigie, "New Dictionary Schemes Presented to the Philological Society" (with Leonard C. Wharton, "Footnote to Sir William Craigie's Paper"), *Transactions of the Philological Society* (1925–30), pp. 6–14.

17. Friend, p. 102.

18. Sledd and Kolb, p. 203.

19. Kennedy, p. 235, no. 6462.

20. Friend, p. 86.

21. Historical Introduction in the *OED's* first supplement (Oxford: Clarendon Press, 1933), p. xii.

22. *Nation*, 48 (May 30, 1889): 450.

23. For details see Frank H. Vizetelly, *The Development of the Dictionary of the English Language* (New York: Funk and Wagnalls, 1915), especially pp. 18, 22 ff.

24. Ibid., p. 22.

25. Quoted in *Business Week* (September 16, 1961), p. 89.

26. For most appetites, a more than adequate sampling of the foolish controversy can be found in James Sledd and Wilma R. Ebbitt, eds., *Dictionaries and That Dictionary* (Chicago: Scott, Foresman, 1962).

27. *OED*, 1:vi.

28. Philip B. Gove, Preface, *W3*, p. 6a.

29. Among conceptual dictionaries, Roget's *Thesaurus* is familiar, but there are many others for other languages, such as Franz Dornseiff, *Der deutsche Wortschatz nach Sachgruppen*, 5th ed. (Berlin: W. deGruyter, 1959), and Julio Casares, *Diccionario ideológico de la lengua española*, 2d ed. (Barcelona: Gustavo Gili, 1959). A good many studies of the French vocabulary have followed R. Hallig and W. von Wartburg, *Begriffssystem als Grundlage für die Lexikographie*, in the *Abhandlungen der Deutschen Akademie der Wissenschaften zu Berlin, Klasse für Sprachen, Literatur und Kunst*, Heft 4, 1952. On fields of meaning and structural semantics, extensive though now somewhat dated bibliographical notes are given in "The Structure of the Vocabulary," chapter 9 in Stephen Ullmann's *Semantics* (Oxford: Basil Blackwell, 1962). A famous essay from the M.I.T. group is Jerrold J. Katz and Jerry A. Fodor, "The Structure of a Semantic Theory," in the Fodor-Katz anthology *The Structure of Language* (Englewood Cliffs, N.J.: Prentice-Hall, 1964). An answer by Uriel Weinreich appeared in Thomas A. Sebeok, ed., *Current Trends in Linguistics*, vol. 3 (The Hague: Mouton, 1966), pp. 395–474. Katz replied in "Recent Issues in Semantic Theory," *Foundations of Language* 3 (1967): 124–94. This

and other discussions continue vigorously; see, for example, James D. McCawley, "The Role of Semantics in a Grammar," in Emmon Bach and Robert T. Harms, *Universals in Linguistic Theory* (New York: Holt, Rinehart and Winston, 1968) or Noam Chomsky, "Deep Structure, Surface Structure, and Semantic Interpretation," a paper dated November 1968 and already widely circulated but apparently still unpublished as this note is written.

30. Uriel Weinreich, "Webster's Third: A Critique of Its Semantics," *IJAL* 30 (1964): 405–9.

31. "The Dictionary's Function," in Philip B. Gove, ed., *The Role of the Dictionary* (Indianapolis: Bobbs-Merrill, 1967), p. 7.

32. *RHD*, p. vi.

33. Ibid.

34. Ibid.

35. Ibid., p. xxi.

36. *Nation* 203 (December 19, 1966): 675–76.

37. *New Republic* 155 (November 26, 1966): 26–28.

38. *Saturday Review* 50 (October 14, 1967): 19–21, 132.

39. *RHD*, p. vi.

40. An *American College Dictionary* of 1959 was opened at random to the column beginning with the word *grass*. Of 20 entries in the column, 19 show some verbal identity with the unabridged *RHD*. Extending the comparison to the college edition of *RHD* (New York, 1968) and a 1966 *American College*, the vexed inquirer found that the college *RHD* had kept 15 of the 20 words, dropped 5, and added 2. If the college edition of *Random House* is based on the unabridged (Laurence Urdang, Preface, College Edition, p. v), then in 14 of the 15 shared entries the unabridged must be based on the *ACD;* for verbal similarity between the *ACD* and both editions of *RH* is very close in the entries *grass, Grasse, grasshopper, grassland, grass tree, grass widow, grass widower, grassy, grate¹, grate², grateful, Gratian, gratification, gratify.* This is precisely the sort of thing that one expects from publishers of dictionaries, and there is nothing wrong with it— except when editors and advertisers say that a book is "entirely new" though obviously it isn't.

41. *Time*, 88 (September 30, 1966): 77.

42. Of course Stein's claim that he has preserved everything that's worth preserving in lexicographic tradition might puzzle a too literal reader. Murray (the naïve student might remember) preserved the distinction between the encyclopedia and the dictionary, as Johnson had done earlier ("my design was a dictionary, common or appellative"), and both Johnson and Murray took special pains with their collections of illustrative citations; but the proportion of proper names on some pages in the unabridged *RHD* is as high as one in three, while Stein's "citations" are apparently not citations at all, but invented

examples, like "He was dubbed a charlatan" (s.v. *dub*). The absence of citations would set Stein equally apart from Webster, Craigie, and Whitney, who must all have thought, like Gove, that citations tell us something about usage; and though Stein makes sweeping claims to sweeping coverage, the "common or appellative" portion of his word-list is much smaller than that in the *Third International,* which itself is not quite outside Websterian tradition.

Such contrasts, misinterpreted, could put an innocent reader into a temper. "The pronunciation system used in the *RHD,*" he will read in Stein's Preface, has "the twofold merit of simplicity and accuracy," and "whenever common variant pronunciations exist," they are shown in the *Random* transcriptions. Turning, therefore, to Bronstein's "Pronunciation of English," to the "Pronunciation Key," and to the text itself, a hypothetical Southerner observes how New Yorkers use the symbol â. He finds it in *air, care, Mary,* and *they're;* but he happens to pronounce all these words with different vowels; and when *Mary* leads him to the derivative *Marist,* he finds still a fifth value for the one transcription. He isn't helped by the confession, in the "Guide to the Dictionary," that the symbol â *is* multiply ambiguous, any more than it helps him to discover that *RHD* doesn't really record or even have symbols for all the variants that Bronstein talks about (cf. Bronstein with the text on words like *sister; hue; hurry* but *curricle, durrie, murrain, murrey, scurrile, scurrilous, turrical; hoarse* and *horse,* but *toro* and *toreador; coral, horrid, orange, sorrow, tomorrow; hog, mock, prong;* etc.). Further discoveries include the facts that the text of *RHD* ignores distinctions which the Southerner carefully preserves between words like *waffle* and *waddle* (so that a Southern child looking up a strange word such as *wattle* wouldn't know which of two vowels to give it), and that *RHD's* symbols for reduction vowels overlap, with ə in both *circus* and *easily* but i in *furnace,* although many Americans keep front and back reduction vowels meticulously distinct.

For Confederates, then, as far as pronunciation is concerned *RHD* is a dubious guide, and there are other instances in which the scholarship of the introductory pages, with their Roman numerals, did not survive the shift to Arabic numerals in the text. So, for example, McDavid says a good deal more than the text does about the geographic distribution of names for the hero sandwich; the text omits the sense "to copulate" under the word *jazz,* though McDavid makes that meaning essential to the etymology; the text omits the terms *northernism* and *proto-English,* which Kemp Malone uses in his "Historical Sketch of the English Language," but includes *proto-Elamite* and *Northernize;* Malone and the text disagree on dates for the Middle English period; Malone rightly recognizes *k* as an Old English letter, though a rare one, while the text asserts flatly that *k* "did not appear in English until after the Norman conquest"; and so forth and so on.

But to get into a temper when scholars say one thing and *RH* editors another, or to sniff out small mistakes (like the failure of explanations B and F, in Stein's third column on p. xxix, to match the adduced examples) would be to carry literalness to an extreme. Stein's quiet appropriation of the finest traditions of English lexicography simply indicates that the functions of editor and advertising man are not always scrupulously distinguished and defined.

43. Sledd and Kolb, p. 245, n. 199.

44. Ibid., pp. 183–91. For Tooke, see the much more elaborate study by Hans Aarsleff, *The Study of Language in England, 1780–1860* (Princeton: Princeton Univ. Press, 1967).

45. Of the familiar history of the *OED*, only those features which are relevant to the present argument are summarized here. More detailed accounts may be found in Murray's Preface in vol. 1, in the Historical Introduction in the first supplement, and in the successive volumes of the *Transactions of the Philological Society*. The completion of the main dictionary in 1928 was duly celebrated: see, for example, "The Completion of the Oxford English Dictionary," *Periodical* 13 (1928): 1–32, Sir William Craigie, *The Oxford English Dictionary: A Short Account* (New York: Oxford Univ. Press, 1928); or E. E. Wardale, "The 'New English Dictionary,'" *Nineteenth Century* 103 (1928): 97–110 (references supplied by Mr. Joseph E. Littlejohn). R. W. Burchfield describes present activity in "*O.E.D.*: A New Supplement," *Essays and Studies 1961* (London: John Murray, 1961), pp. 35–51.

46. A. Kluyver, "Das niederländische Wörterbuch," *Zeitschrift für deutsche Wortforschung* 7 (1906): 334–40.

47. "On Some Deficiencies in Our English Dictionaries," *Transactions of the Philological Society*, 1857, p. 47.

48. *Transactions of the Philological Society*, 1873–74, p. 442.

49. Henry Bradley, "The Oxford English Dictionary," *Zeitschrift für deutsche Wortforschung* 7 (1906): 312–13.

50. The account of Passow follows Aarsleff, pp. 252–63.

51. *Transactions of the Philological Society*, 1857, Appendix, p. 72.

52. *OED*, 1:vi.

53. Cf. Aarsleff, pp. 252, 255.

54. For Littré, cf. especially "Comment j'ai fait mon Dictionnaire," in his *Dictionnaire de la langue française*, édition intégrale (Paris: J. J. Pauvert, 1959), 1:73–113.

55. *Transactions of the Philological Society*, 1868–69, p. 16.

56. *Transactions of the Philological Society*, 1873–74, p. 355.

57. *OED*, 1:vi.

58. *Lexicologie et lexicographie françaises et romanes* (Paris: Centre nationale de la recherche scientifique, 1961), Avant-Propos, pp. 21–27, 34, 41.

59. Burchfield, p. 37, n. 1.

60. Bradley, p. 314.

61. "New Dictionary Schemes," *Transactions of the Philological Society,* 1925–30, pp. 6–14.

62. David Murison, "A Survey of Scottish Language Studies," *Forum for Modern Language Studies* 3 (1967): 276–85.

63. *Old English Newsletter* 2 (December, 1968): 1.

64. Ibid.

65. *Lexicologie et lexicographie françaises et romanes,* p. 269.

66. *Australian Language Research Centre, Third Annual Report* (for 1967).

67. Aldo Duro, "Les nouvelles méthodes du dictionnaire historique de la langue italienne," *Cahiers de lexicologie* 8 (1966): 95–112; Lucio Felici, "Presente e avvenire della lessicografia italiana," *Nuova antologia* 495 (1965): 355–64.

The Sociology of Dictionaries and of Words   BAKER

1. McLuhan's many public pronouncements overwhelm and nullify the bibliographer; see Walter J. Ong, "Hostility, Literacy, and *Webster III,*" *College English,* 26 (1964): 106–11.

2. Quoted in an advertisement, from *War and Peace in the Global Village,* (New York: McGraw-Hill, 1968).

3. McLuhan has overlooked the computer's regression toward printing: it does not speak because, when it is not quantifying, it prints out its answers in teletype. Our research requires "print-outs"; "speak-outs" would be useless.

4. Charles C. Fries, *What Is Good English?* (Ann Arbor: G. Wahr Publishing Co., 1949), p. 44, copyrighted as *Teaching of the English Language* (New York: T. Nelson and Sons, 1927).

5. "A large number of verbal illustrations mostly from the mid-twentieth century has been woven into the defining pattern with a view to contributing considerably to the user's interest and understanding by showing a word used in context. . . .
"In definitions of words of many meanings the earliest ascertainable meaning is given first. Meanings of later derivation are arranged in the order shown to be most probable by dated evidence and semantic development." (Philip B. Gove, Preface, *Webster's Third New International Dictionary* [Springfield: G. & C. Merriam, 1961], p. 6a.) Placing etymology first also greatly strengthens the historical presentation.

6. Richard W. Bailey, "Language and Literature: A Rejoinder," *Style* 1 (1967): 221–22; but see de Saussure's pronouncement that "the synchronic 'phenomenon' has nothing in common with the diachronic one" (*Cours de linguistique générale* [Paris: Payot, 1949], p. 128, trans.

and qtd. by William Labov, *The Social Stratification of English in New York City* [Washington, D.C.: Center for Applied Linguistics, 1966], p. 9).

7. In contesting the idea that "speech" comprises the totality of language, to the apparent exclusion of reading and writing, Dwight Macdonald remarks: "I wonder whether the fact that Structural Linguists have evolved their theories from the study of primitive languages is perhaps significant" ("Three Questions for Structural Linguists, Or Webster 3 Revised," in *Dictionaries and That Dictionary*, ed. James Sledd and Wilma R. Ebbitt (Chicago: Scott, Foresman, 1962), p. 259.

8. See my *The New English*, Occasional Papers: Number Twelve Council for Basic Education (Washington, D.C.: Council for Basic Education, 1967), pp. 6–7.

9. Philip B. Gove, "Lexicography and the Teacher of English," *College English* 25 (1964): 346.

10. Donald J. Lloyd and Harry R. Warfel, *American English in Its Cultural Setting* (New York: Alfred A. Knopf, 1956), pp. 63, 65, 83.

11. "Linguistics and the Prospective Teachers of English," *Changes in Teacher Education: An Appraisal*, Official Report of the Columbus Conference, Eighteenth National TEPS Conference (Washington, D.C.: National Education Association, 1964), p. 495.

12. American Council of Learned Societies, *Handbook of the Linguistic Geography of New England* (Providence, R.I.: Brown Univ., 1939), Preface, p. ix.

13. *Handbook*, pp. 41–45. Note also Clyde T. Hankey's phrase "the expressions prominent in cultured or younger speech" (*A Colorado Word Geography*, Publication of the American Dialect Society, no. 34 [November 1960], p. 66).

14. "Harvard, Yale, and the Educated Colonial," *Michigan Quarterly Review* 7 (1968): 177.

15. "Linguistic Advances and Lexicography," *Word Study*, October 1961, p. 3.

16. Bernard Bloch and George L. Trager, *Outline of Linguistic Analysis* (Baltimore: Linguistic Society of America, 1942), p. 40, qtd. in Labov, p. 11.

17. Introductory Note, by Alfred S. Hays, Director, Education and Research Program, Center for Applied Linguistics.

18. "The Lexicographer's Uneasy Chair," *College English* 23 (1962): 684–85.

19. Ibid., p. 685.

20. *The Philosophy of Language* (New York: Harper and Row, 1966), pp. 244, 269.

21. *Speaker's Meaning* (Middletown, Conn.: Wesleyan Univ. Press, 1967), pp. 49–50.

22. "The Current Scene in Linguistics: Present Directions," *College English* 27 (1966): 587–95.

23. Sledd and Ebbitt, p. 268.

English Dictionaries of the Future   GOVE

1. John R. Bartlett, *Dictionary of Americanisms* (1848; rpt. Boston: Little, Brown, 1877), p. [xxi]: "The natural tendency of language is to improve."

2. "Based on" here refers to a process of cutting out each definition and pasting it on a 3x5 slip so that the definition can be revised or rewritten in the light of new citations and accumulated notes.

3. See, for example, Talmy Givón, 'Some Noun-to-Noun Derivational Affixes," SP–2893, System Development Corp. (July 1967), in which words in *-hood, -dom, -ship,* and *-age* are studied.

4. See Henry Kučera and W. Nelson Francis, *Computational Analysis of Present-Day American English* (Providence, R.I.: Brown Univ. Press, 1967).

5. M. E. Maron, "A Logician's View of Language-Data Processing," *Natural Language and the Computer,* ed. Paul L. Garvin (New York: McGraw-Hill, 1963), p. 150.

6. "Some Linguistic Studies of 1937 and 1938," *MLN* 54 (1939): 533.

7. Some of these directives I have published. See "Subject Orientation within the Definition," *Twelfth Annual Round Table Meeting,* ed. Michael Zarechnak, Monograph Series on Languages and Linguistics, no. 14 (Washington, D.C.: Georgetown Univ., 1961), pp. 95–107; " 'Noun Often Attributive' and 'Adjective'," *American Speech* 39 (1964): [163]–75; " 'Gerund/Noun' and 'Participle/Adjective'," *American Speech* 40 (1965): [40]–46; "The Nonlexical and the Encyclopedic," *Names* 13 (1965): 103–15; "Self-Explanatory Words," *American Speech* 41 (1966): [182]–98.

8. Joseph Aurbach et al., *Transformational Grammar* (Washington, D.C.: Washington Educational Research Associates, 1968), p. 46.

9. Noam Chomsky, *Aspects of the Theory of Syntax* (Cambridge: M.I.T. Press, 1965), p. 104.

10. *Webster's Third New International Dictionary,* (Springfield, G. & C. Merriam, 1961), p. 6a.

11. *Philosophy of Rhetoric* (New York: Oxford Univ. Press, 1965), p. 73.

12. Mills F. Edgerton, Jr., "A Linguistic Definition of Literature," *Foreign Language Annals* 1 (1967): 125.

13. Review of Sydney M. Lamb, *Outline of Stratificational Grammar*, *Language* 44 (1968): 602.

14. M. H. Scargill, "Shifting the Gears," *Looking at Language*, ed. M. H. Scargill and P. G. Penner (Toronto: W. G. Gage, 1966), p. 90.

15. Edgerton, Jr., p. 126.

16. "The History of Linguistics: New Lamps for Old," *Seventeenth Annual Round Table Meeting*, ed. F. P. Dinneen, Monograph Series on Languages and Linguistics, no. 19 (Washington, D.C.: Georgetown Univ., 1966), p. 84.

17. *Linguistic Reporter* 9 (1967): 1.

18. T. A. Sebeok, "Linguistics Here and Now," *Language Sciences* 1 (1968): 5.

19. "On the Form of Rules in a Generative Grammar," *Eighteenth Annual Round Table Meeting*, ed. E. L. Blansitt, Jr., Monograph Series on Languages and Linguistics, no. 20 (Washington, D.C.: Georgetown Univ., 1967), p. 44. Cf. Bruce Fraser, "Some Remarks on the Verb-Particle Construction in English," *Seventeenth Annual Round Table Meeting*, p. [45]: "Recent work on the theory of grammar within the framework of transformational grammars has resulted in the characterization of a grammar as consisting of a lexicon and three major rule components: a syntactic component, consisting of a base and a transformational subcomponent; a semantic component, and a phonological component, where only the syntactic set of rules is generative, the other two sets applying to syntactical constructs to provide the appropriate semantic and phonological interpretation of the sentence."

20. Jerrold J. Katz and Jerry A. Fodor, "The Structure of a Semantic Theory," *Language* 39 (1963): 170.

21. *Sense and Sense Development* (New York: Oxford Univ. Press, 1967), p. 76 f.

22. Paul L. Garvin, Jocelyn Brewer, and Madeleine Mathiot, "Predication-Typing: a Pilot Study in Semantic Analysis," *Language* 43, no. 2, pt. 2 (1967), Language Monograph no. 27, p. 1.

23. A clearly-stated 1956–57 statement is chapter 9, "Syntax and Semantics" of Noam Chomsky's *Syntactic Structures* (The Hague: Mouton, 1957), pp. [92]–105. Compare the following paragraph in a review of Chomsky: "So far we have said nothing at all about the vexed question of semantic criteria in linguistics (Chap. 9). There is a very simple explanation for this neglect: if the term 'meaning' is taken in its ordinary, everyday sense, this notion turns out to be simply irrelevant to grammatical theory and analysis. It is however not at all irrelevant to language study, and it may even be that part of linguistic studies which is of the greatest interest to the majority of our profession. But the study of meaning and its relation to grammar has been woefully confused by the widespread confounding of reference, meaning, synonymy, 'differential meaning', informant response, amount of 'information', sig-

nificance, grammatical equivalence, truth-preserving equivalence, and mutual substitutability. No single concept involved in linguistic tradition has caused such widespread misunderstanding and entailed such a plethora of polemic as has that of meaning, with the possible exception of the 'phonetic law' of the Junggrammatiker. The linguist not only is beset, as is any other behavioral scientist, with all the classical philosophical problems inherent in the notion of meaning, but also must now deal with the added difficulty of identification with one or another of the several schools of linguistic philosophy at odds with one another over the question of whether and (if so) how meaning enters into linguistic analysis."—Robert B. Lees, *Language* 33 (July–Sept. 1957): 393.

24. *The English Verb* (Madison: Univ. of Wisconsin Press, 1964). See also his "A Chapter of Semology in the English Verb," *Fifteenth Annual Round Table Meeting*, ed. C. I. J. M. Stuart, Monograph Series on Languages and Linguistics, no. 17 (Washington, D.C.: Georgetown Univ., 1964), pp. 59–72.

25. *A Short History of Literary English* (London: Edward Arnold, 1967), p. 28.

26. Wallace L. Chafe, "Language as Symbolization," *Language* 43 (1967): 89. "I take it," writes Chafe, "that facts about language such as these [the four resulting analyses] are every bit as important as facts which arise from the observation of sound."

27. Noam Chomsky, "Current [1962] Issues in Linguistic Theory," *The Structure of Language*, ed. Jerry A. Fodor and Jerrold J. Katz (Englewood Cliffs, N.J.: Prentice-Hall, 1964), p. 66.

28. Robert B. Lees, *The Grammar of English Nominalizations*, supplement to *IJAL* 26 (1960): xxi.

29. Katz and Fodor, p. 186.

30. Givón, p. 1.

31. Charles J. Fillmore, "The Grammar of *Hitting* and *Breaking*," *Working Papers in Linguistics*, Ohio State Univ. Research Foundation, December 1967, p. 17.

32. Gerald L. Cohen, "An Attempted Explanation of English 'take sick', 'get sick', and 'keep smiling'," paper read at the 43d annual meeting of the Linguistic Society of America, New York, 1968.

33. Lowell Bouma, "The Semantics of the Modal System in Contemporary German," paper read at 43d annual meeting of the Linguistic Society of America, 1968.

34. Edward P. Lanning, *Peru before the Incas* (Englewood Cliffs, N.J.: Prentice-Hall, 1967), p. 58 f.

35. "Affixal Derivation, Zero Derivation, and 'Semantic Transformations'," TM–3835, System Development Corporation (February 1968).

36. Fillmore, p. 3. Obviously he did not expect his statement to be so isolated.

37. "Inference Expressed by *Should* and *Must*," *Tesol Quarterly* 1 (1967): 47–51.

38. *The Verb System of Present-Day American English* (The Hague: Mouton, 1966) p. 236.

39. "On So-Called 'Pronouns' in English," *Seventeenth Annual Round Table Meeting*, pp. [177]–206.

40. "A Chapter of Semology in the English Verb," p. 69 (see n. 24).

41. *Adverbial Positions in English* (Stockholm: AB Studentbok, 1964); reviewed by Samuel J. Keyser, *Language* 44 (1968): 357–74.

42. Robin Lakoff, paper read at the 43d meeting of Linguistic Society of America, 1968.

43. *Journal of Linguistics* 3 (1967): 37–81, 199–244.

44. Michael A. K. Halliday, "Syntax and the Consumer," *Fifteenth Annual Round Table Meeting*, p. 22.

45. "A Stratificational View of Polysemy," paper read at the 43d meeting of the Linguistic Society of America, 1968.

46. Robert M. Hutchins, "Doing What Comes Scientifically," *Center Magazine* 2 (1969): 57.

47. TV commercial, January 1, 1969.

48. *Britannica Perspectives*, ed. Harry Ashmore, 3 vols. (Chicago: Encyclopaedia Britannica, 1968), 3:91.

49. George Lakoff, "Selectional Restrictions and Beliefs about the World," paper read at the 43d annual meeting of the Linguistic Society of America, 1968.

50. Jerrold J. Katz, "Analyticity and Contradiction in Natural Language," *The Structure of Language*, p. 537 (see n. 27).

51. (New York: Popular Library, 1967), p. 271.

Index